BACKWARD COMMUNITIES

BACKWARD COMMUNITIES:
Identity, Development and Transformation

Editors
V.K. Pant; B.S. Bisht

GYAN PUBLISHING HOUSE
NEW DELHI - 110002

BACKWARD COMMUNITIES:

Identity, Development and Transformation

[*Tribal Studies, Sociology*]

ISBN: 81-212-0625-1

Published in 1999 in India by
Gyan Publishing House
5, Ansari Road
New Delhi 110 002

Laser Typeset at Alphabet, Delhi
Printed at Mehra Offset Press, New Delhi.

Contents

Preface

The present volume is the result of the National Seminar on, 'Backward Communities: Identity, Development and Transformation' held on 15th 17th, Nov..1998 at Haldwani. The Seminar was organized under the auspices of the Research Project entitled, 'Society and Culture of the Eloped pairs: A case study of the Anwals of Indo-Tibetan Border of Uttarakhand, '(sanctioned to Dr. B.S. Bisht, Department of Sociology, M.B. Govt. P.G. College, HALDWANI) in collaboration with the Department of Sociology, Kumaon University, Nainital. The Seminar was inaugurated by Dr. R.S. Tolia, I.A.S, Director Uttar Pradesh, Academy of Administration, Nainital; and eminent sociologist Prof. S.P. Nagendra was the Chief Guest. The Seminar was presided over by Prof. B.K. Joshi, the then Vice-Chancellor of Kumaon University, Nainital.

Although the question of 'Backward Communities is very important particularly in the context of 'Transformation and Development' yet the question of their identity is equally important. In the context the process of transformation and development of the 'Backward Communities' becomes very important, because transformation and development, should in no way destroy the identity of the 'Backward Communities'. It will not be out of the place to mention here that it is not only desirable to give proper thinking to the transformation and develoment of the 'Backward Communities' but in the present circumstances it has assumed the form of a necessity. Classification of castes is due to political reasons which has increased the problems and worries of sociologists. Socio-cultural transformation through law is desirable, but law can not alone achieve the desirable goals in this context. Transformation and development has to be done within the institutional frame work of the community in question. The Seminar was a step towards this objectives and we hope the papers presented, will be useful not only for the academicians but for the planners also.

We thank all the participants in the 'Seminar and special thanks are due to Prof. S.P. Nagendra, who was kind enough to present the key note address. We are also thankful to Dr. R.S. Tolia, I.A.S.; Prof. B.K. Joshi and Prof. P.C. Barakoti not only for their co-operation but also for their academic participation in the Seminar. Our special thanks are also due to the contributors who presented the papers, without their co-operation and academic contribution, this volume would not have seen the light of the day.

B.S. Bisht

List of Tables

List of Contributors

1. Prof. S.P. Nagendra,
   Ex-Director, G.B. Pant Institute of Social Sciences, Allahabad;
   Ex. Pro-Vice-Chancellor, Gorakhpur University;
   Ex. Vice-Chancellor, Lucknow University, Lucknow.
2. Prof. Satyendra Tripathi,
   Former Head Deptt. of Sociology,
   Former Director, Centre for I.R.D.P.,
   Banaras Hindu University, Varanasi .
3. Prof. Surendra Singh,
   Head Deptt. of Social Work &
   Pro-Vice-Chancellor, Lucknow University, Lucknow.
4. Dr B.S. Bisht, D. Lit.
   Reader, Post Graduate Deptt. of Sociology,
   M.B. Govt. P.G. College, Haldwani (Nainital).
5. Dr C.L. Sharma,
   Department of Sociology,
   Mohanlal Sukhadia University, Udaipur.
6. Dr A.K. Kapoor,
   Department of Anthropology,
   University of Delhi.
7. Dr G.S. Saun,
   Asstt. Director, ICSSR, New Delhi - 67.
8. Dr Tarachand G. Meshram,
   Head, Deptt. of Sociology,
   Nagpur University, Nagpur.
9. Dr B.K. Singh,
   Reader & Head, Deptt. of Sociology,
   B.R.A. Bihar University, Muzaffarpur, Bihar.

10. Dr N. Kumar,
Reader, P.G. Deptt. of Sociology,
K.S. College,
L.N. Mithila University, Darbhanga, Bihar.
11. Dr (Mrs) Sarojini Devi Bisht,
Head, Deptt. of Sociology,
G.K.K. Degree College, Kichha, Nainital.
12. Dr J.K. Pundir,
Reader, Deptt. of Sociology,
C.C.S. University, Meerut - 250005.
13. Dr Mohammad Ghufran,
Deptt. of Psychology,
Govt. M.B.P.G. College, Haldwani - Nainital.
14. Dr D. Rajeshwar,
Associate Project Director (CSD),
HIRD - Rajendra Nagar, Hyderabad, Andhra Pradesh
15. Dr K. Suman Chandra,
Asstt. Director (CSD),
N.I.R.D., Rajendra Nagar,
Hyderabad (Andhra Pradesh) - 500030
16. Dr J.B. Ambekar,
Reader, Deptt. of Sociology,
Shivaji University, Kolhapur,
Maharashtra.
17. Dr A.K. Srivastava,
Reader, Deptt. of Sociology,
Lucknow University, Lucknow. (U.P.)
18. Dr T.K. Vaishnav,
Research Officer,
M.P. Govt. Tribal Research and Development Institute,
Shyamala Hill, Bhopal - 462002 (M.P.).
19. Dr P.K. Kar,
Reader and Head, P.G. Deptt. of Sociology,
Ravenshaw College (Autonomous)
Cuttack - Orissa - 753003.

One

Backward Communities: Identity, Development and Transformation

S.P. NAGENDRA

Birth is no longer the validating principle of being the privileged in an Indian society. Not only has the traditional distinction between the *Dwijas* and *Sudras* or the *Savaranas* and *Panchamas* been abolished but untouchability as a basis of exclusion and separation has also been banished from, at least, the public realm. In fact, all exclusionary practices on race, sex, ethnicity, religion, etc, have become untenable in India today.

A modern state has emerged armed with full panoply of power and has conferred a new status upon the individual who is first and foremost a 'citizen' and then anything else like a person with a caste or religious name in his private life.

If homoequalis is the ideal man whose full emergence is awaited in India, then the contours of the social organization are required to be reframed, replacing the hierarchy with stratification based on equality. But, since the change requires overturning the axis, the State cannot be the appropriate agency to bring it about. What is needed is, in fact, transformation of values, a change almost total in our *Weltanschauung* which even law is incapable of carrying into effect, especially when the change in India is for the maintenance of permanence[1]. According to the Sociologists, social mobility in India down the ages, has taken the form of 'Sanskritization' or 'Brahmanization' with the embracing of Hinduism by adopting a caste name and the lower castes climbing up the social ladder by imitating the lifestyle and rituals of the upper castes, both raising their status within the same hierarchy [2], which testifies to the stubborn resistance on the part of Indian society to retain its basic form.

There has been a change, so to say, 'in' the society but not 'of' the society. Even the induced social changes brought about by the law have so far not touched its axis i.e. the value system - in substance. Caste has been excluded from the public discourse, but the exclusion has only taken place to use a Freudian term the form of repression[3]. Like all social taboos, the public taboo on caste conceals behind it an ambivalence of emotions; the repulsion against caste is as strong as the attraction for it. The repulsion is conscious but the attraction is unconscious. Also like all repressed desires, caste invades the conscious or the public space in numerous disguised or surrogate forms like, a parapolitical community,[4] Dalits backward classes, etc.

Take for example the Indian Constitution, which distinguishes between backward, non-backward or advanced classes of citizens on one hand, and between casteless citizens, Scheduled Castes, and Scheduled Tribes, on the other, as if even for describing the secular self of India we have no better idiom than caste. The schism in the traditional non-secular self of India is understandable. It is a reflection of the bipartite division of the society into *Dwijas* and Sudras or the *Savarnas* and *Panchamas*. But, it is not easy to understand the schism in her secular self, reflecting the division of the citizens into casteless and caste-based people (Scheduled Castes). If the grand narrative to rationalize the traditional schism in India's self was borrowed from myths, the narrative to justify the split in her secular self is borrowed from the rational legal code. The typical argument to justify the retention of the caste for a particular class of citizens who deserve special consideration in the form of compensation is that, since caste was the basis of discrimination between the privileged and the underprivileged in the traditional Indian society, there can be no other more appropriate basis of selecting the citizens of the modern State for positive action than caste. But granting that there can be no better substitute for the various sub-castes, for social identification in contemporary India, be it only for making out the underdogs, we cannot afford to shun the sinister fall out of this separation.

In the prevailing distinction between the private and public realm, the latter has come to be associated with urbanity, caste-neutrality, secularism, rationality and sophistication and by the same token the private realm has become a byword for casteism, boorishness, non-secularism and irrationality. The public realm is again correlated with the urban social space and an elitist discourse based on English and the private realm with the rural social space and the commoners' dialect based on the vernacular. The backward classes/communities, including the so-called socially and educationally backward classes, the Scheduled Castes and the Scheduled Tribes tend to be located in the caste-based rural space, irrespective of their actual location while the urban space is supposed to be the preservatory of the advanced or elite classes. This partly explains the elitist attitude of pity and commiseration usually adopted by the '*Savarna*' or even 'non-*Savarna*' planners and administrators while dispensing social justice to the OBC's, SC's and the ST's. And this also explains the growing distance between the elites and the masses even among the so-called backwards.

A truly secular self will never look upon its alter ego, in casteist terms except when it is under the influence of its darker side namely its 'shadow' or the non-secular self which constantly shirks its normal development as if in a dream[5]. The process of secularism through repression of the non-secular (other) as reflected in caste and religion, cannot lead to a normal growth of the secular self. A more positive method for this process is not possible within the framework of a social change through State action. Even a set of bureaucrats, however smart and intelligent sitting round a table and drawing up plans for the development of the people whom they have known only through files, cannot come up with anything more than new versions of aborted plans and programmes. Since this is not an apt place to examine the archaeology of bureaucratic organizations in India, it is enough to say that like its counterparts in the other parts of the world, bureaucracy in India is totally alienated from the people. And as a part of the ruling class, it has to follow a particular method of validating statements to call it truth. It is not for nothing then, that Weber could foresee the emergence of a dictatorship of the bureaucracy rather than the proletariat much against Marx's belief in highly formal organization.

Again the so-called elected representatives of the people fails to do justice by not getting any plan for the development of the backward communities effectively implemented. As the modern democracy has no respect either for its 'people' or for their elected representatives, it has reduced them as an abstract quantifiable mass, who mechanically vote for candidate having no organic relationship with them and play as puppets into the hands of the powerful and the power brokers.

It is against this background that the development of the backward communities is to be viewed. We have already alluded to the distinctions drawn by the Indian Constitution between the backward and non-backward classes. As an exception to Articles 14-18 dealing with equality, Article 15(4) empowers the State to make special provisions for the advancement of any socially and educationally backward classes or for the Scheduled Castes and Scheduled Tribes. Article 16(4) likewise gives the state unfettered powers to make provisions for the reservation of appointments or posts in favour of any backward classes who in the opinion of the State are not adequately represented in the service under the state and Article 340. It also empowers the President to appoint a commission to investigate the conditions of the socially and educationally backward classes and the difficulties under which they labour and make recommendations as to the steps that should be taken by the Union or the States to remove such difficulties and to improve their condition (the order appointing such commission shall define the procedure to be followed by the commission).

It is noteworthy that the noun which the adjective 'backward' (socially and educationally) qualifies is 'classes' and not castes. After Articles 15(2) and 16(2) which totally invalidates religion, race, caste and place of birth as a principle of social exclusion, the terms caste appears only in the limited context of the Scheduled Castes. The terms 'classes' used in Articles 15(4) and 16(4) should not therefore be misconstrued as isomorphic and should not be related with any social reality which the term caste represents. Classes, in other words, should not be defined in terms of caste. But, ironically enough, both the commissions appointed by the Government of India, as well as those appointed by the State Governments to identify the backward classes and recommend measures for the improvement of their lot, used caste as the principal criterion to determine backwardness.

The Kaka Kalelkar Commission appointed by the Government of India which submitted its report in 1953 identified 3,939 castes as SEBs. However, since the commission did not rely on any objective tests to determine backwardness, the Government of India did not accept its recommendations. The Government in fact did not approve of the idea of using caste as a criterion of backwardness, retaining its preference for an economic or means test. The second backward classes commission known as the Mandal Commission which was appointed by the then Prime Minister, Mr Morarji Desai, in January 1979 submitted its report in December 1980. The commission rejected the idea of a means test or any criteria to determine backwardness on view of the language of Article 340. According to the panel, the Article 340 and the reservation envisaged in the Article 16(4) applied only to socially and educationally backward classes and not to economically backward classes. The commission accordingly concluded that: "in view of the permanent stratification of the society in a hierarchical caste order, low ritual caste status has a direct bearing on a person's social backwardness."

Both the commissions, thus, made caste the sole basis for identifying backwardness and in the absence of latest census data on the caste composition of the Indian society, they made use of the 1931 census, the last census to give a castewise break-up of the country's population. This projected the latest percentages of different castes in the total population of the country basing their calculations on the decadal rate of growth of the population. By their hard work the commission produced startling figures. They estimated that in addition to the SCs/STs whose percentage was 22.5, there were 52 per cent SEBC, in India while in Government services and public employment their percentage was only 13 and in plum posts only 4.7. The commission listed 3,743 castes/communities among the Hindus alone as SEBCs.

The report of the Mandal Commission was put into cold storage for several years after its submission in 1980 as the Janta Party, which had appointed it, went out of power before the commission could submit its report. And neither Mrs Indira Gandhi nor Mr Rajiv Gandhi, who headed the successive Governments after the fall of the Janata Government, were inclined to 'play ball with Mandal' as in their opinion the recommendations of the commission had a casteist bias. It actually fell into the hands of Mr V.P. Singh to resurrect the report after 10 years when he became the Prime Minister of the National Front Government. Thus, it was Mr V.P. Singh who announced in Parliament on 7 August, 1990 his government's firm resolve to implement the report, starting with reservation of 27 per cent of the jobs in the Central services and the public sector/undertakings for the SEBCs, in addition to the already existing 22.7 per cent reservation for the SC's and ST's.

The violent backlash against the implementation of the Mandal Commission recommendations which virtually sent the whole of north burning is now a part of history. The Supreme Court in the meanwhile was made to intervene and the operation of the Government notification dated October 1, 1990 was stayed. The development of events eventually saw Mr P.V. Narasimha Rao as the head of the minority Government in 1991, who, following the Supreme Court's directive to the Government to make their stand clear on the Mandal Commission recommendations, announced a new reservation formula in which besides 27 per cent reservations for SEBCs, 10 per cent reservation was given also to the economically backward groups among the Hindus. The formula included also the filling of the unfilled quotas in the services, in the event of non-availability of requisite number of candidates in the poorer sections, by the affluent sections of the SEBCs.

Besides these two national commissions, Gujarat and Karnataka Governments had appointed their own commissions to identify SEBCs in their States. The Rane Commissions in Gujarat used both caste status and income as a basis for inclusion of classes in the list of beneficiaries under Articles 15(4) and 16(4) of the Constitution. The Government of Gujarat accepted the recommendations of the Commissions and raised the reservation of appointments from 30 per cent to 50 per cent. But as this sparked off a fierce agitation, the Government appointed another commission namely the Mankad Commission to examine the matter again.

Similarly, the Karnataka Government had appointed such commissions one of which was headed by Justice O. Chinapppa

Reddy whose report was submitted in April, 1990. The package recommended by the Chinappa Reddy Commission excluded all those from reservation, either of whose parents is/was employed in higher grades (class I or II) of the Government or related services or is a qualified professional (Doctor or Engineer, etc.) paying income-tax or sales-tax or is the owner of more than eight hectares of rainfed dry land or its equivalent and also all those whose parents are graduates. The Commission had also recommended eligibility for the reservation benefit to any member of the SEBCs only on production of a certificate from a Tahsildar issued on affidavit by the parents and by a responsible resident of the locality and punishment by imprisonment upto six months for all those who obtain a false certificate and their accomplices, including the issuing officers extending the limits of punishment to forfeiture of all benefits secured through false certificates.

The Havanur Commission had earlier classified OBCs into: (i) backward communities (15 castes), (ii) backward castes (128 castes) and (iii) backward tribes and recommended 16 per cent reservation for OBC's and 6 per cent for the backward tribes.

A division bench of the Supreme Court of India comprising Justice V.R. Krishna Iyer, Justice R.S. Pathak and Justice Chinappa Reddy way back in 1980 had observed that 50 per cent of the total number of posts should be kept open to attract the best of the nations talent to ensure efficiency of administration through the governing criteria of excellence and quality in the matter of appointments. They, therefore, laid down that the maximum of 50 per cent of the reserved quota for SEBCs and the SCs and STs combined, is fair, reasonable, just and equitable. The Supreme Court in its latest judgement has again laid down that the creamy layer among the SEBC to be determined by each State has to be excluded from the category of those eligible for reservation.

The reservation policy announced by the Government for the SEBCs has come in for a lot of criticism and there is much point in some of the arguments put forward against it. We are not concerned with the politics behind the reservation policy or what has come to be termed as 'Mandalisation of politics'.

Reservation so far as it promotes the welfare of the backward classes or is conducive to their development is welcome, provided it is within the four walls of the Constitution. In other words, if reservations under Sections 16(1) and 16(4) are consistent with the principles of—equality i.e. equality before law or equal protection of the laws (Article 14); non-discrimination by the State against a citizen only on the grounds of religion, race, sex or place of birth (Article 15), equality of opportunity, subject to reservations in favour of the deprived; abolition of untouchability and abolition of titles not being a military or academic distinction (Article 17 and 18) and distributive justice and reasonable classification — then they are all right. Whether the Mandal Commission recommendations are in keeping with the letter and spirit of the Constitutional provisions is not for us to determine. The judgement handed down by the apex court of the country in this matter is the final word as far as the question of their being formally just and fair is concerned. There may be a gap, no doubt, between formal and substantive justice. But in the absence of any foolproof method of bridging the gulf between the two, what is formally just is substantially just too.

Since the court has found reservation of 50 per cent appointments in the services just and reasonable, we have to take it that the reservation package announced by the Government is fair. The only point of contention is whether the 'ritual status' or 'birth' as basis of classification adopted by the Mandal Commission and as accepted by the then Narasimha Rao Government is fair and reasonable.

To say that 'low ritual caste status' has a direct bearing on a person's social backwardness is to support the manner of Lassalle that "Justice is manifest". Nevertheless if it goes awry, the malevolence of its administrators is to blame[6]. This conspiracy theory of historical wrongs has been at the back of all the opinionated ideologies of all modern totalitarian States where a single concept of what is right manifests, justice-prevails and the regime succeeds in suppressing all alternative opinions. And, there is hardly anything to choose except the degree of cynicism between national socialism and Bolshevism, as both try to eliminate casteism and opposition. The danger in a welfare measure based on a conspiracy theory of wrongs, as seems to be the case with the policy of reverse discrimination or political mobilization against particular caste groups, is that it may end up in isolation and elimination of such groups.

However, let us grant that within the framework of the Indian Constitution there is no place, for any such apprehension. In that case we have to see whether and how far is the policy of reverse or positive discrimination in favour of the deprived groups conducive to their development. Development unfortunately has come to be equated with 'empowerment' and upward social mobility, including a steady improvement in ones economic status. It has been argued that empowerment will ensure access to privilege that can provide the necessary leverage to ones' social upliftment.

But development is not empowerment; it is on the other hand becoming according to the law of ones' being. A just and healthy society will ensure that every one is allowed to 'become' and by no misfortune prevented from becoming what he has in him 'to become' i.e. to develop according to his 'psyche' or '*swabhava*'. Equality here lies in hitting the mark or executing the task assigned to the individual according to his natural abilities. No body is more or less equal here except in doing his job more or less skilfully or with greater or lesser degree of excellence. This is not the place to expound the theory of development. If the "unjust" as Aristotle said "is unequal, just is equal, as all men suppose it to be even apart from argument"[7] or if equalities as Rawls said "are to be arranged so that they are both (i) to the greatest benefit of the least advantaged and (ii) attached to offices and positions open to all under conditions of fair equality of opportunity". But then justice and equality cannot be guaranteed in a system based on a cut throat competition for acquisition of power and privilege.

Economic backwardness is a less value loaded concept than social backwardness: less because even though one may differ on what constitutes absolute economic backwardness, there cannot be any two opinions about the meaning of relative backwardness; at least no poor man will detest being considered less affluent than the other. But social backwardness is a culturally relative notion and, therefore, no cultural or social group can be called socially backward by any other group without assuming a false air or superiority.

In fact no caste conceded the cultural superiority over another caste. Nor were castes in India ever lumped together as depressed, or socially backward or forward except when it became politically expedient to classify them as such. During the colonial rule or after independence, 'The Peoples of India' project of the Anthropological Survey of India, has identified 4,635 communities in India using the term community as a substitute for caste. The assumption on which the POI project proceeds is that the Portuguese term 'casta' from which the word 'caste' is derived means 'community'. Castes then are to be treated as communities-organic cultural wholes with their own individual identities. The POI project goes some way in restoring the term 'Jati' to its essential connotation of an organic community.

The development of the so-called backward communities, including the SEBCs, SCs and STs has, therefore, to be viewed independently of the political and economic concessions being extended to them. They must be considered in relation to their traditional 'metier' if the question of their identity and development is to be correctly answered. The traditional 'metier' was an activity or trade which was ones' own and which when properly executed, nourished the whole man — *corpus anima et spirtus*. As against the 'metier', the modern trade or occupation is an activity which is not ones' own but could be of anyone elses that is, which has a market and which one chooses mainly because of its market value. Man's modern trade or activity can nourish only his corpus and not his spirit.

Delinking the development of the so-called backward communities from the political question of their empowerment through measures like protective and reverse discrimination, sociologist will do well to study their history and culture, including the mythic accounts of their origin, which will give them a better perspective to approach the problems related to their development.

In fact their identity was never so much in danger of being wiped out as today by the political moves to homogenize their cultures in the name of empowerment to raise their economic and social status. This is not to suggest that what is being done to improve their lot should not be done; only that it should be done respecting their own cultural and economic aspirations and not out of any political or populist considerations.

NOTES and REFERENCES

1. See especially Domont Louis: *Homo-Hierarchicus-The caste System and Its Implications*, University of Chicago Press, London, 1970.
2. See Srinivas, M.N. *Social Change in India and other Essays*. Even Dr B.R. Ambedkar considers the Sudras as Kshatriyas who had nothing to do with the untouchables. The latter according to him who on account of their conversion to Buddhism had broken off from the villages, had started eating beef and had been declared as untouchables by the upper castes. Dr Ambedkar's own interpretation of the Vedas confers a status on the Sudras as high as that of the Kshatriyas. Thus, there is hardly anything new even in his own interpretation of the Hindu tradition, as the social taxonomy validated by the Vedic episteme which was based on the distinction between the Dwijas and Sudras remains intact in form, Dr Ambedkar only tampers with its contents. See Dr Ambedkar's *'Who were the Sudras'*?
3. See Dhareshwar Vivek: *Journal of Art and Ideas*: No.25-30.
4. The role of caste as a pressure group or what the Rudolfs call a parapolitical community in India, today is increasingly being emphasized even by serious minded social scientists. The behaviour of the caste as a pressure group in the limited context of an election or mobilized political group at the local or national level to exact or bargain a concession in favour from or with the Government in its role as a surrogate caste and not as castes versus caste.
5. We owe this term to Jung, C.G. The 'shadow' according to him is the dark half of the conscious which always thwarts its plan even in his dreams. Man's darker side or shadow, is the female 'anima' and the woman's darker side of 'shadow' the male 'animus'.
6. See, Dahrendorf R.: Uncertainty, Science and Democracy, in *Essays in the Theory of Society*. Routeledge and Kegan Paul., London, p. 248.
7. See, Sivaramaya, B.: *Inequalities and the Law*, Eastern Book Co., Lucknow, 1984, p. 17.

agriculture by providing a piece of land are still not able to cultivate their allotted land properly as to make it fit for their sustenance till the last [illegible]. For instance every Raji (Ban-Raut) family has so far not been rehabilitated on agriculture. Since a considerable number of the Raji families (26.13%) has no land for agricultural pursuits [illegible] the size of the landholding among Rajis is very low (below [illegible] of land) in comparison to the average landholding of other [illegible] U.P. (Bisht, 1993: 102-103). The latest observation (May [illegible] 1994 to June 10th, 1994) conducted for preparing this study [illegible] that even after the period of about half century of independence and in spite of declaring the Rajis as the primitive tribe [illegible] and as the Scheduled Tribe in 1967 [illegible] developmental measures and the welfare policies [illegible] even [illegible] character of Raji tribe. Even today there are families which still dwell in caves and follow the primitive mode of cultivation [illegible] the shifting cultivation [illegible] terrain [illegible] and Kanalichhina [illegible] and [illegible] jungles [illegible] whatever small game they can trap and [illegible] as [illegible] On the contrary the land [illegible] and [illegible] village which was allotted to some [illegible] during [illegible] now completely wasted. Even the Raji families [illegible] left [illegible] only the ashes of their [illegible] their [illegible] past.

[illegible] the rehabilitation scheme [illegible] failed [illegible] of [illegible] significant [illegible] people [illegible] death [illegible] village [illegible] families and the [illegible] the Government under rehabilitation scheme and [illegible] unknown place and, thus, preferred to lead a nomadic life [illegible] today [illegible] so superstitious that they leave their [illegible] and [illegible] their residence treating it ominous particularly when [illegible] casualty of any youngster in the family [illegible] that [illegible] need a proper psychological treatment to banish the [illegible] from their mind rather than any scheme like rehabilitation to restrain their nomadic character.

[illegible] flaw in the rehabilitation scheme is related to its execution pattern. It is often observed that without making any

Two

Impact of Globalization on Tribals

SURENDRA SINGH

Every society in course of its evolution develops unique form of art and culture. In India, different types of tribal clans live in various parts of the country and the village communities inhabited by non-tribal population throughout the nation have been having their typical tribal/folk art and culture. India has been known for its 'unity in diversity' with special reference to the multi culture which its peoples have been following and maintaining despite varied kinds of onslaughts, including cultural invasion by foreign invaders. Jawaharlal Nehru, the builder of modern India (Fanthome and Shaw, 1995: 143) had rightly observed: "India is a cultural unity amidst diversity".[1] He writes further. "The past of India, with all its cultural variety and greatness was a common heritage of all the Indian people (Sharma, 1994: 4)".[2]

Differently viewed by different anthropologists and sociologists, culture is a very wide term denoting all the kinds/patterns of their thinking, feeling, conduct and behaviours. It is so comprehensive that all the various forms of art i.e. drawing, painting, sculpture, song, dance, drama, etc, are included within it. As observed by K.M. Rao (1996 : 191). "The Tribals of our country have fascinating dresses, ornaments and handicrafts, in addition to their rich folklore, folk songs and robust and enchanting folk dances. The complex social organization with associated ritual ceremonies, practices, religious belief systems, faiths and festivals are other inseparable components of cultural heritage of our country".[3] Change is an ongoing process and it must take place whether people want it or not, due to operation of a multiplicity of factors such as political, legal, economic, technological, demographic, forces, etc, societies and cultures do undergo change leading to degeneration and regeneration. However, when the change is evolutionary, spontaneous and natural, changes in art and culture do not produce any kind of cultural upheaval giving shock to the people. But when it is induced in a deliberate, planned and organized manner with specific intention of producing a particular kind of impact, especially with a view to change their ideas, thoughts, likes and dislikes, habits, modes of behaviour and conduct, etc, there is bound to be a drastic and rapid change or a revolution in art and culture, creating an identity crisis in which there is "an acute loss of the sense of one's identity, a lack of the normal feeling that one has historical continuity".[4] (Reber, 1986 : 341).

In the annals of history of India which has been committed to democratic socialism with its goals of equality, justice, liberty and fraternity as clearly stated in the Preamble of the Constitution, a new chapter of liberalization, privatization and globalization (herein after referred to as LPG) began on 24th July, 1991 when the Government of India announced major changes in its industrial policy which *inter-alia* provided for:

(i) delicensing with certain exceptions;
(ii) liberalization of foreign investment and technological participation;
(iii) scrapping of the MRTP regulations pertaining to concentration of power; and
(iv) redefining of the role of public sector.

The natural fall-out of this new policy was globalization which refers to adoption of a global outlook for the business and business strategies aimed at enhancing competitiveness at the global level. Kotler and Armstrong (1996 : 631) have pointed out that : "A global firm is one that, by operating in more than one country, gains marketing, production, R&D and financial advantages that are not available to purely domestic competitors. The global company sees the world as one market. It minimizes the importance of national boundaries and raises capital, source materials and components and manufactures and markets its goods wherever it can do the best job".[5]

In this connection Kotler et.al (1996 : 3) have also observed:

Companies worldwide are not only increasingly sourcing

their components, supplies, and goods from abroad, they are also trying to sell more of their locally made goods abroad. But they are recognizing that to do this well, they cannot do it alone. So they are forming strategic alliances with foreign companies who serve as suppliers, distributors, technological partners, joint-venture partners, even competitors.[6]

Globalization implies the adoption of varied kinds of methods and means, including the use of mass media of communication to bring along changes in attitudes, beliefs, values and patterns of conduct and behaviour so that the products of multinational corporations are purchased by people on a preferential basis as compared to those which are produced by industrial organizations within the country.

Communication as a process of transmission of thoughts and ideas is a *sine qua non* of all the varied kinds of social relationships that may exist in a given society at any point of time. It is through the process of communication that parties involved in any kind of relationship be it primary or secondary, communitarian or associative, come to know not only about the mutual expectations but also about the extent to which these expectations are met.

There are different types of communications such as two-person communication, small-group communication, public communication and mass communication, (Tubbs and Moss, 1977 : 7-13).[7] Mass communication being a special kind of social communication in which the source, instead of working in isolation, operates within a framework of complex organization; communication experiences are rapid and are made public where receivers are large, heterogeneous and anonymous to the source; and the feedback is neither immediate nor complete and is likely to reach a person other than the one to whom it is actually intended (Singh, 1984 : 83-84)[8], is generally used by the corporations operating in different parts of the world.

There is a multiplicity of mass media. The oldest media are the pictures and printed words — drawings, paintings, pamphlets, leaflets, handbills, books, newspapers, magazines, journals, etc., which carry their messages through the sense of sight. Radio is the mass communication medium which transmits messages through the sense of sound. Television and motion pictures as medium of mass communication make use of both the senses of sight and sound - they are audio-visual. (Agee et al., 1985 : 22).[9]

The power of mass media in terms of its influence on people has been a subject of debate some considering that : "The media are quite powerful" (Dennis and Merrill, 1984 : 74-79) while others advocating that : "The media are not so powerful" (Dennis and Merrill, 1984 : 80-83).[10] But the fact remains that mass media like television, radio, newspapers do provide information of varied kinds and create new needs relating to the possession of various consumption goods, especially those which may be instrumental in adding to the comforts and luxuries of people in contemporary materialistic society. Repeated exposure to the media, particularly to audio-visual ones, does reinforce the beliefs, attitudes, values and behaviour patterns which are in conformity with the morals and lessons disseminated through these media. Not only do these media act as reinforcement agents but they also create new beliefs, attitudes, values, skills, and patterns of social conduct and behaviour.

Encouraged by the New Economic Policy announced in 1991, various multinational corporations are making use of various methods, means and media of communication, including aggressive advertising to create a favourable market to promote the sale of their products and thereby to earn profits. Availability of various commercialized programme providing organizations such as Star TV, Zee TV, Sony TV, EL TV, etc, which are giving their programmes on various channels through satellites and making it possible for people to watch programmes of their choice all the twenty four hours has thus provided a fillip to their exposure to new kinds of art and culture. Varied kinds of print media are pouring in different type of printed material of various forms, exposing people to new patterns of art and culture.

Organizations of specifically designed film shows and other wide variety of cultural programmes by government departments, NGOs, etc, aimed at producing a particular kind of impact on people has also played a significant role in exposing people to new patterns of art and culture.

Exposure of rural/tribal population to new patterns of art and culture through varied medium, specially the mass media, particularly radio, television and newspapers, has not only endangered traditional art and culture which used to prevail in rural/tribal society in India, but, it has also created a kind of feeling among rural folk/tribals that perhaps their art and culture are of inferior level as compared to the so-called modern art and culture flourishing in the form of fashion parades, 'Miss India' and 'Miss Universe' contests, Yanni show (organized in Agra), etc., organized under the aegis of highly westernized organizations or at the instance of the so-called broad-minded people, has, therefore, led to a degeneration and decay in rural/tribal art and culture. Tribal/folk dances, songs, art, etc, are being rapidly replaced by their westernized counterparts, mainly because of exposure of the villagers/tribals to mass media like radio/transistors, television, newspapers, books, etc.

Justice Grover (1989:20) has beautifully summarized the role of mass media in these words:

> Turning to mass media, there is quite a common conception that at times they act more like a villain than a beneficial friend because of their destructive influence on our traditional culture. The exaggerated and highly unreal demonstrative effects of consumer goods which are advertised can have a deleterious effect on unsophisticated minds. The marriage scenes that are shown on the TV marked by lavish pomp and show can make the have-nots angry and may particularly affect those who can expect to actualize them either through dowry or by corrupt means and to unprincipled and even prospective criminals. The scenes of violence, crime and drug addiction in stories yielding an ultimate good moral lesson leads to fantasies and ideas which can turn immature persons into callous, brutal creatures who revel in causing pain torture and death.[11]

Singh (1989 : 64) has also pointed out: "knowledge of new methods and techniques of flouting social norms is provided by various means of communication, particularly to young and impressionistic minds, many of whom also venture to put it into practice. Films have played a significant role in this regard.[12]

Pathak (1985:17) while commenting upon the magnitude of violence portrayed through films, has concluded that the content or realism in modern films accounts for only one per cent whereas depicting violence in multifarious forms and regions rates as high as 17 per cent.[13] In this connection Luthra (1985 : 12) has observed that the acts of terrorism, hijacking, sex-scandals, drug abuse and other anti social activities sometimes do borrow from film stories, defective acting and poor censorship standards.[14]

Films and now commercial advertisements on television, have very badly affected dress and fashion. Many young girls and women put on such exciting dresses that it becomes difficult for many young boys to restrain themselves from indulging in eve-teasing and making efforts to take undue liberties with them and a lot of public nuisance is created when these efforts take the form of molestations and rapes.[15] (Singh, 1989 : 65).

In addition to inculcating of unhealthy attitude and values and development of indecent and undesirable behaviour patterns, films and other means of recreation have considerably deformed the traditional art and culture, especially through unwanted eroticism, vulgarity and nudity in songs and dances, and even in dialogues.

As a result of fast decay in cultural values and norms of tribals/villagers, a kind of vaccum has been created particularly because of their inability to fully assimilate the so-called modern values which are alien to them. Today, serious kind of cultural crisis as also economic underdevelopment and exploitation are engulfing the tribal and village communities; and special kinds of efforts are required to promote their desired sociocultural and economic development.

A multipronged strategy is required to be adopted to preserve the intrinsic and valuable facets of tribal/rural heritage, which is full of 'great traditions' and from which several generations have to learn lessons throughout the human history. First and foremost priority should be given to rewrite the textbooks of the schools and colleges to incorporate nicely written lessons on different aspects of tribal/rural art and culture, including their folklore, artistic forms, performing arts, etc, in order to curb the ethnocentric and temporocentric tendencies. This should also be done to promote harmonious integration of various ethnic groups as equal and respectable partners in shaping the destiny of this great country which has shown the way to the entire humanity, teaching the lessons of truth and non-violence. One has to always bear in mind that many traditional patterns of art and culture have evolved over a long period of time in accordance with the requirements of the surrounding environments and all of them are not necessarily useless and out of date, and, therefore, not necessarily the objects to be discarded with any kind of inferiority complex. Planned, conscious, deliberate and organized efforts are required to identify such facets of tribal art and culture as they are in no way harmful to people and society and a national policy on tribal and rural art and culture should be developed in order to promote sustainable development of tribal/rural population and to conserve their ethnic and cultural identity, particularly by incorporating those elements in this policy which may be instrumental in operationalizing the various directives given in the Constitution of India in a systematic and evolutionary manner.

The national policy must envisage such measures as may be helpful in mechanizing the villages and ruralizing the tribal villages so that ultimately the Indian population may be divisible into two broad categories of 'rural' and 'urban'.[16] (Majumdar and Madan, 1994 : 243).

NOTES and REFERENCES

1. Fanthome, Francis and Shaw, D.E.W., Selections from Nehru's *Discovery of India: Concept and Presentation*, Oxford University Press, Delhi, 1995.
2. Sharma, K.N., *Indian Society*, National Council for Educational Research and Training, New Delhi, 1994.
3. Rao, K. Mohan, "Perspective of Tribal Culture", *The Eastern Anthropologist*, Vol. 49, No. 2, April-June, 1996.
4. Reber, Arthur S., *The Penguin Dictionary of Psychology*, Penguin Books Ltd., Harmonds Worth, 1986.
5. Kotler, Philip and Armstrong, Gary, *Principles of Marketing*, Prentice-Hall of India Private Ltd., New Delhi, 1986.
6. Kotler, Phillip, Leong Siew Meng, Ang, Swee Hoom and Tan, Chin Tiong, *Marketing Management: An Asian Perspective*, Prentice-Hall of Simon and Schuster (Asia) Pvt. Ltd., Singapore, 1996.

7. Tubbs & Moss.
8. Singh, Surendra, Communication in Organisations, Unpublished D. Litt. Thesis, Department of Social Work, Lucknow University, Lucknow, 1984.
9. Agee, Warren & Ault, Philip H. and Emery Edwin, *Introduction to Mass Communication*, Herper and How Publishers, New York, 1985.
10. Dennis & Merrill.
11. Grover, A.N., Social Development and Communication, in Loomba, Ram Murti and Singh, Anand Bahadur (eds.), *Report of the National Seminar on Social Development and Communication*, Indian Council of Social Welfare, Lucknow 1989 (Mimeograph).
12. Singh, Surendra, "Positive Negative Impact of Communication on Social Development", in Loomba, Ram Murti and Singh, Anand Bahadur (eds.), op. cit.
13. Pathak, R.L., "Children on Violence in Visuals", *Social Welfare*, Vol. XXXII, No. 8-9, Nov.- Dec., 1985.
14. Luthra, P.N. : "Child Problems in Developing Countries and Mass Media", *Social Welfare*, Vol. XXXII, No. 8-9, Nov.-Dec., 1985.
15. Singh.
16. Majumdar, D.N. and Madan, T.N., *An Introduction to Social Anthropology*, Mayoor Paperbacks, NOIDA, 1994.

Three

Globalization and Tribal Problematique

SATYENDRA TRIPATHI

Liberalization is the catchword of an economy and the economic policy today. There is so much euphoria about it that we tend to ignore the ground realities. It is desirable that an objective and balanced study of this impact of liberalization should be made from the viewpoint of the country so that we do not fall in a blind alley. There is a marked difference between the impact of British influence in the pre-1947 period and influence of developed nations during the post -1947 period. After the break-up of the Soviet Union, a sea-change has occurred so far as the influence of developed nations is concerned. Globalization on a big scale has emerged during this intervening period. The pre-1947 period influenced a small section of this populace but the new phase is now influencing (bulldozing) a very large percentage, thanks to TV and electronic media. In the new phase, consumerism is being propagated along with undesirable moral values while this was not so in the pre-1947 period, since whatever was good in British system was also transmitted, particularly to the spirit of patriotism. Self-confidence was generated in this period but in this new phase this is going to be completely lost.

Liberalization, as the basic strategy guiding the economic reforms in India, aims at the opening up of the economy towards larger international trade, more foreign investment and greater inflow of technology which are served under lesser governmental intervention through controls, licenses and regulations and a greater reliance on undisturbed market signals for resource allocation. This strategy, thus, aims at converting a hitherto introvert, autocentric, import substituting, costly and wasteful economy to an extrovert, export promoting, efficient and competitive economy.

As part of a conscious polity, and also as a result of forces beyond its control, the Indian economy is becoming increasingly globalized. Globalization is a process which involves increasing integration of the domestic economy into the world economy. The influence of globalization is much deeper than mere increase in trade and investment flows between countries. It leads to changes in tastes and preferences of individuals, even their thought patterns and aspirations. Thus, consumption patterns get globalized, wages and incomes across jobs begin to reflect global patterns, institutional structures begin to take shapes recognizable elsewhere in the world, technologies become common and legal governance systems become comparable across countries. There are common concerns for the world population, global environment and a common emphasis on human values.

The globalizing process is not predicted only on such instrumentalities as the World Trade Organization, or the conscious decision of an economy to export and import more. Globalization rules on waves that emanate from the modern technologies of processing and communication of information, technologies of telephone, television, satellites and computers. Transmission of information is far more important than the transhipment of goods across countries and this makes the globalization an inevitable and irreversible process. The option is not 'whether to globalize', but 'how to globalize', not as to 'what we receive from the rest of the world', but also 'what we can contribute'.

Liberalization - A Salient Revolution

If 1947 brought the freedom, through non-violent revolution, 1950 brought basic structural ideological transition in the State's value system and functional agenda "warfare to welfare", "night-watchmanship to kinsmanship", "authoritarianism to democratism", "individualism to communitarianism" and "laissez faire-ism to socialism", 1991 brought into being another salient revolution — a new freedom from the past, orthodox and strait-jacketed ideology and protective economic strategy. Liberalization broke the barrier — it opened up the economy, it exposed the world market, it unleashed competitions, it made India one of the world players. The new policy has in one stroke, brought in an environment characterized by, among others: (1) Decontrol and delicencing, (2) De-bureaucratization, (3) De-nationalization and privatization, (4) Internationalization - fluidity in geo-economic reality, (5) Globalization of competition, (6) Financialization, (7) Technology invasion, (8) Information explosion, (9) Communications revolution, (10) Transitional organizations, (11) Newer skill generation and diversifications, (12) Quality concerns, (13) Time-cost schedulization, (14) Organizational restructurization, and (15) Human administration.

There are many other influencing factors which must follow the trail of liberalization. A recent, fashionable acronym to describe the post - 1991 economic situation is LPG (Liberalization, Privatization and Globalization). If it has offered, through imponderables and unknowns, new challenges, it has also opened up new vistas of opportunities. It not only needs restructuring of organizations to cope with the vastly different environment of operation, but also calls for realignment in the human systems of organizations.

Development of India

The 73rd and 74th Constitutional Amendments mark the culmination of concerns that have dominated India's search for an alternative paradigm of development and of governance. This search, as is well known has not been exclusive to this country. It has, on the other hand, developed on a global scale over the last 20 years when, in the 70s an equity emerged as a prime value in the development process. A grossly iniquitous pattern of development, following an entirely new light on poverty, was attributed to an unequal distribution of political power in society. It is in this context that efforts have been mounted world over to reorder the societal power structure in a way which will permit a realignment of power equations in favour of the oppressed and the excluded. Efforts aimed at revamping and revitalization of the local self-governing institutions have been at the centre of this redistributive strategy, although other, market-based, strategies have also been extensively mooted.

There has been a paradigm shift in development thinking since around mid-70s. The point at the centre of the debate was that development had become capital-centred, as opposed to people-centred. That is by becoming exclusively concerned with producing physical assets, it has pushed people to the periphery. That, in capital-centred development - which was concomitantly technology-dominated, bureaucracy-controlled and a top-down variety - people had been reduced to the status of passive spectators, concerned largely with receiving whatever benefits this professional-dominated model was able to bestow upon them.

Those who advocated alternative development or people-centred development, acknowledged the improvements in physical environment (e.g. new crop varieties, health facilities) which the professional-dominated development had helped to achieve for the rural poor, but it was argued that this was a distorted and self-defeating view of development insofar as the people had been marginalized. That, unless the people and their education and organization became the prime focus, the development effort will come to a nought.

A two-fold argument was advanced. One, poverty is structural in nature with its roots in the economic and political conditions which influence the livelihoods of the rural people. And, in order to tackle this poverty, it is important to provide the rural population a say in controlling the forces which shape their lives and livelihoods. It is important that they are enabled to develop necessary abilities to exercise a voice in developing, designing and implementing as well as in monitoring and evaluating a host of developmental projects where heretofore, under the traditional development strategy, the bureaucrat-expert-professional trio has dominated. The traditional approach in herding people to new projects is conspicuously deficient and wanting. Powerlessness or inability to exert an influence on the decisions which determine access to assets and resources, is an important dimension of poverty, and a cause of it, that poverty does not arise from just lack of physical resources or assets. Two, the State-initiated development process, while benefiting some, has bypassed a large majority of the rural people. There is, in this context, the need to re-examine and redesign the development strategy to ensure that the neglected majority has a chance to benefit from development initiatives.

This reappraisal attributed poverty not just to a violently iniquitous distribution of wealth and resources but equally to an oppressive system of governance in which power was unequally distributed. This it was asserted, prevented the majority from participating in the political processes, and, therefore, this majority has no opportunity to influence the decisions which affect them. The silent majority remains an object of development initiatives.

The recognition of the inadequacies of the traditional capital-centred development and the re-examination which such recognition triggered, has led to the emergence of a new perspective, referred to as 'alternative development'. It is also identified by other labels such as people oriented development, participatory development, bottom-up development, and so on.

The concerns of the advocates of alternative development converge most prominently on the rural poor. The reasons for this need to be dealt further, even if briefly.

Focus on Rural Poor

Development via modernization — an alternative characterization of development initiatives under the traditional paradigm — which undermined virtually all that was 'local' and 'native' and, in the Third World context, mainly rural, working for the process of nation-building through 'imported' knowledge, technologies and capital; engendered a set of socio-economic forces. These forces included industrialization, urbanization, monetization, markets that brought about a rapid destruction of the rural economies and pushed the rural poor to the margins of the political arena where battles for resources and opportunities are fought. In producing what were patently region-specific efforts, e.g., depletion of resources from which the rural poor derived their income and employment, redundancy of traditional skills, failure to incorporate wisdom and indigenous management practices in designing development projects, massive dislocations of populations to accommodate gigantic development projects, rural migration to urban areas. The process of modernization in a very real sense fractured the society, with a handful of people cornering the benefits of development while a large majority remained excluded from achieving access to the same. Because scarce resources (land, industries) became concentrated increasingly in fewer hands, the net benefits of even growing public investments in the concerned sectors were effectively cornered by the rich peasants and entrepreneurs. The actual producers — the tillers of soil (tenant farmers, landless workers) and the industrial workers — did not benefit from this pattern of State intervention. The traditional modernization model, in this sense actually supported and maintained a highly iniquitous and non-egalitarian system.

With the emergence of new structures, institutions and agencies in the rural areas (e.g. markets, bureaucracy, contractors), situation on the ground turned effectively against the rural poor and their control over the local resources - to which previously they had ready access - was transferred to the outsiders, because under the new dispensation, the very same local products must be routed to them via the impersonal market and that too at infinitely higher prices. This is how the rural areas were progressively subordinated to subserve the needs of the urban areas and more generally, interests of the poor (tribals, rural artisans) marginalized to promote those whose economic status provided them ready access to market and political power.

Consequences of Liberalization: Threats to Tribals

The process is neither neutrality of class or nationality. The presumption of liberalization and globalization process as for the entire humanity is abstract and, thus, supra-class and supra-nation/community advocacy is misleading and conceals the dominant class and national interests. Assumed neutrality of liberalization at macro-economic level forbids any serious analysis of the relationship between the State and the structured society, on the one hand and obfuscates the nature of world capitalism and its segmentized impacts on different regions, sectors, classes and communities, on the other. Thus, the entire debate on liberalization must necessarily be coloured by ideological discourses. In a class-structured and community-divided society, any effective policy cannot but have diverse and often contradictory consequences on different classes and communities, as well as on regions and sectors. Perhaps this gives some justification to the title of the present article. Indeed the available evidence suggests that the underdeveloped poorest regions and the oppressed classes and nationalities tend to suffer most and experience absolute economic decline and deterioration in their economic levels and further unequal exchanges of their produces. The attempt here is to deal briefly and a bit ineptly, the consequences of liberalization on the tribal peoples of India, precisely because they happen to be the hardest hit.

Liberalization can only be understood with reference to the so-called globalization and new world order. Both move together. Marginalization is a necessary precondition of liberalization while globalization provides an existential framework in which millions are marginalized and considered dispensable. Speculative finance capital, SAP, adverse terms of trade for primary goods, intellectual property rights and the World Trade Organisation (WTO) allowing the emerging oligopolistic and conglomerate forms of global capitalism to work freely without interference from national governments, demand adequate committed reflection. Likewise, the overriding power of the Brettonwoods institution in controlling the decision-making process of the South, rendering the States as puppets of the global system. In other words, it is not the transitional corporation (TNCs) alone, but the support of multilateral banks and G-7 countries (US, UK, Germany, France, Italy, Japan and Canada) that dictate terms to the sovereign State. These processes are clearly threatening the general viability of the States in their present form and substance, except with respect to law and order so as to facilitate TNCs into their territories. As a reaction, there have been several localized, communal/nationality struggles. But the TNCs use several tactics to avoid any organized militant opposition through high publicity of themselves, co-optation of a few opponent leaders and recalling several unjust international agreements. The two aforesaid propositions on liberalization lead us to turn to the issue of 'why the tribals should be of any special interest for the international capital.'

A common feature shared by most of the tribal habitats is their remoteness and marginal quality of territorial resources. Earlier exploitation of such poor regions was considered both difficult and uneconomic. But the recent technological advancements, unrivalled economic and political strength of world capitalism, the rising powers of new-colonialism and liberalization have created favourable conditions for the invasion and extraction of natural resources from the ecologically fragile regions of the tribal peoples. Accordingly the mammoth capital-intensive development prospects have become distressingly routine and an ever-increasing phenomenon. The zealously extracted water and sub-surface resources accentuated the tribal dispossession. The Land Acquisition Act, 1894, as amended in 1984, is indiscriminately invoked to alienate tribal lands in the name of public interest. No wonder there is a heavy concentration of industrial and mining activities in the central tribal belt. These projects are intrinsically associated with the predatory activities of giant corporations and other project-seeking agencies, connected with an undercurrent of authoritarian and ethnocentric values and political institutions.

It is true that this process predates liberalization, but given the fact that the tribals constituting only eight per cent of the Indian population occupy nearly 20 per cent of the geographical area, containing over 70 per cent of minerals, bulk of forests and water resources — especially the 40 contiguous districts in Central and Eastern India — the region must be the choicest one for neo-colonial interests. Moreover, the limited official articulation of the tribal grievances, the liberal provision of land acquisition under the colonial doctrine i.e. the Doctrine of *Laissez Faire* and its further market-led liberalization, the local Bearing (Acquisition and Development) Act, 1957, that provides no guaranteed compensation to the displaced, weaknesses in the land ceiling legislations, availability of cheap dispensable labour, plus State subsidies on land, water, electricity and raw materials in these areas, attract the imperialists and their agents. Every State government attracts them with more and more concessions, subsidies and tax exemptions to establish massive plants of dams in tribal regions. The strategy has contributed to a greater displacement of tribals and forced them on to low paid, insecure, transient and destitute urban labour market. This is nothing short of ethnocide as at the State level lies their economic and cultural survival.

As part of liberalization and privatization, landownership is shifting from small tribal peasants to private companies, including the TNCs. The land-ceiling laws are slowly getting amended to allow the corporate sectors to acquire vast tracts of land for horticultural, agricultural, floriculture, industrial, vegetable oil seeds production and plantations of tea, coffee, cashewnut, rubber, etc. Trade liberalization will also displace landless tribals, artisans, fishermen and others who would loose their traditional markets and linkages with the agro-sector as well as by the loss of food entitlement.

Anyway, despite intense liberalizational activities in the central Indian tribal belt, the tribal productive employment is negligible. Apart from the provisions of Apprenticeship Act, there is no stipulation for recruitment of displaced tribals in private and joint venture sectors. Meanwhile, they are forced to live in juxtaposition with alien capitalist relations and cultures that often lead to traumatic results. With respect to hydroelectric projects, mostly supported by the World Bank, most of them are located in the tribal regions, but no more than five per cent of tribal lands are arable. In fact, the traditional methods of water harvesting and spreading are rendered non-viable. The World Bank estimates that two million tribals are displaced. No wonder that poverty, malnutrition, mortality, morbidity, debt bondage, serfdom, under-employment and illiteracy among the tribals is higher. Notwithstanding the unfathomable gravity of the sufferings of the involuntarily displaced, India is yet to formulate a national policy for relocation and rehabilitation of project oustees.

Thus, the opening of mines, industries and ecological projects to the TNC's will not only aggravate physical displacement of an increasing number of tribals from their territorial resources but also destroy their very identity. The hegemony erodes the reproduction of collective existence.

Turning to the question of forests, it may be asserted that, for the tribals, forest is an essential part of his or her being and becoming. Whereas, since the colonial period, the State has been depriving the tribals of their ancestral forest resources, the recent imposition of the market liberalization process - with provision to lease out forest lands to private entrepreneurs, expanded social forestry and farm forestry to cater to forest-based industries, etc, - will not only degrade the forest resources but intensify marginalization of the tribal poor. The predatory green capitalism has indeed a sway. Likewise, the State monopoly on forest produce is geared to serve both local and foreign capitalists at the cost of the tribal collectors.

Patents under the WTO regime and its IPR and TRIPs do not merely deny the creativity of tribal peoples' traditional knowledge, but also deny the creativity of nature. The IPR will spread monocultures, herbicides and undermine the tribal concern for bio-diversity. The TRIPs will not legally recognize the tribal knowledge of forestry, medicine and agriculture, whereas the transitional pharmaceutical and agri-business corporations will gain enormous profit.

The TNCs not only dominate in the trade of natural resources and commodities resulting in depletion and degradation of forests, soil, water, marine resources and bio-diversity, but also dominate in activities that pollute the atmosphere, prone to industrial and occupational hazards, toxic wastes and other lethal products.

In short, multilateral banks and the G-7 countries are largely responsible for the brutal impoverishment of the tribals. The denunciation of their macro-economic therapy should not be solely based on moral or ethical grounds, for world capitalism has the innate logic of searching for maximum profit.

Alongwith liberalization, there is the northern cultural invasion. The present mass media and ardent display of films, music, games, toys, T-shirts fantasies, etc, will disseminate global dreams, which cannot but undermine the tribal institutions, values and culture and interpersonal and inter-community relations and their cultural heritage. Global tourism and selective cultural exhibitionism deforms the tribal cultures and displaces people from their heritage. Commodification of cultures according to alien tastes generate an ornamental hoax. As a reaction to the sale of tribal cultures, the domestic religious revivalist organizations and others contribute to their further debasement and destruction.

Prospects and Issues

Despite Constitutional safeguards and government policy of special protection to Scheduled Tribes, insulation of tribal areas from the negative impact of liberalization is not possible. Examples of liberalization elsewhere point to an increase in poverty which exposes vulnerable groups like tribals to greater risk. Recent studies in India point to the adverse effect of the economic reforms like liberalization on the poor, such as increasing prices and reduction in the consumption of nutritious items, like cereals. Transitional costs in terms of increase in prices, increase in unemployment, reduced social services, problem in shifting to new occupations and new relations and equations are going to have maximum adverse effect on the Scheduled Tribes.

Liberalization, privatization and commercialization form a major threat to the economic survival of many tribal groups. Liberalization encourages privatization in the name of curtailment of public expenditure. The Scheduled Tribes are lagging behind despite all Constitutional protection and welfare and developmental measures. They will be adversely affected with the curtailment of public expenditure which leads to privatization of services. Reduction and elimination of subsidies has been built into the liberalization process. Subsidies have been a part of the schemes implemented in tribal areas in view of the poverty and vulnerability of the tribals. Increased cost of foodgrains aggravated by the reduction of subsidies on fuel, power, etc., are affecting the consumption pattern of the people. Anthropologists have pointed out to the effects of commercial crops on nutrition in traditional societies. The thrust on exports lead to further shift towards cash crops resulting in failure to grow sufficient amount of basic food-grains. With large enterprises venturing in having large capital and advanced technology, individual enterprises, such as coffee plantations, orchards, small-scale production units are not going to be viable and competitive. The tribal communities living on ecologically and economically vulnerable areas are more likely to be marginalized. Pressure is already on the dwindling natural resources, neglecting long-term environmental needs. If MNCs enter into tie-ups even with State forest development corporations, it may not be possible to safeguard the interests of the tribals and offer them protection.

Studies have highlighted the plight of the tribals in terms of indebtedness and land alienation with the opening up of tribal areas during the British period. Being largely unskilled, endowed with primitive technologies and poverty stricken, tribals are at a disadvantage to enter into any kind of market, labour market, product market and credit market. Even if they enter, they may not be in a position to receive fair returns.

The existing rural industries are becoming enviable. Disruption of traditional crafts and small-scale industries is predictable as capital efficiency factor throwing out small-scale units. The entry of joint-ventures with multinational participation will be affecting small-scale production because of capital intensive export oriented enterprises. There will be more unemployment as traditional labour intensive small-scale industries will be displaced by new technologies. The new technologies are not going to be labour-intensive and hence will render people jobless. Liberalization of imports is bringing to the doorsteps of the people even basic goods required for their needs of daily use. Consumer tastes and preferences are being influenced by the market. Even in remote areas, processed foods are making inroads. Tribal workers are mostly engaged in the unorganized sector, like forest works, casual labour in factories, construction work, laying of roads, etc. Effects of liberalization include increase in unemployment and rise in the number of those employed in unorganized sector. The international market orientation is not likely to open up many opportunities because of the existing social clauses and sanitary measures under GATT. Work participation among Scheduled Tribe women is very high even when compared to Scheduled Caste women. Experience shows that whenever new opportunities arose, women did not get their due. Women are likely to be displaced from traditional roles which gave them a more or less equal status with men.

The tribal groups are known for their collective spirit in all spheres of life and this is steadily being eroded. The implications of a shift from common rights to private rights need to be considered with regard to tribal communities. The preamble of TRIPs Agreement states that intellectuals property rights are recognized only as private rights. This excludes all kinds of traditional collective knowledge, ideas, and innovations of the tribal population.

Conclusion

Therefore, the explicitly market-friendly liberalization process has little to offer to the tribal people and their regions, except in the negative. The renewed visibility of the tribal question, will hopefully speak the collapse of the major political and economic ideologies. And those looking forward for an alternative paradigm should assess the issue in the matrix of the decisive struggles against imperialism and their domestic allies aimed at a viable vision of socio-economic-cultural and ecological harmony. The task is formidable but unavoidable. To alter the structural reality, we need an appropriate political programme, overhauling and also overthrowing the economic and political power of the dominant classes and nations.

Four

Tribal Development: A Case Study of Himalayan Tribes of Uttarakhand

B.S. BISHT

Today it has become a moot question, whether the plans, strategies and the programmes adopted for the overall development of the tribals are relevant and adequate or is there any need to reformulate the same as to make them more and more suited to the tribals and in the realm of their development.

Keeping in view the question, the present study aims at producing an evaluative scientific note on the existing level and the nature of the tribal development, particularly with reference to the developmental measures adopted under the Constitutional frame of reference for the tribal communities. For the attainment of the scientific results the paper has been prepared on the following hypothesis formulated with the help of the past experiences, existing literature related to the prevailing conceptual analysis of the development paradigm and the relevant scientific findings presented by the previous scholars on the basis of their studies conducted on tribal development in different times.

Hypothesis

"The existing development paradigm which is predominantly economic in nature will be incompatible with the desired objectives of overall development unless it does not take its cues from the humane dimensions and the ecological background of the given community."

To verify the hypothesis, this study is based on the impacts of the various protective/supportive measures, family-oriented programmes, infrastructural developmental plans and the reservation policies meant for the tribal communities namely; the

Khasas, the Bhotiyas, the Rajis (i.e. the hill tribes) and the Tharus & Buxas (the plain tribes) of Uttarakhand Himalayas in Uttar Pradesh. The first-hand field information, collected through participant observation about the various aspects of the tribal communities under reference and the secondary information available in different public records, governments reports, books, journals, etc, are scientifically used to substantiate the hypothesis.

Ecology of the Region

Along with the northern part of Uttar Pradesh, the region of Uttarakhand, has an area of 51,122 sq. kms. Geographically, the region can be divided into three parts namely, the greater Himalaya, the lower Himalaya and the sub-Himalaya. The height of the different parts of the region ranges from 300 m to 7,800 m from the sea level. Except the Tarai Bhabar's plain belt of Dehradun and Nainital district and some of the river and foothill plain valleys, the whole of the region is uneven in altitude, inaccessible and abstruse. The region consists of eight hill districts namely Almora, Nainital, Pithoragarh, Chamoli, Paurhi, Tehri, Uttar Kashi and Dehradun. The first three districts constitute Kumaun Commissionary while the rest five districts form Garhwal Commissionary. The region is the main concentration of the tribal population as all the five Scheduled tribal communities of the State are the habitants of this very region. The district wise area and the break-up of the tribal population is given in Table 4.1.

The region is politically important, as it is situated on the fringe of the two political communities i.e. the Nepal and the Tibet respectively in east and north. The eastern-most district of the region i.e. Pithoragarh makes the international boundary with Nepal in the east while the western part of the region is demarcated by Himachal Pradesh. The northern parts of Uttar Kashi, Chamoli and Pithoragarh district jointly constitute the international boundary with Tibet (China) in north, while the southern boundary of the region is constituted by the district boundaries of Saharanpur, Bijnor, Moradabad, Rampur, Bareilly and Pilibhit. The region of Uttarakhand is famous for its natural beauties of tourists spots, sacred rivers, lakes and snow covered mountain peaks on the one hand and diversified cultural complexes of various ethnic groups in the varied geographical and corresponding sociocultural varieties of the region on the other. Due to topographical reasons the climate of the region differs vastly from one place to another.

TABLE - 4.1
DISTRICT-WISE BREAK-UP OF THE AREA AND THE POPULATION OF UTTARAKHAND : (1992 : STATISTICAL PERIODICAL KUMAUN & GARHWAL REGION).

Name of the Region	*Districts*	*Area Sq. Km.*	*Total Population*	*Scheduled Tribe*			*Percentage*
				M	*F*	*Total*	
Kumaun	Almora	7023	836617	1405	1334	27399	0.32
	Nainital, (including U.S. Nagar)	6792	1540174	46313	43707	90020	5.84
	Pithoragarh, (including Champawat)	7217	566409	9181	9132	18383	3.23
Garhwal	Chamoli	9125	454871	4982	5291	10273	2.25
	Paurhi	5440	682535	861	641	1502	0.22
	Tehri	4421	580153	266	349	615	0.10
	Uttarakashi	8016	239709	1205	1095	2300	0.95
	Dehradun	2088	1025679	44510	39566	84076	8.19
Grand Total		30090	5926147	108723	101115	209838	3.54

The temperature of the extremely northern snow covered mountain peaks always remains below freezing point, while the lower hill slopes have temperate climate with approximately 300-cm annual rainfall. During summer, there is sometime heavy hail falling in the hilly terrain of the region. But climatic conditions of the Tarai Bhabar belt of the region are quite different. Here, during summer it is extremely hot while it is very cold in winter. The rainfall ranges between 152 and 229cm per year. With the variations of the land structures and climatic conditions in the region, there grow a variety of species of flora and fauna. Thus, the region contains diversified ecological features and geographical conditions, with a number of ethnic groups domiciled with their peculiar cultural traits in different parts of the region. The people from different castes, creeds, class and race form the distinct cultural complex of the region and the tribal culture is one of the manifestations of its distinctiveness (Bisht, 1994: 18-21).

Habitat, Ethnography and Sociocultural Traits of the Tribal Communities

The tribal communities under reference with 2,09,838 population are scattered over seven districts of Uttarakhand. The district and the blockwise distribution of the tribal population of Uttarakhand is given in Table 4.2.

TABLE - 4.2
THE DISTRICT AND THE BLOCK-WISE DISTRIBUTION OF SCHEDULED TRIBAL POPULATION

District	*Block*	*Bhotiyas*	*Buxas*	*Tharus*	*Rajis*	*Jaunsaris*
Pithoragarh	Dharchula	8004			168	
	Munsyari	8192				
	Didihat	584			99	
	Berinag	542				
	Kanalichhina				71	
	Champawat				48	
	Bina	605				
	Total	17927 (52.21%)			386 (100%)	
Almora	Kapkot	2289				
	Garurh Baijnath	137				
	Bageswar	292				
	Takula	21				
	Total	2739 (7.98%)				
Nainital	Kathgharia	265				
	Kashipur		156			
	Bajpur		9426			
	Gadarpur		10148			
	Ramnagar		1250			
	Sitarganj			26878		
	Nainital	220				
	Khatima			41677		
	Total	485 (1.40%)	20980 (72.72%)	68555 (100%)		
Uttarkashi	Bhatwari	2124				
	Rajgarhi	176				
	Total	2300 (6.70%)				
Chamoli	Joshimath/ Badrinath	10273				
	Total	10273 (29.92%)				
Tehri	Tehri	615				
	Total	615 (1.79%)				

(Contd.)

District	*Block*	*Bhotiyas*	*Buxas*	*Tharus*	*Rajis*	*Jaunsaris*
Pauri Garhwal	Dogadda		1502			
	Total		1502 (5.20%)			
Dehradun	Chaukrata					40876
	Kalsi					36830
	Doiwala		1285			
	Sahaspur		5085			
	Total		6370 (22.08%)			77706 (100%)
Grand Total		34339	28852	68555	386	77706

According to the territorial groupings, (Burman, 1972:39) the tribal communities of Uttarakhand may be classified as the tribes of the sub-Himalayan region of north and north-west India. The ethonographic notes of various eminent scholars depict that the Mongoloid racial traits are very common among the Bhotiyas, Tharus, Buxas and Rajis while the Khasas or the Jaunsaris belong to the Mediterranean racial stock. In particular, the Bhotiyas who have been residing alongside seven river valleys, after which they have derived their names Joharis, Darmias, Vyansis, Chaudansis, Marchhas, Tolchhas and Jads are not of the common origin (Chatterjee, 1975: 138). It is, however, irrefutable that the Bhotiyas are of the Mongolian origin and belong to the 'Sino-Tibetan' language family (Bisht, 1992:20). The physical appearance and the dialect they speak, evidently show their social balance with Tibetans, the most representative group of the Mongolian stock. Tharus, the habitants of Nainital Tarai, claim Rajput origin on the mother's side and Bhil on the father's, but the Mongolian features are definite among them and even the skin colour is yellow brown and oblique eyes are numerous (Majumdar, 1942: 33). Even today, inspite of the intermingling of the various ethnic groups, there are every possible traces of countenance and physical features having semblance to the Tharus of Mongolian origin (Bisht, 1994:30). Though the Buxas, the aboriginals of Tarai plain of the region, claim that they belong to Panwar clan of Dharanagar, yet they do not reflect on any particular clue in their countenance and physique to trace their racial origin. Appearance wise an average Buxa possesses an average height and is stout by built. Both the male and female are of wheatish or dark complexion with broad face, oblique eyes, flat nose, thick lips and black hair. The beard and moustaches of Buxas are very scanty. Such a countenance and the physique eventually gives no clue of the particular racial origin. It is rather an appearance of a mixed racial trait which came into existence as an outcome of the mixtures of different ethnic groups in Uttarakhand in remote past (Bisht, 1994: 33-34). Similarly, the Ban Raut or the Rajis, the modern representatives of the Raj Kirat has the racial mixture of the Tibetans and the Khasas (Atkinson, 1882:365-66), while Majumdar has related them with Mongolian affinity (Majumdar, 1944:148). But today no Mongolian traits can be observed in the countenance and physique of Rajis. They are very much like the low Hindu castes in countenance and unlike to that of Bhotiyas. It appears that the medley of different ethnic elements for ages has caused the disappearance of the original racial elements among Rajis (Bisht, 1992:17). It is, however, debatable that, they at present exhibit a mixed racial trait of Aryo-Dravidians and Mongoloids in common. Besides this, Khasas the polyandrous people, despite some intermixture with Mongoloids of the Upper Himalayas or with the Doms of the lower region, are clearly distinguishable from the 'Proto-Australoid' or Mongoloids and form the bulk of the tribal people with the true Mediterranean features (Majumdar, 1940).

Thus, we observe that the tribal communities of Uttarakhand Himalaya differ from one another in racial traits as well as in language, social organization, cultural patterns and economy. Yet, they all regard themselves as Hindus by religion. The close familiarity with the scholarly references of the early academician prove the Bhotiyas and the Khasas have been the herdsmen, and the Bhotiyas in particular, were the itinerant traders who with the help of animals like sheep, mule and Jhibus (Yaks) conducted international trade between India and China. On the contrary, the Tharus and the Buxas, the omnivorous people of Tarai-plain, are known as the agriculturist tribes, while Rajis, the cave-dwellers are still known for their nomadism and the corresponding way of life.

Plans, Strategies and Programmes of Tribal Development

For centuries, the tribal population of Uttarakhand has persisted in the forest and isolated terrains with its age-old patterns of life and the means of subsistence. In view of their socio-economic backwardness, the welfare Government of free India by its Constitutional Order 1967, declared them as the Scheduled Tribes. Since then, all possible efforts have been made through various developmental agencies of the Government for the socio-economic development of the tribals.

In reality, the concept of tribal development is not new. The past experience and the close familiarity with the history of tribal development process prove that the existence of the 'Adivasi' or the 'aboriginals' some of them in the nineteenth century onward, were constitutionally recognized as the Scheduled Tribes or the primitives in order to uplift their socio-economic standard as to bring them together in the mainstream of national life, was of course acknowledged during all the periods of the entire historical era and the concern for their well-being may be traced as far back as Maurya empire. For a long time the tribals and the areas of their habitations remained inaccessible due to the lack of communication and transportation. The Britishers were, however, the first to administer a planned and systematic policy for the administration of the tribal areas but with various vested interests in mind. In fact, they never wished to bring the tribals into the mainstream of the national life, since the mode of tribal administration was basically law and order oriented and also they wanted to keep the tribals isolated from the mainstream of society. It was their primary object to exploit the forest products and to use the forest for the defence and security purposes. Thus, in view of the vested interests in mind they tried to make accessible the tribal regions by keeping their inhabitants isolated. Later on they started providing some relief to the poor and downtrodden tribals but their attitude always remained as usual. In post-Independent India the entire approach towards tribal problems underwent radical changes. The late Jawaharlal Nehru, the first Prime Minister of free India, had deep sympathy for the tribals. Viewing the overall development of tribals, he then laid down the foundation of the new development policy under the Constitution of free India and stated that the development in various fields such as communication, medical facilities, education and better agriculture should be pursued. In view of the overall development of some of the tribal groups the Constitution of India has specified some tribes as the 'Scheduled

Tribes'. In the list of 'Scheduled Tribes' prepared in 1950, the primitiveness and backwardness were the tests applied for specifying a 'Scheduled Tribe'. The main characteristics which are common to all the 'Scheduled Tribes' are; (i) tribal origin; (ii) primitive way of life; (iii) habitation in remote and less easily accessible areas and (iv) general backwardness in all respects (Chandra, 1968: 27-28). Under the Article 342 of the Constitution of India, the President, may with respect to any State or union territory and where it is a State, after consultation with the Governor, thereof, by public notification, specify the tribes or tribal communities or parts of or groups within tribes or tribal communities which shall for the purposes of this Constitution be deemed to be Scheduled Tribes in relation to that State or Union territory, as the case may be (Constitution of India, 1986: 117). Thus, for the Scheduled Tribes, as constitutionally specified, the Constitution has also prescribed protections and safeguards with object of promoting their socio-economic and educational interests and removing their social disabilities they are subject to. The safeguards contained in different Articles and the Schedules of the Constitution are as follows :

(i) The Article 46 of the Constitution has the provision for the promotion of educational and economic interest of SCs and STs and other weaker sections and declares that the State shall promote with special care the educational and economic interests of the weaker sections of the people and in particular, of the Scheduled Castes and Scheduled Tribes and also protect them from social injustice and all forms of exploitation (1986:15).

(ii) The Article 244(1) of the Fifth Schedule of the Constitution has the provision as to administration and control of Scheduled areas and Scheduled Tribes. Part 'B' (4) of the same Article has also the provision for 'Tribes Advisory Council' to advise on such matters pertaining to the welfare and advancement of the Scheduled Tribes in the State as may be referred to them by the Governor. Part B (95-2a) has also regulations to prohibit or restrict the transfer of land by or among members of the Scheduled Tribes in such areas (1986: 166).

(iii) The Articles 330, 332 & 334 of the XVI Part of the Constitution have the provision for the reservation of seats for SCs and STs in the House of People and in the legislative assemblies of the States (1986:113-114).

(iv) The Article 335 defines the claims of SCs and STs to service and posts (1986:115).

(v) The Article 338 has special provision for the Special Officer for SCs and STs . The Article defines that: (a) there shall be a special officer for the Scheduled Castes and Scheduled Tribes to be appointed by President; (b) it shall be the duty of the special officer to investigate all matters relating to the safeguards provided for the SCs and STs under this Constitution and report to the President upon the working of those safeguards at such intervals as the President may direct and the President shall cause all such reports to be laid before each House of Parliament (1986:115).

Thus, within the frame, reference of the various Constitutional provisions and the Government orders passed from time to time, the State Government of UP, like other States and Union Territories is constantly striving to frame the policies regarding the various protective and supportive measures, family-oriented programmes and reservation facilities and also trying to implement them effectively and tactfully as to achieve the ultimate goal of allround development of the tribals. But, how far the developmental policies and the sustained efforts of the Government have been successful in achieving the desired objectives, the following delineation presents an objective appraisement of this concern.

Development schemes

Rehabilitation of Landless Tribals on Agriculture

Under the general scheme of rehabilitation, there is a provision of apportioning a piece of land for agricultural purposes to the landless tribals at their habitations, but the field observations exhibit that the results of the efforts made under the rehabilitation scheme can not be cited positively as; (i) all the landless tribal families have not been allotted the land for agricultural purposes so far; and (ii) the tribal families which have been rehabilitated on agriculture by providing a piece of land are still not able to cultivate their allotted land properly as to make it fit for their sustenance as the land is fallow. For instance every Raji (Ban-Raut) family has so far not been rehabilitated on agriculture. Since, a considerable number of the Raji families (26.13%) has no land for agricultural pursuits even the size of the landholding among Rajis is very low (below 1 acre of land) in comparison to the average landholding in other parts of UP (Bisht, 1993: 102-103). The latest observation (May 16th, 1994 to June 10th, 1994) conducted for preparing this study also proves that even after the period of about half century of independence and in spite of declaring the Rajis as the primitive tribe in 1965, and as the Scheduled Tribe in 1967, the various development measures and the welfare policies could not restrain even the nomadic character of Raji tribe. Even today there are Raji families which still dwell in caves and follow the primitive pattern of cultivation i.e. the shifting cultivation in the hilly and forest terrains of Dharchula and Kanalichhina blocks and subsist on the jungle products, whatever small game they can trap and survive as the landless labourer. On the contrary, the land in Madanbori and Bhaktirwa village, which was allotted to some Raji families during 70s is now completely wasted. Even the Raji families have left these villages, only the ashes of their abodes make the clue of their settlements in past.

In fact, the rehabilitation scheme is in itself the cause of its failure. It has no commensurating functional and motivational significance to the superstitious people like Rajis. With the untimely death of some persons caused due to landslide in Madanbori village they left their houses and the agricultural land allotted by the Government under rehabilitation scheme and fled to some unknown place and, thus, preferred to lead a nomadic life. Even today the Rajis are so superstitious that they leave their abodes and the place of their residence treating it omnious particularly when there is a casualty of any youngster in the family. It appears that first they need a proper psychological treatment in banishing the superstitions from their mind rather than any scheme like rehabilitation to restrain their nomadic character.

Another flaw in the rehabilitation scheme is related to its execution pattern. It is often observed that without making any assessment of its agricultural prospects, the land which is allotted to the people after sometime does not give full satisfaction to the allottees because of its unfavourable agro-climatic conditions and low, insufficient productivity and, thus, ultimately compells them to leave in search of a new suitable place. Recently, the migration of ten Raji families from their age-old forest habitations to the Tarai plain of Tanakpur in Nainital district, is a living example.

Agricultural Development

The economy of the tribes under reference, largely depends on agriculture which is by and large practised on primitive lines. Today about 90 per cent of the tribal working force is engaged in agriculture and allied occupations. This dependence on agriculture is existing not because it is highly remunerative but because other sectors of the economy are either absent or inadequately developed in the tribal areas. The major limiting factors for agricultural development are: (i) lesser area for cultivation, (ii) unfavourable agro-climatic conditions (particularly in high hills of tribal habitations), (iii) unavailability of irrigation facilities and (iv) the primitive way of cultivation pattern. Thus, in order to provide a proper conceptual framework for developing agriculture sector, various plans according to the suitability of the corresponding tribal areas have been launched with considerable financial outlay. For instance, in Bhotiya tract the main emphasis was given in the promotion of herb cultivation and also for some beans like soyabeans and *rajma*. For its viability, an essential financial assistance was also provided under various schemes like land development, Gul construction (minor irrigation) and also for the chemical fertilizers and pesticides. In Rajis areas too, the Government for promoting agricultural potential, has also provided subsidy for improved agricultural implements, soyabean cultivation, horticulture development and fertilizers and pesticides. While in Tharwat and Buxar (i.e. the habitation of Tharu and Buxa tribe) areas, the main emphasis was given in the cultivation of high yielding varieties of major cereal crops, oilseeds and sugar cane. For this purpose almost all possible facilities like irrigation, establishment of seed and fertilizer centres, organization of plant protection measures, establishment of processing units of raw materials available and creation of proper marketing facilities for marketable surplus of agricultural produce, etc, were made available in the tribal areas.

But so far as the provision of land development and 'Gul construction' (minor irrigation) is concerned, the real target-oriented areas are still depriving these facilities. For instance, in order to develop the tribal land of high altitude, there is a provision of making terraces on the steep hill terrains with the help of the supporting walls. But in real practice it is observed that the beneficiaries in general cases took the subsidies under the land development scheme and spent it on some other items like staple food, narcotics, alcoholic drinks and beverages, providing false report to the concerning department for the proper utilization of the grants-in-aid. In the next season, the same beneficiaries again applied for the subsidy by stating that the supporting walls of the terraces have eroded due to the heavy rainfall in the rainy season. While the personnels bearing the responsibilities of the execution of this scheme seem not so sincere even for the location survey due to the inaccessibility of the tribal habitations. In some other cases it is also observed that owing to the communication gap between the real beneficiaries and the personnels, the subsidy is sanctioned to those people who of course do not belong to the target-oriented families and the benefit, thus, could not reach the real hands with the result, the problem of land development in general is still at the same place as before.

The same is the case of 'Gul Construction' scheme. It is observed that the 'Guls' have been constructed only in those areas where the traditional natural source of water supply through traditional 'Guls' is already in practice, while the areas lacking natural sources of water supply are still away from the irrigation facilities. Most of the land particularly in the Khasa, Raji and Bhotiya tracts is, therefore, non-irrigated so far. In this way the 'Gul Construction' scheme as such, has no viability to the tribal areas in general. Even in the Tarai plain areas, where there is a provision for making available the artisan tubewells for irrigation purposes, the Tharus and the Buxas in general are still deprived of this irrigation facility not because of the unavailability of the artisan tubewells there, but because of their improper upkeep and maintenance. For this reason the beneficiaries as well as the personnels are responsible. As the former do not bother about the proper upkeep of the artisan tubewells assuming it to be an exclusive duty of the latter while the latter always expect the 'Subidha Shulk' as an incentive from the tribals for putting the wells in working order. Thus, due to the lack of work spirit, sincerity and positive outlook of both the parties, which is an evident outcome of the improper socialization, the scheme has failed. Most of the artisan tube wells throughout the Tarai tribal areas are not in functioning order today due to this.

Besides this, there is also a Government provision for providing improved agricultural implements, seeds, chemical fertilizers and pesticides on subsidized basis in order to boost the agricultural production in tribal areas. But the field observations in general have contrary experiences about these subsidized items. As there is no receptivity of the majority of the tribal people towards these items because till date the tribal population particularly living in the farthest remote and inaccessible hill areas could not make up its mind in favour of this scheme. It is really difficult, if not impossible for the tribals to approach the officials concerned and more complicated is the pattern of fulfilling the formalities for getting these subsidized items. Hence, they prefer to be confined to their age-old pattern of agriculture rather than to invite the troubles to be shoved about. The majority of the tribals are still of the opinion that these items are incompatible with the agro-climatic and the land formation of the tribal areas of high altitude. That is why they do not wish even to test the feasibility of these items. For example, Rajis are accustomed to cultivate with their crude type of hoes and spades and, therefore, the improved agricultural implements are meaningless to them. However, some Raji families were granted aid for this purpose which they spent for the fulfilment of their daily needs. Because the so-called improved agricultural implements were available neither in the local markets nor known to the people. As a result, the subsidized amount could not be adequately utilized for the purpose it was really sanctioned (Bisht, 1993:10). More so, the Rajis are skilled and experienced in using the burnt ashes of shrubs and the organic manure as the fertilizers and so the chemical fertilizers have no meaning for them as they may scorch the crops. Besides, the hill tribes have no liking for the improved varieties of seeds as they are not mentally prepared to take the risk even for an initiation of sowing the improved quality on trial basis. For instance, the Rajis in place of Soya cultivation still prefer to grow a crude variety of traditional soya called 'Bhatt' as a supplementary crop with maize and 'Kodan'. While the Bhotiyas prefer to grow 'Palthu' and 'Uwa', the traditional crops rather than the 'Soyabean' and other crops of improved variety. The general opinion of the people is that the crops of improved variety, other than their traditional ones have no adaptability with the agro-climatic conditions of the tribal areas, while the 'Soya' as such is astringent in taste and so they do not prefer its growth. Even in Tarai tribal areas where the agro-climatic conditions are favourable for these items, the majority of the tribal population consisting of the small and the marginal farmers in particular do not have receptivity with those items. So far as the acceptability of improved seeds is concerned, the Buxas and the Tharus of the Tarai plain are not at all ready to accept the condition laid down by seed providing agencies and, thus they use their own agricultural produce even for sowing the seeds. Only a handful of big tribal farmers have shown their acceptability towards these items, but their number is decreasing day by day with the fragmentation of landholdings due to generation growth.

Pesticides have functional importance for all agriculturists in protecting their crops from the destruction caused by the infection of pestiferous pests. But in spite of being cent per cent subsidized, the use of pesticides throughout the tribal areas is almost nil for them. It is so, not because of the fury of pests but by the wrath of the supernatural being or the evil spirits. Therefore, they prefer to follow the traditional method i.e. the superstitious device, sorcery and enchantment, etc., to eradicate the pestilent seasonal crop diseases. For instance, among Tharus, "Bharare" the traditional priest has the skill to throw a magic spell to the soil infected by pestilential diseases and it is assumed that unless there is effect of these magical verses, the pests causing crop diseases will not be effective. Even, they have the tenets that the birds and the beasts can never harm the standing crops by the effect of the magic practices done by the 'Bharare'. The birds can fly over the field but will never sit on the crops, the beast may come around the fields but not harm the crops unless there is the effect of the magical practices. But whenever any person tries to drive off the birds or to shunt away the beasts by beating drums or by making hullaballoo, from the fields the effect of the magical spell vanishes and this would harm the crops in the near future. Such erroneous assumptions and postulations have nullified the use of the pesticides and other means of protecting the crops from pests, birds and beasts.

For tribes there is a general scheme of providing subsidized loan for horticulture development purposes. In every Annual Plan there is a certain financial outlay meant for this end. But the field observations show that in spite of favourable climatic conditions and the special schemes like soil testing, soil preservation and plant protection nothing has been done in this sector throughout the tribal areas. For example, in the Bhot tract there are many conditions suitable for herb cultivation, the Government through its various schemes is also desirous to promote this sector but the tribal people seem reluctant and pessimistic towards this long-term process. Similar is the case of the Rajis. There are also suitable agro-climatic conditions particularly for yielding some fruits like peach, pears, apricots, etc, but the poor people have no interest in this sector, because this sector does not provide any immediate return to the poor Rajis whose everyday labour is the base of setting their hearth on. Similarly other tribal communities under study, do not have any interest towards horticulture development. However, the most interesting aspect is that, the horticulture scheme still exists in the area.

Housing Scheme and the Tribals

In order to achieve the object of overall development of the tribals, the government has another scheme for providing necessary assistance to the houseless tribal families for constructing *pucca* houses. In every Annual Plan a certain outlay meant for providing some shelter i.e. the *pucca* house to the houseless tribal families, is made to achieve the target. For this purpose, an outlay of Rs. 3,000 was fixed during the seventies as the cost of the house, which now due to the increase in cost of the building materials has been raised to Rs, 10,000 per house. But the field observations exhibit that every houseless tribal family has not been able to get the necessary assistance for constructing a house. There is still great variation in housing conditions within every tribal community under reference. Some well-off tribal families hardly manage the essential material for constructing their hutments. For instance, only the 50% Raji families have owned *pucca* houses so far while the rest families dwell either in their selfmade hutments or sometimes take shelter in the caves located in the contiguous rocks of their habitations. The same is the condition of the majority of the Koltas in Jaunsar Bawar, Bhotiya Harijans and the Bhotiya artisans as well as of the Buxas and Tharus who generally construct their own hutments. But that part of the tribal population is facing harassment even for procuring the wooden logs to erect the structure of the hut and procuring the grass to thatch the roof due to the legal ban laid down by the forest department. In the 'Buxar' and 'Tharuwat' tribal areas the species of grass i.e. the 'Bharai', 'Dabaina' and 'Jhau' which used to be available in forest and swamp areas of the Tarai have disappeared with the disappearance of the swamp areas (on account of decreasing the water level), and the plantation system followed by the forest department.

It doesn't mean that the target-oriented families are not getting necessary assistance under housing schemes. They do avail it but (i) the improper utilization pattern of the subsidy; (ii) lack of technical knowhow and the managerial capacity of the beneficiaries; (iii) unavailability of building material within the approach of the tribal areas; and (iv) the apathy and the lack of supervision of the concerning department, have posed some unavoidable impediments in the smooth running of the housing scheme in tribal areas. In most of the cases it is observed that the beneficiaries have failed in producing proper utilization on account of the first instalment of the subsidized grant. This causes failure in receiving the next and the final instalment of the grants-in-aid, because of which the construction of houses remains almost incomplete which after some time collapses due to heavy rainfall and other causes. Today a number of incomplete houses can be viewed in Raji settlements. Even the condition of the *pucca* houses constructed completely under housing schemes is pitiable and rather hazardous, because the material used in the construction of these houses always remains of low quality. In general the beneficiaries themselves erect the walls by laying the hard stones with clay. The outer part of the walls are unplastered, which, within the short period of time fall down into pieces and demand repair work. But due to the lack of proper upkeep and repair, the house collapses and the family again steps down to its original hutments.

On the contrary the superstitious nature and primitive mental set-up of the Rajis, which ascertain the nature of their stay in any place, are the responsible factors to a very large extent of the state of their houselessness. There are still a number of *pucca* houses throughout the Raji settlements left desolated not because they are not worth living but because these houses have been labelled the stigma of being ominous for taking the lives of the youngsters particularly of the infants. Therefore, the Raji families prefer to accommodate themselves in a suitable place may be in their selfmade huts or the caves, rather than occupy any *pucca* house of omnious nature.

Animal Husbandry

Animal husbandry is an important subsidiary and supportive unit in agricultural economy in general and in some tribal economy in particular. For instance, the Khasas are known for keeping the sheep, horses and the milching cattle like cows and buffaloes, while the Bhotiyas are famous for sheep rearing and also for raising the mule, horse and the yaks as transport animals. In the post -Independent India, the Government has made a scheme for providing different animals of different varieties to the tribals according to the viability and the need of the people. The Government has also come out with a policy to facilitate the natural services in the tribal areas for improving the breed of local cows and buffaloes by providing a Jarsi bull and a Murra bull respectively because there was no artificial insemination center available in the tribal areas. Similarly, in order to achieve the objective of augmenting the sheep population, the Government has a scheme for providing subsidized sheep flock with a ram to the beneficiaries. But the field observations are still contrary in comparison to the schemes and the financial outlays ascertained for this purpose. The beneficiaries are always inclined to achieve the subsidized benefits both in kind and cash but never succeeded in getting the commensurable results. It is so because of the in-acceptability of the schemes by the tribals. For example, an aged and well educated Bhotiya tribal man narrated that in order to increase the quality of wool, the Government had a scheme of distributing an Australian breed of long tailed merino sheep flock in Bhot tract, but the Bhotiyas who were Hindu by religion, could not accept this breed of the long tailed sheep, only because of its very much resemblances with that of the calf. As the local proverb i.e. *'Sag Dhowe Bhat'* means the sheep (*Sag*) i.e. the vegetable, being a transport animal carries (*Dhowe*) the rice (*Bhat*), proves the multipurpose uses of the sheep. As long as it is alive it earns the money for the masters and when it dies it becomes the meal for them. But the long tailed sheep resembling with calf cannot be used for eating purposes. Thus the cultural ethos were the main hurdle in accepting the high breed sheep by the tribals.

Another instance which proves the failure of the sheep rearing scheme is related with 'Sheep Sawai Loan' scheme. Under this scheme the beneficiaries were distributed the flocks consisting 20 to 25 sheep with a ram, in each flock, which were to be returned to the Government with the interest of 1/4 time more sheep. At the early stage of its implementation the scheme ran smoothly commensurating its objectives. But later on the tempted beneficiaries began to play a false game pretending that sheep are either killed or devoured by the lion or hyena in the jungle and, thus, requested the Government officials for recovering the loan in cash, as the cost of the sheep. The officials too have preferred this procedure particularly escaping from the troubles of approaching the sheep-herds located in high altitudes and collecting them to redistribute to the new beneficiaries. But with this false practice, the sheep could not be provided to other needful beneficiaries, resultantly the 'scheme,' in spite of being viable became dead due to the false play of both the parties.

Even today, in Bhot and Jaunsar Bawar areas the scheme for goat and sheep rearing can be beneficial as well as successful in providing the earning to the tribals by increasing indigenous wool production and other allied practices because the geographical conditions of this area are suitable for goat and sheep rearing. But (i) viewing the environmental dangers, the goat rearing has been harmful in hill areas, and (ii) on the contrary the Government has declared the forest area even of the tribal region where the traditional pastures for goat and sheep grazing were located as the 'Mrig-Vihar'. Thus, the non-availability of pastures for grazing goat and sheep in general has ended the economic prospects of sheep and goat rearing in tribal areas, affecting adversely not only the traditional occupation of sheep rearing but also its allied production and multiple uses.

Besides, the sector also has the provision for supplying of milching and draught animals for their respective uses. Particularly viewing the nutrition problems, the cows and the buffaloes are meant for providing the milk to the children, while the milk is produced for the use of whole of the family members. But it is observed that the majority of the tribal population, particularly in Raji, Tharu and Buxa areas, still abstains from the use of the milk and its allied products for some superstitions prevalent in the tribal areas. For them, milking the cows is an offence against the calf, the only claimant of the milk of one's mother and might be the cause of the sufferings of the off-springs in future. Therefore, they do not prefer to feed the calf other than its mother. Another prevalent cause of not milking the cow is out of the fear of being kicked or hit by the horn. However, whenever they needed bullocks for agricultural and other allied purposes, they used to rear the cows. For example, the Rajis, Buxas and the Tharus, in general, prefer to raise the bullocks for their multiple uses, namely, for ploughing the field for selling them and pulling the cart (only in Tarai plains), etc. Therefore, the tribals preferably demand oxen and other draught animals like horse and mule rather than the milching cattle like cow and buffaloes. There are still 75 per cent tribal population, particularly in Raji, Tharu and Buxas area being deprived of the milk and allied produces. Thus, it is evident that the scheme for providing milching cattle to the tribals could not be proved as target oriented due to some indigenous erroneous assumptions. In fact cultures make their choices according to their ethos and idiom and determine how best they can adapt and absorb innovation (Dube, 1991: 24). The livestock they are raising today is of inferior quality even though they get subsidized grant for purchasing the milching cattle of high breed, they have satisfaction only by buying the local inferior breed, at a cheaper cost. There is no one to bother about the assessment of the utilization pattern of the subsidized grant as the "Subidha Shulk" is already gulped down by the concerned personnel and the mediators who play an important role in sanctioning the subsidized grant to the beneficiaries.

Employment Generation Schemes

Viewing the acceleration of tribal economic development, the Government has been imparting training to the tribals in various trades and cottage industries under the employment generation schemes. This is also true in the case of the tribal communities of Uttarakhand, because they are still backward in the field of industrial development and self employment. Today, there are many schemes like: spinning, weaving, knitting, tailoring, 'ringal' weaving, carpentry, blacksmithy, basket and cane furniture making, mat weaving, rope and *sutali* making, pottery making, sericulture and bee keeping, etc., for the tribals according to their viabilities. The Government has also made arrangements to impart training to the tribal beneficiaries in their respective and viable trades with certain amount of stipend during the training period and providing subsidized grants after passing out the training as an incentive. In this process, it is evident that a massive expenditure has been incurred by the Government. But the information bearing the reality of the output of the various efforts made in this sector exhibit that in spite of having a reformatory and creative approach, the employment generation schemes have not been able to gain optimum success in imparting the settled economic base to the tribals in general. For example, the Rajis asserted that, the Government has undoubtedly provided them training on carpentry alone with implements to carry on the job. But, at the same time the Rajis were legally forbidden from procuring the timber from the forest. Thus, due to the lack of the raw material the Raji carpenters in general could not establish their jobs. However, there are some Raji carpenters, who could manage the raw material by hook or crook and prepared some wooden items, but due to the lack of marketing facilities, the items could not be sold. (Bisht, 1993:114). Thus the training as well as the subsidized equipments proved almost useless. Today most of the Rajis have sold their equipment for petty sums while the remaining are rusting day by day. Same is the case of Tharus and Buxas. Today they are trained carpenters, blacksmiths, tailors, *ban*, rope and *sutali* makers, pottery makers, mat and *dari* weavers, but nowhere they get success in establishing any employment generating unit on their own account. In fact, the traditionally agriculturist tribal communities like Tharus and Buxas are already trained artisans on the various jobs they are now being trained. The basket making art, rope, *ban* and *sutali* making, fine weaving of cots, *dari* and mat making, shoulder bags and hand fans are some of their inherent specialities. But socially and culturally they are not inclined to sell their art and skill and it is a common notion that those who sell one's art or skill for the sake of earning their livings are looked down upon by the people in the community. This is only due to the failure of the employment generation scheme, particularly in Tharuwat and Buzarh areas.

On the contrary in Jaunsar Bawar and Bhot tract, the tribal people have inherent art and skill in the preparation of woollen goods like, carpet (Dan), Chutka, Tulma, Sweater, Shawl, etc. In addition, they became refined in their inherent art after getting the training through employment generation schemes by virtue of which they are able to compete in the market. But the unavailability of the raw material and the facilities of marketing of the woollen products have placed impediments on the feasibility of the employment generation scheme. For instance, some trained beneficiaries are employed, in production activity in the training-cum-production centers on wages on piece rate basis. While under another scheme the wool slivers are distributed to individuals who return it after spinning. The payment is made on piece rate basis after ascertaining the count of the spun wool. But both the schemes as such could not provide either self-employment to the beneficiaries or in getting commensurate benefits from their labour. Thus, the employment generation schemes as such are not successful in achieveing the desired objectives due to some indigenous sociocultural and infrastructural reasons of the tribals.

Infrastructural Facilities

Corporation: In tribal areas the 'Large Areas Multi-Purpose Societies (LAMPS) have also been formed as a part of Government policy so that the tribals must get all services at one point and the societies should be viable and efficient in delivering the package services. The LAMPS, in general, cover the provision of credit for developmental activities, including agriculture, horticulture and cottage industries and also serve for the consumption needs. Besides, the LAMPS also cover various other sectors of indigenous nature of the respective tribal communities. But in spite of the sufficient outlays meant for LAMPS for meeting the credit needs of local tribals, the money is not utilized properly. The major shortcomings of cooperative movement in the tribal areas under study has been that: (i) those who are actually in need of loan are hardly able to secure it; (ii) the utilization pattern of loaned money being unplanned always gives unfruitful results to borrower; (iii) people have no trust in the cooperative system because it does not fulfil their instant crying requirements; (iv) the tribal people are of the view that the cooperative loaning system is comparatively more complicated than the private money lending system; (v) for tribals, the cooperative credits cannot be utilized according to the choice of the borrower, because the loan is to be invested only in that item for which it has really been sanctioned and, thus, according to the tribals, the cooperative system is not viable to satisfy their casual pressing needs and (vi) the tribal people as well as their habitations absolutely lack the essential prerequisites needed to make the production possible. For example, the unfavourable agroclimatic conditions, lack of technical know-how, pervaded illiteracy, lack of entrepreneurship, indolence among the people are some of the constraints in the proper utilization pattern of the cooperative credits. In spite of this, there are tribals who have been sanctioned the cooperative credits, but the agony is that the actual amount sanctioned for a particular person does not reach his hand because the machinery involved in the process of sanctioning the loan grabs at least 25 to 50 per cent of it, and the remaining, which the borrower receives is spent by him in some unproductive purposes such as catering, narcotics, clothing, etc., for which it has not actually been sanctioned. Resultantly, the loan is hardly refunded to the cooperatives and in some cases the land and the property of the borrower is to be attached for recovering the loan.

Thus, because of the shortcomings of the present cooperative system, the tribals are still compelled to approach the private moneylenders for procuring loan. The money lenders sometime grab their cultivable land or the standing crops, but provide the required loan without any complication. Further, the borrowers are free to spend the loaned money according to their choice. This procedure as the tribals assume, is, however, more convenient for the people, therefore, they prefer to follow it rather than the cooperatives.

Social Services: In order to make full use of the development-oriented programmes, it is essentially important to improve the quality of life of the tribal people. The programmes, related directly to the quality of life include the provisions like medical, health and nutrition, child and women welfare, education, drinking water, shelter, fuel and light and also the means of communication and transportation in general. But in the tribal areas, the availability of these social services or the infrastructural facilities vary from place to place.

Medical, Health and Nutrition: It is observed that the medical and health services have not been able to produce any desired impact because of the erroneous assumptions regarding health and diseases prevalent amongst the tribals. Even today the tribals living in the farthest, remote and isolated areas have no sense of health care, nutrition and cleanliness. The filthy surroundings of living (except Tharus), dirty, pugnacious and ragged dress of the tribals, stinking thick layer of filth on the body, people suffering from cough and colds the deep cracks on heals and fungal infection between toes and a lean and thin body tell the story of their unhealthy nutrition pattern and also the unavailability of proper medical and health services. Diseases like tuberculosis, whooping cough, paralysis, venereal diseases, diarrhoea, iodine deficiency disorder related diseases, neonatal tetanus, etc, are very common throughout the tribal settlement.

Actually it is observed that (i) the Government could not make available the essential medical and health facilities in the tribal areas which are spread over in a large area; (ii) the tribals even today, rely on the traditional pattern of treatment. For them the illness of any sort of psycho-physical disorder is caused due to the wrath of the supernatural being or the spirits or due to somebody's curse or the evil eye or the magical practices, hence, the magico-religious practices and the use of the indigenous herbs are regarded as the best suitable methods of treatment. In this way they do not attach any seriousness to the disease and think of having medical advice or treatment only when the disease becomes almost fatal; (iii) the primary health centres, which bear the responsibility of providing necessary medical and health facilities to the tribals are lacking every sort of equipment, medicines and the vaccines. These are the shortcomings responsible for the failure of the medical health and nutrition schemes launched in tribal areas.

Child and Women Welfare: The Government has taken a number of initiatives for eradicating the amenable root causes of malnutrition, the most responsible factor of infant mortality. Under the Integrated Child Development Services Scheme (ICDS) there has been a provision of inputs like nutritional and pre-primary education and non-formal education for women which help in improving the quality of life especially of the vulnerable groups of the society, i.e., the children and women. The Government has also made the provision for providing the essential adequate nutritive food and milk to the children and also to the lactating mothers. But none of the schemes could produce any fruitful results, becuase the food could not reach the needy families owing to the inaccessible regions of the habitations. In view of the women welfare, the Government has also the provision to carry out adult education as well as training for cutting, tailoring, handicraft and sericulture. No doubt, some tribal women particularly in Bhotiya, Tharu and Khasa communities have got training in different trade particularly to avail the incentives but soon they found the schemes as useless, uneconomic and time consuming. Hence, the welfare programmes could not be carried out successfully in tribal areas.

For instance, among Rajis, during the day time none of the tribal women who play an important part in tribal economy can devote their valuable time for any uneconomic task because this act may deprive the whole of the family of the food scarcely managed by the day-long labour of the earning members of the family. While at night the day-long physical fatigue compels the tribal women for taking shelter of the patched quilt and dreaming for the coming day's activity. Similarly the excessive preoccupation of the tribal woman in their day to day routine work, do not provide any leisure time for joining any scheme related to the welfare of the womenfolk. Thus, in such a backward area, any programmes like adult education, cutting, tailoring, handicraft, etc., may not be able to attain the desired objectives.

Education: In view of illiteracy pervading throughout the tribal area, the Government has framed a strategy for the extension of the educational facilities at the doorsteps of the tribal settlements. For gaining the desired objectives, every tribal child has been motivated by providing certain incentives like mid-day meal, stationery, school dress or uniform, etc. For this purpose some pre-primary and primary schools have been opened in tribal areas. Besides this, there are Ashram Type Schools (ATS) located in the tribal areas. Most of the ATS are run by the Harijan and social welfare departments. These institutions are meant exclusively for the tribal children. The Government has made all the arrangements, free of cost, for lodging and boarding of the tribal children.

But field observations exhibit that in spite of various educational facilities, the tribal people in general are still unable to get the desired education for making it job-oriented. For instance, in the Raji community almost all the pre-primary and the primary schools which were being run by the Harijan and other social welfare departments of UP have been closed for last two years due to the problem of mass drop out among the Raji children. In fact among Rajis, the children as soon as they attain the age of six years, become a part of the economy and thus, they are deputed either with the cattle to graze them or left at home for taking care of the household activities. Hence, school going for Rajis is an uneconomic pursuit. On the contrary, there are ample examples among the Tharus and Buxas community, when the educated tribal youth do not get jobs in spite of being from the reservation quota, and, thus, the sheer unemployment of the tribal youths becomes the reference to discourage the next coming line for schooling.

The scheme for ATS, as learned and aged tribal man admitted, is the main hurdle in developing a feeling of social integration, coherence and coexistence among the tribal children. Because in such schooling pattern, the children since childhood, begin to feel some sort of segregation and could not avail the company of non-tribal children and ultimately the grownup tribals felt themselves alienated, segregated and aloof from the rest of the society. Thus, the ATS system is not helpful in bringing the tribals in the mainstream of society and also in developing the feeling of social integration among them.

Schemes for drinking water, electricity and road communication: Though the tribals have been accustomed to fetching of the drinking water from its natural source, in olden days too as the scholarly references prove, the tribals used to settle themselves only in such places where the natural water sources were abundantly available. Gradually the natural water sources began to dry-up, therefore the Government particularly in the post-Independence era has made the provision of drinking water facility in the tribal areas. Under this provision, as the field observations show, the drinking water was made available through pipelines and the tanks were constructed for the storage of water in tribal settlements. This is particularly in hill areas, while in Tarai plains, public hand pumps were installed in the tribal villages. But, today it is observed that the pipelines, water tanks and the hand pumps are physically present at their places but are not in working order. The hill tribes, living in the remotest areas are still using ageold pattern of fetching water from the long distant natural water sources, while the plain tribes have managed by hook or by crook, their own hand pumps at their places. In fact, the pipelines, as in the case of Rajis, Bhotiyas and Khasas, were mostly spread out on the surface of the land which needed more care and maintenance as most of them were not in working order. The pipes are damaged while the empty tanks have become the place for merry making for the children. In the Tarai plain, the tribals assume that the boring was not up to the mark and the material used for installing the hand pumps were not of good quality, for that reason after some time the pumps stopped functioning. It is then obvious that the apathy of the personnels shouldering the liabilities of the maintenance and their attitude for 'serving the purpose for time-being' as well as the lack of the awareness, and ignorance of the tribals are altogether the main causes of the failure of the schemes.

Same is the position of electrification of these tribal areas. There are some tribal villages where the electric lines are spread out, but the tribals are not in a position of taking electric connections at their own cost. They either pursue their age-old system of making light by burning the thin sticks of pine wood called *chhula* in Raji and Bhotiya tracts, or otherwise, and sometime through earthen lamps or kerosene lamps while some cunning tribes steal the electricity at night by laying the anchor on the line. It is observed that most of the electrified tribal villages have no legal connections taken by the tribals in general. On the contrary, the tribal villages located in the remote areas, particularly in Bhotiya, Rajis and Khasas settlements are still deprived electric lines. Electricity for them is still an awe-inspiring thing. For instance, when electric line was first spread out in the Raji settlements, a Raji youth just clung on the wire for fun, but died instantly by electric current. Thus, they still have a deep rooted fear of electricity and feel that it may cause the death of any person at any time, and therefore, even today they are not mentally prepared to avail of the facility of electricity. Thus, the poverty as well as the ignorance of the tribals are the main constraints on the way of the scheme.

So far as the facility of roadways, is concerned, most of the accessible tribal areas are connected by bridle paths (in hill areas) and roads in Tarai plains. While the naturally inaccessible remotest tribal areas particularly in the hills are still deprived of this facility not because of the absence of the provisions but because of the improper implementation of the schemes. The bridle paths therefore exist on records as well as on the signboard showing the bridle paths but actually don't exist. The Jaulajibee -Ganagaun bridle path is an example of this sort.

Reservation policy: In view of the overall development of the tribal communities, the present reservation policy as such is not viable in achieving its desired objectives. No doubt, the tribal communities under reference, had opportunities in the various aspects of their life to avail of their socio-economic development as well as in flowing in the mainstream of the social life by abandoning their primitive way of life. They were quite hopeful to achieve every benefit, every facility and every opportunity as was laid down under the Constitutional provisions through reservation policies. But, in reality as the field sources prove, only that part of the tribal population could be successful in availing the benefits of the reservation policies, that was already economically well-off and inhabited in some accessible and favourable ecological conditions (see for details Bisht, 1992: 37-56). For example, the Bhotiya tribe, which is known as the traditional trader was economically sound, and, therefore, immediately after the ban on the international trade with Tibet-China, it turned its children to education and tried to avail the maximum benefits meant constitutionally for them (STs). In this process too only that part of the Bhotiya population could have the success of availing the benefits, which was already economically well off. Same was the case with other tribal communities.

Today, the position even of the tribals under the reserved category has become worst because there are two clear cut groups within the tribals. The first group is constituted by those handful of tribal families who have been availing the reservation benefits from the very beginning, while the second group, which subsumes the majority of the tribal population has been too late to gain the benefits meant for the Scheduled Tribes as a whole due to some indigenous socio-economic and ecological problems. Gradually, the gap between both the groups broadened with the passage of time and today the position is quite irreversible and complicated too. Because the offsprings of both the groups are competitors in availing the benefits reserved under different sectors of life for the tribals in general. In this process the offsprings of the later group can hardly achieve the benefits, because they are not able to compete with the former. Thus, it can be concluded that the reservation policy, as such, meant for the Scheduled Tribes will never be successful in achieveing the target of overall development of the tribals rather its results will be quite squint and lopsided in nature, evident from the field study of the tribal communities under reference.

Resume

In view of the afore delineation, it is pertinent to state that the developmental schemes as such are predominantly commercial in nature. The humane dimensions in the social, cultural, psychological, moral and spiritual fields are almost missing in the existing development paradigm and, thus, have become an epi-phenomenon dependent upon the economic variable. Even the social development schemes which subsume some specific social categories like age, sex and social class are of economic nature. Because the development policies by and large without awakening the will power, work spirit and the feeling of merits and demerits, morality and immorality among the people aim at achieving the objectives by providing sheer economic assistance as an incentive to the categories concerned. It seems that the existing development paradigm has turned man into an economic species by making him more and more materialistic, individualistic and selfcentered. The human traits like morality that cherished the ideals, honesty that inspires for fair dealing, sympathy which implied the feeling of worldliness and brotherhood and sincerity that represents the fidelity and devotion to one's duty are all at a discount. Evidently, a man, whether he is planner, an executor, a beneficiary or a mediator in the spectrum of development planning, has his sheer single-point programme as to remain vigorously in search of an opportunity as to satisfy one's ego at any cost. Therefore, the results of the existing developmental plans particularly in tribal areas are not commensurate with the outlay fixed and incurred in different sectors. In reality, only a nominal part of the grant sanctioned for development is utilized in its proper cause, while the maximum part of it is outlayed in switching over the machinery for work. On the contrary, the false trick which the so-called simple, honest, ingenuous tribals have learnt for economic gains through Government subsidies side by side with the newly emerged indigenous leadership, mediators, as well as the personnels shouldering the liabilities of implementing the development schemes, is nothing but a repercussion of this system, bearing exclusively the economic concern. Today, for tribals the thumb impression, that pays beyond expectation, costs nothing but generates a latent passion and a lasting ambition to achieve this without much of hardship. This tendency has made them indolent, idle, inactive and cunning in order, to grab the subsidies.

The other aspect of existing development planning, as the text proves, is its incompatibility with the sociocultural ethos and the ecological surroundings of the tribals. It seems that the planners and the policy-makers through their round table discussion have formulated the development schemes and injected them without making any diagnostic analysis of the sociocultural ethos of the tribals, their ecological background and psychology. The imposition of such incompatible and contrary schemes has also caused counter results as compared to the desired ones. Thus, as regards the verification of the hypothesis, it is asserted that the existing development paradigm might be commensurable only when it essentially takes its cues from: (i) the compatible humane dimension, which includes the sociocultural ethos and the inherent humane traits of human beings; and (ii) the ecological background of the given community.

REFERENCES

Atkinson, E.T., 1882, *Himalayan Gazeteer*, Cosmo Publications, New Delhi.

Bisht, B.S., 1992, *Uttarakhand Ki Bhotiya Janjati*, Vivek Prakashan, Delhi.

———, 1993, *Rajis: A Tribe of Indo-Nepal Border of Uttarakhand*, Vivek Prakashan, Delhi.

———, 1994, *Tribes of India, Nepal, Tibet Border land*. Gyan Publishing House, Delhi.

Burman, B.K. Roy, 1972 Tribal Demography, In *Tribal Situation in India* (K.S. Singh ed) Indian Institute of Advanced Study. Simla.

Chandra, B., 1968, *Hand Book on Scheduled Castes and Scheduled Tribes*, Office of the Commissioner for Scheduled Castes and Scheduled Tribes. Govt. of India, New Delhi.

Chatterjee, B.B., 1975, Bhotiyas of Indo-Tibetan border of Uttarakhand, Unpublished Project report.

Dube, S.C., 1991, Cultural Dimensions of Development; In *culture Development Interface* (Yogesh, Atal, ed), Vikas Publishing House, Delhi.

Majumdar, D.N., 1940, Some Aspects of the cultural life of the Cis-Himalayan Region, In *Journal and Proceeding of the Royal Asiatic Society of Bengal* IIIrd series, Vol. VI.

———, 1942, The Tharus and their blood group. In *Journal of Royal Asiatic Society of Bengal* Vol. VIII, Part-I.

———, 1944, *Races and Cultures of India*, Asia Publishing House, Bombay.

Five

Ritualistic Implications of Chyakti: A Microcosm of Shauka Identity and the Trends of Transformation

B.S. BISHT

Ferguson (1966) has aptly remarked that India is a socio-linguistic giant. It accommodates several linguistic, racial, territorial sociocultural and heterogeneous communities. The culture of the different ethnic groups is thus an integral part of the diversified cultural system of India. Hence, for a comprehensive understanding of the Indian sociocultural system, an adequate knowledge of the social and cultural set-ups of the various ethnic groups which altogether constitute the composite culture of India is essentially important. With this aim in mind the studies of the various cultural patterns of different ethnic groups have largely been conducted by the social scientists. Yet there exist the tribal pockets which are beyond the microscopic sight of the researchers. There is still a gap of knowledge in comprehending the diversified cultural system of India. Even the curiosity of the comparatively more cautious and awakened social scientists is unsatisfied and in the absence of the first hand field information, they are relentlessly experiencing this void. Out of the various such tribal pockets, the 'Shauka' of Uttarakhand is one and the other includes the trait 'Chyakti' which is still beyond the scientific look of the social scientists.

'Chyakti' as such implies a number of ritualistic uses or functions under the observance of the different life cycles, rituals and religious ceremonies in Shauka Community and is an important cultural trait and, therefore, is termed as a microcosm of the 'Shauka identity' in Uttarakhand region of Uttar Pradesh.

It is observed that during the past decades the Shaukas

borrowed much of the cultural traits and the ways of life particularly for economic gains from the outside world, yet despite frequent cultural contacts and the growing influences from outside, they have maintained their own customs, beliefs and practices. The Chyakti and the ritualistic implications for ages are an example that 'Shaukas' have maintained in the same frame of reference. Invariably, there are still several other cultural traits which the Shaukas are determined to retain as their distinct identity which can exist alongside various other ethnic groups of the contiguous regions.

Though a number of scholars namely, Sherring (1907), Chattopadhyay (1934), Pant (1935), Panna Lal (1942), Dabral (1965), Srivastava (1960), Rahul (1970), etc, have made intensive studies on the different aspects of Shauka community, yet there are still some more components of the cultural traits like the Chyakti in particular, which are to be studied in the frame reference of the whole of the Shauka community under reference.

Method of Study

The study has been limited to three Shauka villages of Kumaun hills selected purposefully on the basis of territorial divisions, high concentration of Shauka population and the permanent ancestral settlements. For collecting field data the standard scientific technique of participant observation is used. Secondary information are compiled from the secondary sources and, thus, the collected data have scientifically been analysed and presented in a descriptive manner.

Shauka Tribe

Etymologically, the word Shauka is used to denote the so-called Bhotiyas of the Darma, Vyans and Chaudans valleys of Pithoragarh, a hilly and border district in the Kumaun region of Uttar Pradesh. The European writers, namely, Crooke (1897), Atkinson (1882), Traill (1980), Walton (1928), etc, were the first to address the Shaukas in terms of Bhotiyas which as (Chatterjee, 1975: 138) states stands for a generic name of several distinct ethnic groups which share many features in common and at the same time each group also exhibits certain sets of distinctive features which may be unique for one or more groups but not shared by the rest. Even the earliest writers, namely, Sherring (1906), and Pant (1935) have also stated that, if a straight line is drawn between Askot and Kapkot, the area to the North-East of this line will constitute the region locally known as the Bhot or the Bhotiya tract and, thus the people residing in this region would be called Bhotiyas. Even in the Constitutional frame of reference, the term Bhotiya has been referred for the seven major ethnic stocks namely Joharis, Darmiyas, Vyanses, Chaudanses Marchha, Tolchha and Jods of the Kumaun and Garhwal hills who are respectively the original habitants of seven river valleys i.e. the Gori, Dhauli, Kutiyangti, Kali (in Kumaun) and the Vishnu Ganga, Dhauliganga and Bhagirathi (in Garhwal). But the Shaukas themselves are not willing in all cases to be known by this appellation i.e. Bhotiya (1906:61). Even today they call themselves Shaukas and feel proud of being called so . Regarding the racial status of the tribe it may be asserted that, they are of the Tibetan origin. It is sufficiently shown by the language that they are of Mongolian origin (1982:397). Sherring (1906:60), Pant (1935:42), Dater (1961:73) and Randhawa (1970:122) are also of this opinion that, they have Mongoloid features.

These people are the traditional traders. In ancient times, Tibet was the main market of Shaukas where the main commodities they sold to the Tibetans were the foodgrains, jaggery (gur), utensils, clothing, instruments, ornaments and other fancy items. They used to barter salt, wool, borax, musk and exotic materials found only in Tibet (1962:230). But due to the ban on the international trade, they confined their business in the contiguous regions and the foothills of Kumaun and Garhwal region. Even today they are the biggest suppliers of woollen stuff like Dan (carpet), Chutaka (a type of blanket), Pankhi, Shawl and the Sweater prepared in their household industries. They also raise sheep, goats, cows and yaks. But the land suitable for cultivation and raising of staple crops is awfully meagre in all the settlements. The settlements are subject to extreme weather conditions like heavy snowfall throughout the winter due to which these people follow the transhumance practices.

Thus, the Shaukas are a distinct racial group, whose physical features, dresses, food habits, occupation, surroundings and the religious rituals and practices are unique in themselves. The ritualistic uses of the Chyakti is the symbolic manifestation of their cultural identity.

Chyakti at the Birth of a Child

In general the naming ceremony of a new born child is considered as the best occasion for merry making in every family. Among Shaukas the naming ceremony called 'Bhomo'* is followed by the Chhosimo* and the Mulinkormo*. The first day of the child birth irrespective of the sex difference, is celebrated with ecstasy. All the deities, spirits and goblins are worshipped with an offering of Chyakti. In the same manner the Chhoshimo rite is also observed on the eleventh day of the child birth. At this ceremony only the 'name' suitable for the child is proposed by the elders of the family. On the twenty-second day of the child birth, the mother takes a sacred bath to purify herself and then the 'Mulinkormo'* rite is observed on the same day. At this occasion the mother is offered Chyakti for sipping, and only after that she is permitted to enter into the hearth, to touch the drinking water and also to cook the food. Because the sense of defilement caused with the delivery of the child is considered to be removed with the sipping of the Chyakti at the ceremonial rite of the 'Mulinkormo'. But the actual naming ceremony called 'Bhumo' takes place with the completion of three months of the birth. At this occasion all the kith and kins are invited. A pair of bottle full of 'Chyakti' duly decorated with green grass and flowers and a 'Dhalan'* are placed in front of some of the village elders and then all the deities, spirits and goblins are worshipped with the offerings of the Chyakti and Dhalan. The mother, the child and all other invitees are offered the Chyakti to sip and then a boy or any of the male person of the same kin group having at least a brother and sister alive, ties the child to his back with the help of a cloth and crosses the threshold of the house nine times wishing for the long life of the child. Then the child is publicly given the name already proposed by its parents at the 'Chhasimo' ceremony. And, thus, the naming

* Refer notes

ceremony is deemed to be completed with a grand feast and with the drink of Chyakti.

Chyakti at the Marriage (Damisyasya)

In ancient period, the available scanty references of the previous scholars depict the way of acquiring mates among 'Shaukas', namely, by capture, by mutual consent and elopement, by purchase. It is customary for girls to get married after adolescence is passed, but the process of marriage is a sort of combination between 'Rakshash' and 'Gandharva' style. It is based upon courtship or premarital acquaintance and love (1939:161). This statement indicates the premarital love between the boy and the girl which leads to the marriage by mutual consent and elopement which is the most prevalent form of marriage still observed by the 'Shaukas' of Darama, Vyans and Chaudans. Besides this, some traces of the 'marriage by purchase' have also been observed among 'Shaukas'. The bride-price is paid either in cash or kind and some times in both. In Shaukas' marriage, there is no priest, no hymns, no Shalgram stone, no *bedi*, no registration, they have learned not to follow any unnatural methods, whoever falls in love with another becomes his or her bride or bridegroom. Only the chosen bridegroom gifts Rs 21 or Rs 19 to the bride to get the ring made. She informs her parents about it. Then on some convenient night absconds with the girl to his own house. Later, there is a feast where a couple of goats or sheep may be sacrificed (1934:162), (Pant, 1935:204-5) says: "Premarital sexual experience and compassionate marriages are quite usual ...." Thus, it may be concluded that the marriage by mutual consent and elopement and the marriage by capture were the most prevalent ways of acquiring mates among the Shaukas.

But the present investigation shows a considerable change in the patterns of acquiring mates. However, the traditional rites are still observed symbolically by the 'Shaukas'. At present the marriage among 'Shaukas' called, "Dhami-Syasya" is preceeded by the 'betrothal' rite called 'Thomo' which is performed after having the consent of the virgin, called Chamai Kharmo*. To have

* Refer notes

the consent of the girl a female mediator called, 'Taram' is appointed indirectly by the proposed groom. Some times the 'Taram' also persuades the girl and makes her agree to marry the man. In case of the positive response of the girl the formal rite of betrothal called, 'Thomo' takes place.

Betrothal (Thomo)

On this occasion the people from the man's side approach the girl's parents with the presentation called, 'Bintee'*. In the presence of the parents and the aged persons from the girl's side, the groom's kin convey the consent of the girl referring to the information gathered through the 'Taram' and thus offer the proposal for the marriage. If the girl's parents and relatives accept the 'Bintee' the proposal is considered to be accepted. The 'Chyakti' then is offered to spirits, deities, Gods and Goddesses symbolically and simultaneously to all the persons present on that occasion as a token of benediction. Thus, the acceptance of 'Chyakti' by the girls' side eventually permits the others to complete the moral and social obligations required for the wedding and decide about the suitable wedding date.

Thus, the 'Chyakti' socially conjoins the two families and their kin into an affinal relation system and also indicates a way out to acquire a life partner in the Shauka culture. For example, in the Shauka community a man's failure to acquire a partner by a socially approved manner leads to the capture of girl in love to his house where he makes her sit on the threshold and then offers her a piece of Dhalan and a cup of Chyakti. The acceptance of Dhalan and sipping of Chyakti by the girl leads to perform the primary rite of the marriage and, thus, in spite of being opposed by the looser the man may have a social sanction to treat her as his wife before the council of elders.

At the marriage ceremony the marriage party before its departure to bride's place observes the 'Shakanu'* rite by devotional offering of 'Chyakti' to the spirits, god, goddesses and goblins. The members joining the marriage procession are also offered 'Chyakti' as the auspicious symbol. The Tisyas* also join

* Refer notes

the procession with a pair of bottle full of 'Chyakti' and the 'Dhalan' in a basket tied to their backs. On arriving at the bride's village, the families on the way, welcome the marriage party with the observance of the 'Shakanu rite'. The marriage procession is offered bottles full of 'Chyakti' duly decorated as the symbol of auspicious omen. A woman of the family places the 'Chyakti' in the middle of those persons sitting around her house. Then she pours the 'Chyakti' in the cup and offers to bridegroom and all the members one by one. In the same way almost all the families of the bride's village either jointly or in a group of two and more or separately perform the 'Shakanu rite' until the procession reaches its destination. At the bride's house, the marriage party is received with great zeal and graceful manner by the bride's side. The 'Bintee-rite' is observed first. Generally, the bride's mother or any woman of the bride's family offers 'Shakanu' to the groom's people sitting in the corridor. The father or the guardian of the groom, the 'Tisyas' and every member from the groom's side are offered 'Chyakti'. Before performing the 'Shakanu' rite, they jointly offer the 'Chyakti' to the spirits and then take it lavishly. Thus the first phase of the marital rite is considered to be completed. After having meal the second phase of the marital rite is performed in a room of the bride's house. Along with other ritualistic performances the exchange of 'Chyakti' between the bride's party and the groom's party (brought by the 'Tisyas') is made. This rite is considered to be the symbol of the completion of the wedding ceremony which is followed by recreational activities which contain the singing and dancing of the people of both parties called 'Ran-ban'.

Chyakti at the Obsequies

At the time of the last journey of a person, when people are grief stricken, 'Chyakti' is offered to pacify the departed soul. At the beginning, the deceased body, covered with shroud, is purified with the spray of 'Chyakti'. Before being taken to the cremation ground the offering of Chyakti is made to all the spirits and goblins. The processionists also take the 'Chyakti' and proceed to the nearest cremation ground where a bottle of 'Chyakti' is placed at the head side of the deceased and then the funeral pyre is lit. After having lit the pyre the processionists come back to their place from where they started and drink 'Chyakti' till the dead body is burnt to ashes. Then they go to the cremation place and collect the ashes of the deceased and again offer the 'Chyakti' to the departed soul as its last offering and dispose off the ashes in a sacred place.

It is, therefore, asserted that the Shaukas have been preserving their cultural heritage and still they are determined to maintain it and its components. This is the reason that in spite of constant cultural contacts and the influence from outside, people have still maintained their cultural identity particularly, in their non-material (site) cultural complexes. Shaukas have a peculiar way of living including their religious beliefs and practices. They have distinct physique, dialect, food habits, customs, occupation, religion, style of life and the world views as compared to the neighbouring tribal and non-tribal groups. The Chyakti and its functional utility in the observance of the different rituals is the miniature representation of the identity of the cultural uniqueness of the Shaukas. The present study, thus, reveals how the Shauka community is distinct in their lifestyle and world views.

Apart from the ritualisitic functions, which can be termed as the 'manifest function' of Chyakti, there have been some latest functions too which are subsequently being transformed into adaptive and commercial functions. In fact the 'Chyakti' as such has been originated from a type of 'Beer' called 'Barchhya' in Shuka dialect. It came into existence as a cultural cum religious commodity in Shauka community and is used in different occasions for performing the cultural and religious ceremonies. The people used to take it as an offering in the name of gods and goddesses. It was basically the manifest function of the 'Barchhya'. Since the 'Barachhya' used to prepare by decomposing the herbs, medicinal plants, seasonal fruits and grains in a certain procedure. Hence the use of the extract obtained through distillation as an offering used to cure a number of bodily diseases of the people, particularly abdominal. It was the latent function of 'Barchhya' about of which the people were practically ignorant. Since the 'Barchhya' had warns property which was experienced by the people through its after effects. Hence they began to take it regularly as to adapt themselves with the high cold attitudinal zones. The 'Barchhya' had a very light alcoholic taste and effect due to less percentage of alcohol in it. But in due course of time some of the business minded people have begun its trade as an alcoholic drink by increasing its alcoholic properties with the addition of some other things like the tablets of Balan, etc, in its preparation. It was the turning point when the 'Barchhya' due to the increase in alcoholic properties transformed into 'Chyakti' means an 'alcoholic drink' i.e. local made wine. Since all the Shauka families used to prepare it for their own use and consumption. But now they started to brew it in more surplus quantity. So that the surplus production can commercially be used by them. Being a frontier zone the defence and para-military forces, other government employees are abundantly deputed in the adjacent areas of the Shaukas. Besides this the non-tribals living in the viscinity of the 'Shaukas' who jointly form a 'consumer group' of 'Chyakti'. The people buy the Chyakti for the sake of intoxication and also to save themselve from severe cold.

In this way the 'Chyakti' by preserving its ritualistic functions has transformed into the commodity for sale. Even today it is one of the various sources of earnings for the 'Shaukas' which is ofcourse a new and latest commercial function of the 'Chyakti'. Besides this, the 'Chyakti' because of its intoxicated properties has also generated a number of social evils like disputes among the people, invectives, adultery and other immoral acts even in the Shauka community. These are the dysfunctions of Chyakti for the Shauka community as a whole. There dysfunctions were better realised by some of the elderly Shauka people and therefore they also initiated a campaign against the production of 'Chyakti', but in vain. Sri Soban Sing Daryal was one who took initiative for prohibition. But keeping itself behind the cover of a cultural cum religious implication the process of brewing Chyakti is going on briskly without any thick and hindrance. Thus we observe how practically the implication of Chyakti are subsequently transforming.

NOTES

Chyakti: The term refers to a kind of intoxicated drink. As an integral culture commodity it is prepared in every Shauka family, and the Shauka people without the difference of age, sex and status take it freely as the token of an offering to the name of the deity. Basically it was known as 'Bachhay' meaning the 'beer' and used only on different occasions. But with the passage of time the so-called 'Bachhay' transformed into 'Chyakti' particularly when Mr. Dalpat Singh Shauka (Rayapa, 1974:148) from Darama valley learned the method of preparing the 'Chyakti' in 1894. Since then the 'Chyakti' has also been used for economic gains by the 'Shauka people'. In fact the ban on the international trade between Shaukas and Tibetans has eventually posed an intricate problem of economic subsistence for the former. Subsequently, the so-called sacred as well as the religious thing, i.e., the Chyakti had to be used as the subsidiary source for economic gains. In spite of that the basic socio-religious tenets or the postulations and inherent social values as well as the ceremonial functions of the 'Chyakti' have been maintained as usual.

Bhomo: The term refers to the ceremonial rite of tying the child with mother's back when working. Infact, this is a unique ritual observed only among Shaukas. It seems that people have developed this rite to adopt themselves with the ecological life conditions. Because the mother alongwith her domestic, agricultural, weaving and knitting works is supposed to rare and care the child. Thus, she in order to look after the child virtually ties it up with her back with the help of the shawl or sari or the bed sheet in such a way that the child can move its hands and feet freely and the mother can also perform her routine work. But the child, it is assumed, remains physically too weak to tie up with mother's back before three months of age, and, therefore, the child, as soon as it completes three months of its birth is supposed to have some bodily strength and then the Bhomo ritual provides ceremonious sanction to the mother to tie the child with her back when working.

Chhoshimo: The term refers to the ritual observed on the eleventh day of the child birth to liberate the mother partly from the pollution caused due to the delivery of the child. At this occasion the mother takes a sacred bath, sips Chyakti and enters into the main house yet not allowed to enter into the hearth, to cook the food and to touch the drinking water.

Mulin Kormo: The term denotes the ritual observed on the twenty second day of the child birth to set the mother free from all sorts of defilement caused due to the child birth and also enable her to get entry into the hearth, to cook the food and also to participate in every religious activity.

Dhalan: Means the cake prepared by the flour of the 'Uwa' a sort of wheat and the seeds of a vegetable called 'Palthi' Dhalan implies certain socio-religious implications for Shaukas particularly in determining the connubial and commensal relations between two or more families. It also embodies the food habits of the people dwelling in high hill ranges.

Chamai Kharmo: In local dialect the term 'Chamai' means virgin and the Kharmo stands for the 'cheating' or the substance of the discussion. Among Shaukas the man desirous to marry a particular virgin (Chamai) appoints a female mediator who tries to captivate the latter by cheating or sometime by eloquence and also conveys the man whatever information she draws about the virgin to form an opinion.

Bintee: It is a cultural complex which consists of the commodities of religious importance namely a bottle full of Chyakti; white cotton cloth, Dhalan and sweets. Before the observance of any religious rituals the 'Bintee' is offered to all the spirits and deities and then distributed to the persons present at the occasion as a token of benediction.

Shakanu: Etymologically, the term implies hundreds of blessings, and the pattern of offering these blessings called the 'Shakanu rite'. Those who offer the blessings are known as 'Shakany Rande'. In every auspicious occasion the people come to observe the 'Shakanu rite' and offer a vessel full of 'Chyakti' duly decorated with flowers and green grass as a token of the blessings.

Tisya: The term refers to the group of unmarried girls, who join the marriage procession. The girls may be the sisters of the groom or the groom's father's sisters which are two to five in number. The girls jointly constitute an essential part of the Shauka marriage. The main function of the 'Tisyas ' is to carry the essential commodities, namely bottles of Chyakti, Dhalan, etc, and also to make recreation in 'Ran-ban' celebration.

REFERENCES

Atkinson, E.T., 1982, *Himalayas Gazetteer*, Delhi: Cosmo Publications.

Chatterjee, B.B., 1975, "Bhotiyas of Indo Tibetan Border of Uttara Khand", Typed Project Report.

Chattopadhyay, P.K., 1934, *Himalayas Pare Mansarover*, Calcutta: Orient Book Co.

Crooke, W., 1897, *Tribes and Castes of the North West Provinces of India*, Calcutta.

Dabral, S.P., 1965, *Uttarakhand Ki Bhotantik*, Dogadda Veergatha Prakashan.

Dater, B.N., 1961, "Himalayas Pilgrimage", Faridabad

Ferguson, A.C., 1966, "National Socio-linguistic profile formula", in W. Bright (ed.), *Socio-linguistics*, Mouton, The Hague.

Lal, P., 1942, *Hindu Customary law in Kumaun*, Allahabad Govt. Press.

Pant, S.D., 1935, *The Social Economy of the Himalayas*, London: George Allen and Unwin.

Randhawa, M.S., 1970, "The Kumaun Himalayas", New Delhi: Oxford I.B.H.

Sherring, C.A., 1906, *Notes on the Bhotiyas of Almora and British Garhwal*, Calcutta: Asiatic Society of Bengal.

Srivastava, R.P., 1962, *Tribe Caste Mobility in India and the Case of Kumaun Bhotiyas*, University of London.

Traill, G.W., 1880, *Statistical Report on the Bhotiya Mahals of Kumaun*, Delhi: Cosmo Publications, (Reprint).

Walton, H.G., 1928, *District Gazetteer of United Provinces, Vol. 35*, Govt. Press.

Six

Constitutional Provisions and Welfare Measures for SCs/STs

C.L. SHARMA

This study provides a sociological analysis of the Constitutional provisions for the Scheduled Castes and Schedules Tribes with a view to explain the welfare measures adopted for their social transformation in the post-Independent Indian society. It is an open fact that the Indian society had been historically fragmented, divided and hierarchically arranged in the forms of 'Varnas' and 'Vargas'. These categories are so intertwined that any one formation crosses the boundaries of others. However, the 'Varna' system has now become a matter of past in this society and what remains is the 'Jati' and the 'Varga', i.e. the caste and class divisions in their all-pervasive forms. The generic term used for both SCs and STs is the "backward classes" in which other weaker sections of society are also included. The credit goes to the British administrators in the second quarter of this century itself so that all such weaker sections have been listed in the different Schedules for providing special treatment to them from the government side. Getting some inkling from the British approach to the backward classes, it would be proper if I offer my sincere tributes to both the Father of the Nation Mahatma Gandhi and the Father of the Indian Constitution, Baba Sahib Ambedkar, for their valuable contributions in introducing the welfare and Constitutional provisions to uplift the social status of the weaker sections in Indian Society.[1] Whereas Gandhi talked and worked for changing the approach of the Hindus i.e. 'Sawarnas' towards their Harijan brothers in the Hindu fold of Varnaashram system while rejecting the segregated caste system; Dr Ambedkar rejected the degenerated

Hindu caste-ridden society and asked them to embrace Buddhism for he believed that the Hindu and untouchability have become synonymous. It would be irrelevant to raise the Gandhi-Ambedkar controversy here. I shall be dealing with the legislative measures[2] for societal transformation with reference to the SCs/STs, during the last five decades. These measures can broadly be categorized as under:

(A) Protective;
(B) Political; and
(C) Developmental

Protective Measures

The Protective measures safeguard the interest of the SCs and STs through the following Articles of the Constitution:

1. Article 15(4) protects them from the discrimination on the grounds of place of birth in the particular low caste or tribe, for providing special educational facilities to SCs/STs Article 29 is also formulated.
2. Articles 16(4), 320(4) and 330 safeguard the employment opportunities for these people for getting benefits of these safeguards. These categories of people are considered as socially and educationally backward. The OBCs are also further benefited under these clauses after the adoption of the Mandal Commission's recommendations.
3. Article 17 which is later amended as the protection of civil rights Act in 1976 makes untouchability behaviour as a cognizable offence. This Act declares following acts as offences and punishments are prescribed for the same i.e.
   (i) Refusing admission to public institutions such as schools/colleges, etc.
   (ii) Preventing any person from worshipping or offering prayers in any place of public worship;
   (iii) Subjecting any person to any disability with regard to any shop, public restaurant, etc;
   (iv) Insulting a member of the SC on the ground of untouchability; and
   (v) Preaching untouchability directly or indirectly.
4. Article 23: It abolishes the forced labour;

5. Article 19: Provides economic safeguards to the STs;
6. Article 46: Provides protection from social injustices and all forms of exploitation. It also promotes the educational and economic interests of the SCs/STs. In the plans also a separate sector namely "Backward classes sector", has been specifically mentioned. In the First Five Year Plan the Budget Provision for SC and ST categories was 1 to 0.35 per cent of the total Plan budget which was subsequently raised upto 4 per cent each in the Seventh Plan.
7. Articles 244 and 339 with the clause 244 A facilitate the special administrative provisions through the Fifth and Sixth Schedules. The Fifth Schedule applies to the administration and control of the Scheduled areas and Scheduled Tribes of any State other than the States of Assam, Meghalaya and Tripura. Whereas the Sixth Schedule applies to the administration of the tribal areas in the States of Assam, Meghalaya and Tripura and the Union Territory of Mizoram.
8. Article 338 makes it obligatory on the part of Central Government to appoint a National Commission for SCs/STs for laying the role of watchdog of their Constitutional safeguards. The duties of the Commission are:
    (a) To investigate and monitor all the matters relating to the Constitutional safeguards for SCs/STs.
    (b) To inquire into specific complaints with respect to the deprivation of their rights and safeguards.
    (c) To participate and advise on the planning process of the socio-economic development of SCs/STs.
    (d) To present to the President of India the annual or fact-finding reports on the contemporary conditions of SCs/STs.
    (e) To make recommendation for effective implementation of Constitutional provisions.
    (f) To discharge such other functions in relation to the protection, welfare, development and overall advancement of SCs/STs.
9. Article 31B protects the interest of SCs/STs included in the Ninth Schedule of the Constitution. Thus, this Article offers a complete cover for any of the fundamental rights.

Political Provisions

Political Provisions are those which provide special protections for SCs/STs in legislative bodies of peoples' representation and reservation of posts in various Government services. They are as under :

1. Article 164 guarantees for the appointment of a Minister-in-charge to look after the welfare of SC/ST selections.
2. Article 330 facilitates the reservation of seats for SC/ST in the House of the People's Representatives in the proportion of their respective population in the nation as a whole or the States as the case may be.
3. Article 334 provides the reservation of seats for SC/ST in the Lok Sabha or State Assemblies upto 2000 A.D.
4. Article 335 protects the claims of SCs/STs to the services and posts in all the Government departments as per their population ratio. This Article removes some of the limitations of Article 16(4). While Article 335 relates to the SCs/STs only, Article 16(4) applies to OBCs generally. As per this Article, the Central Government provides 15 and 7.5 per cent reservation quota for all the services and posts for the SCs and STs respectively. The State Governments are directed to follow the same reservation principle as per the ratio of their populations. For example, Rajasthan Government provides 12 per cent reservation of posts in all Government services to the STs and 16 per cent to the SCs.
5. Articles 341 and 342 provide for the Presidential Notification of the lists (Schedules) of SCs and STs respectively. All the Constitutional provisions are applicable to the castes and tribes mentioned in these respective Schedules only. The Parliament may include or exclude any caste or tribe from these Schedules by specific notifications. In pursuance of these two Articles of 341 and 342, specified castes and tribes have been declared in those Schedules and time-to-time some modification of the SCs/STs have also been made.

Developmental Provisions

Developmental provisions are made for both the SCs/STs to promote their interests of social change. They are as under:

1. Article 46 gives directions to the States for promotion of special care of the educational and economic interests of SCs/STs. These sections have to be protected from the social injustice of any sort and all forms of exploitation.
2. Article 275 provides grants from the Central Government to the States for welfare of Scheduled Tribes and raising the level of administration of the scheduled areas.
3. Article 39 A provides for equal justice and free legal aid to all the SCs/STs and OBCs. This Article is under the Directive Principles of State Policy.

Apart from these categories of Constitutional provisions, there are some temporary, transitional and special provisions for the welfare of the SCs/STs as per the 13th Amendment Act 1962. They are as under :-

1. Article 371, 371-A, 371-B, 371-C,371-G and 371-H covering the States of Maharashtra, Gujarat, Nagaland, Assam, Manipur and Arunachal Pradesh.

It would be proper if some light is thrown on the Fifth and Sixth Schedules. The former has four parts, i.e. part A,B,C and D. Part A makes it amply clear that the States of Assam, Meghalaya, Tripura and Mizoram are excluded from the provisions of the Schedule. For proper administration and control of the Scheduled areas and Scheduled Tribes, the Tribal Advisory Councils have been constituted by the Governors of the respective States. The Scheduled areas are also declared by the President on the Governor's recommendations. And there are provisions for amendments to those orders. The Sixth Schedule, in pursuance of the Articles 244(2) and 275(1), provides the rules of administration of Tribal Areas in the States of Assam, Meghalaya, Tripura and Mizoram. This provides for the formation of the following systems by the Governors of the respective States :

(a) Autonomous districts and autonomous regions;
(b) District Councils and Regional Councils on the basis of election.

These councils are given full powers of local and regional governance in almost all the fields — social, economic, political religious, etc. The District Councils also have powers to establish schools, dispensaries, markets, etc, in their areas of jurisdiction. The funds are provided by the Centre and the States directly to these Councils which have all kinds of autonomous powers. They are also empowered to assess property taxes and collection of revenues of various sorts. The moneylending procedures are also controlled by these District councils. All the laws and bye-laws are also created by them which are published in the State gazzetier.

TABLE - 6.1
SOME DETAILS OF SCHEDULES CONSTITUTED ON 1.5.1976

Parts of the Schedules	*Names of States*	*Total Number of Categories Castes/Tribes declared for all Kinds of Benefits.*	
		S.C.	*S.T.*
I	Andhra Pradesh	59	33
II	Assam	16	23 (14+9)
III	Bihar	23	30
IV	Gujarat	30	29
V	Haryana	37	-
VI	Himachal Pradesh	56	08
VII	Karnataka	101	49
VIII	Kerala	68	35
IX	Madhya Pradesh	47	46
X	Maharashtra	59	47
XI	Manipur	07	29
XII	Meghalaya	16	07
XIII	Orissa	93	62
XIV	Punjab	37	-
XV	Rajasthan	59	12
XVI	Tamil Nadu	76	36
XVII	Tripura	32	19
XVIII	Uttar Pradesh	66	-
XIX	West Bengal	59	38
	Total	839	503

As per the sections 3 and 4 of the Constitution-order, two separate Schedules have been published to facilitate the State-wise lists of all the SCs and STs respectively. Table 6.1 gives some details about these two Schedules constituted as on 1.5.1976. It is amply clear that the States like Karnataka, Orissa, Tamil Nadu, Kerala and Uttar Pradesh have larger number of SC categories whereas the States like Orissa, Karnataka, Maharashtra and Madhya Pradesh have larger number of tribal categories. Roughly, around one-fourth of the total seats of MPs or MLAs are reserved for SC/ST categories as per the constitutional provisions. In some States, this ratio is higher whereas in others it is lower. But, the States where either only they represent or their MP/MLAs are larger than the non -SC/STs are Arunachal Pradesh, Meghalaya, Nagaland and Mizoram.

A few Amendment Acts after 1987 in relation to the Scheduled Tribes and Castes are also worth mentioning here. They are:

1. The Constitution (Scheduled Tribes) Order Amendment Act 1987 provides for the inclusion of certain tribes in the list of STs specified in relation to the State of Meghalaya. A few more tribes have been added to the list making it 17 in all.
2. The Constitution (Scheduled Tribes) Order (Amendment) Act 1991 provides for inclusion of certain tribes in the list of Scheduled Tribes specified in relation to the State of Jammu and Kashmir. It was an amendment in the Constitution (Jammu and Kashmir) ST Order 1989, through which four more tribes are added to the original list.
3. The Constitution (Scheduled Tribes) Order (Second Amendment) Act, 1991, provides for inclusion of certain tribes in the STs original list in the State of Karnataka. Six more names are added by this amendment.
4. The Scheduled Castes and Scheduled Tribes (Prevention of Atrocities) Act, 1989, prevents the commission of offences like atrocities against the members of the SCs and STs; and it also provides for special courts for the tribal, of such offences and for the relief and rehabilitation of the victims of such offences. This is applicable to the whole of India except Jammu and Kashmir. This Act has five chapters. After giving preliminary in the Chapter - I, the provision for punishment for offences of atrocities are given in Chapter-II. It's experiment part is also given in Chapter-III. There is a special provision for the special courts and the special Public Prosecutor can be appointed by the State Government.

Further State Government's power has been enhanced to convict and impose collective fine on the offenders.

Apart from the above-mentioned constitutional provisions, let us dwell upon the government policies toward SCs/STs in the post-independent period. According to C. Parvathamma[3] it can be well said that the Gandhian approach has largely been followed to uplift these weaker sections. The reservation on the basis of quota system has been extended till the end of this century. The untouchability factor is totally given up at all the public and official places of work. The Government both at the Central and the State levels have extended economic and educational facilities to the SC/ST section to their maximum capacities. Parvathmma rightly observed[4]:

> The Government rightly recognised the needs of SCs and STs in the field of education. In fact one of the criteria in considering them as backwards is connected with their educational backwardness. Formal education, money and power go hand in hand. The latter buttress the former ..... the Union Government has a national policy in implementing certain measures in favour of SCs/STs. Accordingly, reservation facilities are extended in the institutions of higher education. Financial incentives are given to the children of SCs/STs in schools and scholarships are given to the students from these communities for their post matric education. In addition, hostel facilities and reimbursement of extra boarding charges are met by the State.

Though the Government has opened its doors for all levels of services for SCs/STs as per their reservation quota, the real achievement targets in providing services to them vary from one level of service to the other, i.e. from class 1 to class 4 categories. Table 6.2 gives comparative figures of better achievements in getting services of different categories from 1982 to 1991. There is a considerable improvement in the share of the SC/STs in the categories of A and B in the last decade. As the education and standard of living of the SC/ST people improves, the share in the upper levels of services will also increase. It is a fact that appointments of SCs and STs in Class A and Class B services are much below the expected quota i.e. 22.5 per cent (both) as they together constitute only 12 and 14 per cent in the Class A and B categories respectively. In the universities, appointments on the teaching posts are far beyond the filling of required quota for SC/ST as there are only less than 5 per cent teachers belonging to these two categories. There has been a special drive for appointments in almost all the Central/State Governments, LIC, Public Sector undertakings and Banks for the recruitment of SCs/STs. The latest appointment drive is announced by the UGC on November 4 this year that all the Central Universities in the country so far appointed only 5 per cent teachers from the SC/ST candidates on their reserve seats of 22.5 per cent quota. The posts lying vacant should be frozen for the appointment from non SC/ST candidates till the required quota is not fulfilled by the SC/STs for all the teaching and non-teaching posts in these universities. This will produce farreaching results to cover the gap between the real position and the Constitutional provision in the case of varsities.

TABLE - 6.2

PERCENTAGE OF SC/ST IN THE TOTAL NUMBER OF SERVICES

Categories of Services of Central/ State Government	*1982*		*1991*		*Difference of Gains*	
	SC	*ST*	*SC*	*ST*	*SC*	*ST*
A Class	5.49	1.17	9.09	2.53	+4	1.36
B Class	9.02	1.43	11.82	2.35	3.8	.92
C Class	13.39	3.47	15.65	4.98	2.26	1.51
D Class	23.41	7.45	38.4	12.0	15.0	4.5
IAS	10.1	5.4	-	-	-	-
IPS	10.02	3.5	-	-	-	-

Source : Year Books of 1984 and 1992, A Government Publication.

As for the economic and social development of SCs/STs, there are separate departments for their welfare measures. To control and monitor the implementation of the welfare measures, there are Samitis of MPs and MLAs in almost all the States. In West Bengal, Tamil Nadu and other States, there are Tribal Advisory Councils. The grants-in-aid are also provided to a host of NGOs in all the States for the developmental programmes and projects adopted by them. For the sectoral development plans, the corporations for SC/STs have been established in the States in which 49 per cent share capital belongs to the Centre and 51 per cent share is from the States. The special assistance is also provided to the States for making investment and extending economic grants to the poor SCs/STs under various schemes. All the banks are also making year-mark provisions for extending loans on subsidized rates to the SC/ST families for enhancing their incomes. The corporations also provide guarantees to the banks for SC/STs housing and schemes. In 1989, SC/ST Finance and Development Corporation has been established at national level which also helps the State level SC/ST Corporations in adopting economic planning.

One important chapter is also opened with the Birth Centenary celebration of Dr B.R. Ambedkar's birthday in 1991 with the establishment of Dr Ambedkar Foundation for starting :

- (a) Ambedkar National Public Library;
- (b) Dr Ambedkar Chairs;
- (c) Dr Ambedkar Memorial Overseas fellowship; and
- (d) Dr Ambedkar National Award.

The benefits of all these programmes will be available largely for the SCs. Many institutions of higher learning and researches have been started in the name of Dr Ambedkar.

Social transformation among the SC/ST sections is a matter of great concern for the social scientists,[5] activists and reformers. Following three dimensions are distinctly visible on this aspect:

- (i) Changes or development of socio-economic conditions within the traditional fold of occupational and religious clinging;
- (ii) Changes in traditional occupations but not changing the religious identity; and
- (iii) Changing the traditional occupations with the changing of one's own religious identities.

If we take the role of two great political activists namely Gandhi and Ambedkar with reference to these three dimensions, the former, i.e. Gandhi stood for the first and second dimensions, whereas Ambedkar struggled for the third one of the transformation. Gandhi followed the path of removal of untouchability, poverty, illiteracy and general backwardness from the Harijans by bringing out attitudinal changes among the non-Harijans, i.e. Swarnas within the Hindu fold of social life. He was confident that the caste-generated stigma of untouchability can be removed only by the caste Hindus by bringing all the ex-untouchables to their own societal network without any segregation. He believed in true Varnashram Dharma in which major division of labour with the concept of dignity to all forms of labour is justified. Gandhiji wished that the free Indian society will be Sarvodayee, Swadeshi, self-ruled, egalitarian, unexploitative and trusteeship-oriented with basic education for all castes. But even after five decades of Gandhiji's death, his wishes are yet to be fulfilled. However, some changes are quite visible and they might also be related to the contributions of Dr Ambedkar who preferred to call the untouchables as 'Dalits' rather than Harijans.

Dr Ambedkar was also conscious of the limited effects of Constitutional provisions on the social transformation process among the untouchables in India. He organized and inspired them to get educated and also motivated them to get their dues in the social system. He was always against the Hindu psyche, based on Brahamanical literature specially *Manusmriti* which was publicly burnt by him in 1927. In Maharashtra, Gujarat, Uttar Pradesh, etc, his influence on the 'Dalits' is now felt when the SCs have become a major force to reckon with for their claims on all the fronts. As Dr Ambedkar himself launched certain movements among the Mehars of Maharashtra for their socio-economic rights and political power, the leaders from within the SCs/STs have spearheaded the process of social transformation on the lines of Dr Ambedkar. This kind of change was significant for religious conversions from Hinduism to Buddhism in the leadership of Dr Ambedkar.

Another activist, social scientist and Action-sociologist Dr Bindeshwar Pathak[6] has also launched a nation-wide movement to liberate the scavengers in particular and untouchables in general from their age-old occupational hazards. Through Sulabh International Foundation, lakhs of scavengers have been freed from their traditional mode of carrying night-soil on their head. Thousands of scavengers are put on the service in the Sulabh Toilet complexes. This has brought radical changes in the lifestyle and psyche of the scavengers for whom no constitutional provisions could have done any thing to help them. Beginning from the State of Bihar now it is a nation-wide programme to transform the social conditions of the SCs in general.

Occupational mobility and social transformation go hand in hand. They certainly raised the social status of the SC/STs in the overall social setup in which the achievement criteria make the persons more privileged and honoured in comparison to their ascribed bases which usually downgrade them due to certain normative value systems. Due to an overall increase in education facilities for masses and selection of new occupations/services available in the market or industrial settings, there has been a sea change in the social conditions of SC/STs in India. However, one should not get an impression that all the sub-castes or groups of these sections have equally been transformed towards better socio-economic conditions. Some of them have really advanced in all respects whereas others have lagged behind. The research studies and SC/ST Commissioner's reports show that these sections are still lacking in education and better economic pursuits.

A major breakthrough in the occupational alliance has been observed for a particular category of SCs in northern Indian States.[7] This kind of occupational mobility is seen among the Regars, Meghwals, Chamars, Bolas and Bairwas of Rajasthan and Uttar Pradesh who were earlier engaged in leather works, skinning and tanning the leather. The 'Mochis' or shoemakers in the urban localities of Rajasthan are an exception to this trend as they are still continuing in that job to a large extent. In Maharashtra and Gujarat, the same phenomenon has been observed. But mere occupational change from leather-related works to other menial jobs, construction work or masoning works has not helped these people to raise their socio-economic status. Education with better services or entrepreneurship could help them but these are still scarce in these castes. Most of the SCs and STs have been benefited by the overall socio-economic developments and educational proliferations in India and consequently, a sizeable number of them have been transformed into the middle-class category.

It is also observed that hardly any family of SC/STs have made any dent to the category or propertied upper class echelon who really control the economy of the country. At the most they have joined upper level of bureaucracy or professional jobs. The process of Sanskritization[8] at the family or individual level has also generated some significant changes over a period of time. As the population of the country is growing very fast the pace of development among these SC/STs is relatively very slow. Poverty begets poverty, at least among the SC/STs because of the simple reason that the meagre resources reserved for them are usurped by those who are already better off and those who can survive without those reservation-benefits, which are literally meant for those who are economically poorest among the poor. Recently in the PET test of Rajasthan it was observed that almost all the reserved seats of SC/STs were taken up by those persons whose fathers and/or grandfathers have already been benefitted through the reservation quota. This means that from now onwards the wretched of the earth among the SC/ST categories will be left out even if the reservation quota continues in the present form on corporate basis for an indefinite period. This does not mean that the reservation policy must be discontinued after 2000 A.D. But there is a need for serious thinking on the criteria of identification of beneficiary persons of the quota system of reservations. The funds or resources should really percolate and reach the poorest among the poor of the SC/ST categories. The Constitutional provisions should be so formulated that a family which is already well-off should be debarred from this policy.

Lastly, a few empirical observations are worth mentioning here for these have become the facts of the modern Indian society. They are:

(a) There is a visible process of caste-based politics or politicization of castes due to the constitutional provision for SCs and STs which are largely misappropriated by the new "middle class" category of the society.

The elections for caste Panchayats/Sabhas are evident of this fact. The candidates success is decided on the basis of caste factors. After being elected the candidate himself also owes more to his own caste rather than to the people at large whom he is really representing. This has generated casteist feeling which further consolidates the caste factor.

(b) There is also the casteist phenomenon among the upper-castes which was already there prior to the modern reservation policy; but it was of a different nature. Now as a counter productive of the caste-based politics of the SC/ST categories, the Brahmins, Rajputs and Vaisyas have also evolved their consolidation strategies to fight unitedly with the so called Dalits. This has gained potential grounds for caste-wars, a sort of civil war, to take place in near future, if not curbed.

(c) The education and class A and B services are supposed to weaken the caste psyche of the people. However, the ground realities in the Indian society are projecting a different scenario. Despite more education, more achievements in higher jobs, still a person clings to his own caste for atleast two considerations : (a) marriage proposals for his children, and (b) consideration for one's own caste in new jobs and opportunities.

(d) The elitist orientation of social formation are still operative as we have found "Harijan elites",[9] "tribal elites", "Backward class elites" to fight for the cause of these people in principle but to gain the benefits for their own families. This is becoming a great stumbling block in the process of having 'sarvodaya' or egalitarian model of social development.

(e) As the individual base of identification for taking benefits of reservation policy is not evolved, the well-off people will continue to get benefits meant for depressed people.

(f) The rural SC/STs of the really poor categories are yet to be freed from the slavery of upper castes and classes for their survival. Whatever sectoral or area development plans are launched so far, they have remained inadequate for the large number of people of such sections.

(g) There is a need to provide more incentives and special treatments to those who opt for intercaste marriages from within the SC/ST sections. People should be appraised of such programmes by local propaganda techniques.

(h) More entrepreneural trainings and facilities should be extended to the SC/STs to promote self employment schemes. This would generate competitive spirit and self confidence among these sections.

(i) There is a need for distribution of basic educational kits and facilities for all the SC/ST boys and girls whose family can not afford even such items.

REFERENCES

1. For details see Madhu Limaye, "Gandhi Versus Ambedkar: A futile Controversy" in his edited book *Gandhi and Ambedkar*, Delhi : Gyan Publishing House, 1995.
2. See for details Giridhar Gomango, *Constitutional Provisions for the Scheduled Castes and Scheduled Tribes*. Bombay : Himalaya Publishing House, 1992; also see Zaheer Hasan, *Gandhi and Harijans*, New Delhi : Shree Publishing House, 1986; K.S. Padha and J. Mahapatra, *Reservation Policy in India*, New Delhi: Ashish Publishing House 1988; A.K. Vakil, *Reservation Policy and Scheduled Castes in India*, New Delhi: Ashish Publishing House, 1985; H.H. Mehta and Patel, *Dynamics of Reservation Policy*, New Delhi : Patriot Pub., 1991.
3. See for details C. Parvathamma. *Scheduled Castes and Tribes: A Socio-Economic Survey*, New Delhi : Ashish Publishing House, 1984.
4. Ibid, p. 23.
5. For details see C. Parvathamma, *Scheduled Castes at the Cross Roads*, New Delhi: Ashish Publishing House, 1989, Also see R.K. Saxena, *The Schedule Caste Voter*, New Delhi : Radha Publications, 1990; S.K. Vyas, *Educational Schemes for Scheduled Castes*, New Delhi : Shree Publishing House 1986; S. Selvanathan, *Status of Scheduled Castes*, New Delhi : Ashish Publishing House.
6. See for details, Bindeshwar Pathak, *Road to Freedom: A Sociological Study on the Abolition of Scavenging in India*, New Delhi : Sulabh Foundation, 1991; Also see his book *Sulabh Shauchalaya: A Study of Directed Change*, Amola Press, Patna, 1982.
7. For details see, C.L. Sharma, *Social Mobility among Scheduled Castes: An Empirical Study in an Indian State*, New Delhi : M.D. Publications, 1996. Also see Sunavela Patwardhan, *Change among India's Harijans*, New Delhi : Orient Longman, 1973; S.K. Lal and U.R. Nahar, *Higher Education: Scheduled Castes and Scheduled Tribes*, Jodhpur: Jondosn, 1978; N.K. Singhi, *Educational Problems of Scheduled Castes and Scheduled Tribes School students in Rajasthan*, Jaipur University of Rajasthan, 1975.
8. For details, see M.N. Srinivas, *Social Change in Modern India*, New Delhi : Allied, 1966.
9. See for details, Sachchidananda, *The Harijan Elite*, Faridabad: Thomson, 1977.

Seven

Culture: A Prerequisite for Economic Development

B.S. BISHT

"As much as the development planning would take the cues of the cultural dimensions and their time and region specific attributes into consideration, so much as it would be commensurable with its presupposed consequences of economic development."

Infact, the dissatisfaction owing to the relentless failure of the existing economy related conception of development paradigm has caused an ebullience in the world of the academicians. The question, how to view culture in the context of economic development, has resounded some other counter questions which are yet to be answered and calls for a healthy academic discussion as to reach to some scientific conclusions about the nature of the culture-development interrelationship.

So far, the different views prevailing in this regard, present a contrary rather a unified canvas. As for instance, Weber (1958)[1] was one of the early thinkers to explain the development of the western societies and the underdevelopment of those in the east in terms of the variation in their cultural patterns. Under the spell of the Weberian thesis, many scholars echoed the beliefs and values provided by Hinduism as the barrier of economic development in India. William Kapp (1963)[2] emphasized the negative role of Hindu culture in economic development. Even the proponents of the earlier development paradigm attribute the failure to the indigenous cultures regarding them as obstacles to development. Marx (1906)[3] called the religion (a major component of culture) as an opium for the society. There are scholars like Rostow (1960)[4], and Dobb[5] who conceived economic development in terms of savings and investment, while Leibenstein (1957)[6] the prominent economist, has emphasized on the non-economic factor derived through the pattern of culture for economic development. On the contrary McCllelland (1961)[7] has correlated the variation of economic development of a nation with the variations of psychological attributes called the need for achievement (n'Ach) present among the members, while Harbison and Myers (1964)[8] stressed on the importance of the role of human factor in economic development. Similarly, Muthayya (1985)[9] considering the human factor as pre-condition to economic development, has also asserted that an improvement in the quality of the human factor is as essential as investment in physical capital. Bisht (1994)[10] has emphasized on the articulation of human traits in development planning and stated that the existing development paradigm which is predominantly economistic in nature might be commensurable only when it takes its cues from the compatible humane dimension which includes the sociocultural ethos and the inherent humane traits of human beings.

Thus, apart from the scholarly writings of the early thinkers, social scientists and the philosophers, this study with the presentation of various instances of the inappropriateness of economic policies and programmes which have completely neglected the culture as a precondition of economic development and thus, aims to synthesize the controversy on culture-development interrelationship.

But, prior to presenting the factual delineation to substantiate the validity of hypothesis, some questions still remained to be answered; they are : (i) what we really mean by culture and its dimensions?; (ii) what is economic development and its major indices?; and (iii) how the culture should be viewed in the context of economic development? Until the appropriate answers of the questions are enunciated particularly in such a situation when the prevalent development paradigm has completely disregarded culture as irrelevant and blamed it for the failure of the model, the correlation between the culture and the economic development cannot be enumerated scientifically.

Infact, numerous thoughts pertaining to the concept "culture" apparently prove the lack of unanimity of the scholars, philosophers, litteratures, social scientists and anthropologists. It is of course injustice to the concept particularly when it is termed in a very limited sense of traditions, customs, beliefs and similar other abstract facets, as we observe in the writings of E.B. Tylor (1874)[11] and other early anthropologists. It is also irrelevant to delimit the concept with social activities and the facts as we find in the thoughts of Benedict (1904)[12]. Even Weber (1958), the prominent social thinker, views culture within the limited sense of beliefs, values and rituals. As a result, a number of scholars also resounded the beliefs and values of Hindu culture as the barrier to economic development in India. There are still the scholars who use the term 'culture' as synonimous of the ethnic groups specially in multi-cultural societies where a discrepancy between the traditional norms and values and the values of industrial life is strictly observed. Besides this, Kluckhohn (1945)[13] observes 'culture in the context of explicit and implicit elements which exist at any given time as potential guides for the behaviour of man, while Kroeber (1952)[14] views culture in terms of two major aspects i.e. the 'eidos' and the 'ethos'.

Thus, it is evident that most of the earlier thoughts present either an unidimensional or an ambiguous picture of the culture. Naturally the unidimensional consideration of culture in developmental planning will produce skewed and lopsided results. Hence, the need of the hour is to conceive the culture in totality of its various inherent paradoxical attributes manifested in different types of culture traits, culture complexes and culture patterns. The culture is infact, a multi dimensional phenomena. The material*, the non-material*, the psychological*, the human* and the humane* are the main dimensions of culture. Every dimension has its own functions may be social, economic, creative, psychic, religious, aesthetic, integrated, adaptive and humanistic. The culture, therefore, must be viewed in terms of the coexistence of its multidimensional frame of reference while framing the plan for economic development.

Conceptually, the dimensions of culture as cited above, though are universal in nature, their attributes are responsive to the specific time and region, on the basis of which the cultures are

---

* See Notes

identified as the national culture (that has a civilized base and reflects the cultural identity of the nation), the regional culture, (that presents the cultural identity of an approximate homogeneous regional group), the local culture (that exhibits the cultural identity of a local community) and the ethnic culture. It is the pre-condition of the economic planning to consider the cultural dimensions in terms of their time and region specific cultural attributes for gleaning the expected positive results of economic development.

Any economic planning obliterating the cultural dimensions and their time and region specific cultural attributes would never achieve its ultimate goal of economic development. But the question: What we really mean by economic development in the present day context? also requires a healthy academic discussion. It is, of course, too indispensable to trace the relevant major indices of economic development to understand the functional inter-relationships between the cultural dimensions and the economic development. Though, in traditional economic thinking some indices like, per capita income, rate of capital formation, reduction of poverty line, proportion of population in non-agricultural sector and urbanization, etc, are conceived as the major indices of economic development. But today these indices cannot be regarded as sufficiently appropriate because the recent development thinking has moved away from the limited objective of raising per capita income and similar other indices and, thus, does not reflect the positive and the balanced picture of the development. Rather, the economic development, refers to the upward movement of the social system and is something more than the economic growth and, therefore, it evolves a social context too. The new concerns: (i) the demographic variables (like population control, fertility, infant mortality rate, sex-ratio, the nature of male-female discrepency); (ii) the natural variables (like environmental conditions, natural resources and their alternates); (iii) the human variable (like the nature of human resource, education); (iv) the social variable — the status and role structure, participation of women in economic activities, the status and role of the masses in national context, the nature of receptivity and resistance of masses towards the traditional and modern value system, the developmental scheme and the pattern of the distribution of their benefits, and the investment and expenditure pattern altogether may be termed as the indices of the economic development in a given society.

In view of the conceptual analysis of the cultural dimensions and the indices of economic development, the valuation of the various protective and supportive measures adopted under the Article 46, (part IV) and the Articles 330, 332, 334, 335 and 338 (part XII) of the Constitution for the Scheduled Tribes in general and the special developmental provisions meant for the overall development of the Khasas, the Bhotiyas, the Rajis (Hill tribes) and Tharus and Buxas (plain tribes) of Uttarakhand Himalaya, is made through observations and available secondary information. In fact, the Government by its Constitution Order, 1967, has declared the tribes of Uttarakhand (as cited above) as the Scheduled Tribes. Since, then relentless efforts are being made through various development agencies of the Government for their all round development. The schemes like, rehabilitation of landless tribals on agriculture, agricultural development, housing scheme for homeless tribals, family oriented programmes, development of infrastructural facilities, namely, cooperation, medical health and nutrition, women welfare, education, drinking water, electrification, road communication, etc, are some of the major developmental efforts which are being taken care of with a massive outlay for achieving the presupposed consequences of tribal development.

But the results of the existing developmental schemes are not commensurating with the outlay fixed and incurred in different sectors. Only a nominal part of the grant sanctioned is utilized in its proper cause while the maximum part is outlayed in switching over the machinery. So far, the tribal people who were already well-off and had favourable ecological background could be able to achieve the benefits of the development programmes while the poors i.e. the real beneficiaries, have been pushed from bad to worse (Bisht : 1993). There are still landless tribal families particularly among Koltas in Jaunsar Bawar, Rajis and Harizan Bhotiyas in Pithoragarh and Tharus and Buxas in Nainital Tarai region, who subsist merely on their day long physical labour and other subsidiary primitive sources. There are tribal families who have subsidized housing grants but no roof, and, therefore, compelled to take shelter of the caves (Bisht : 1993), while about 40 to 40 per cent tribal families still dwell in their self made hutments. In general, the tribals are still adhering to their age old crude type of cultivation pattern. The advanced agricultural equipments and improved quality of seeds, fertilizers, and the use of pesticides have no meaning for them. Even today, they are guided by their religious beliefs, practices and cultural ethos (Bisht : 1993). The tribal areas still deprive them of proper irrigation facilities. Under family oriented programmes they have subsidized loan for buffalo/ bullock cart, milching cattle, goat and sheep rearing but in practice they are yet to get these.

A number of tribal men and women are being trained in different trades with Rs 150 as scholarship per month under the employment generation schemes but so far only few tribal men and women could be able to establish any occupation for self-employment. Even the infrastructural facilities like cooperation, road communication, electrification, drinking water and education, have no compatibility, with the outlay incurred. The educational facilities in spite of different incentives, could not attract and motivate the tribal children towards schools. As a result, the schools in Raji tribal areas are out of function for the last three years. The Ashram type schools, exclusively meant for tribals, have no doubt functional utility but have caused the problem of social integration by segregating the tribal children from the rest of the society since their childhood. Medical health and nutritional programmes have no meaning for them, as they are being governed by the traditions full of supernatural beliefs and magical practices. Thus, the results of the existing developmental plans particularly in tribal areas are not commensurating with the outlay fixed and incurred in different sectors.

In fact the development policies, as such, have no concern with the stimulation of will power, work spirit, skill, entrepreneurship and features of merits and demerits, morality and immorality among the different parts of development organization, but it aims at achieving its objectives by providing sheer economic assistance. The excessive emphasis on investment and subsidized grant has fumigated the culture and its dimensions. It seems that economic planning has vanished from the notion of humane traits, human factors and the psychological implications which are in real sense the preconditions of economic development. Even the human resource development programme merely on account of its economic nature could not produce the desired results. The tribals are inclined to get admission in different job-oriented programmes not because they really want to become self-reliant by developing workmanship and entrepreneurship in themselves but out of the greed for availing of the scholarships, subsidized equipments and raw materials provided to the beneficiaries while completing the training. Same is the case with the "incentives" which are generally in the form of economic assistance and which could not leave any lasting motivational impression on the beneficiaries rather it generates a latent passion and lasting ambition to achieve it without toil.

In brief, it can be asserted that various developmental schemes, which are predominantly economic in nature have disregarded the culture and its dimensions. Neither the ecological background nor the inherent skill, mental set-up and the cultural ethos of the tribes have been taken into consideration while framing the economic planning, resultantly the schemes could not produce its presupposed results. Even the personnel shouldering the liabilities of implementing the schemes in remote and inaccessible tribal areas are not bothered about the valuation of development works. It seems, that humane traits like morality that cherished the ideals, honesty that inspires for fair dealing, sympathy which implied the feeling of worldliness and brotherhood and sincerity that represents the fidelity and devotion to one's duty are all at a discount. That's why a man whether he is a planner, an executor, a beneficiary or a mediator in the spectrum of development planning has its sheer single-point programme as to remain vigorously in search of an opportunity as to satisfy one's ego at any cost. Even the false trick which the so called simple, honest ingenuous tribals have learnt to play for economic gains through Government subsidies with the help of the newly emerged indigenous leaders, mediators and the personnel, is nothing but a repercussion of this system, bearing exclusively the economic concern. It is because of this reason only that the existing development plans could not get positive results.

Thus, it is asserted that economic planning can be commensurable with its presupposed consequences of development only when it takes cues from cultural dimensions and their time and region specific attributes in consideration. In this way the culture as such is not an obstacle but a precondition for economic development.

NOTES

Material: It consists of the different instruments, equipments and the means used for satiating the human needs, may be biological, metabolic, reproductive, bodily comfort, safety, movement, growth and health.
Non-Material: It subsumes the traditions, norms, values, beliefs and many other abstract facets having functional importance for group living.
The Psychological: It includes motivations, attitudes, thinking, ideology etc.
The Human: It contains the skill, the entrepreneurship, willingness, risk taking capacity, knowledge, technical know how, experience, education, etc.
The Humane: It deals with the morality, honesty, sympathy & sincerity etc.

REFERENCES

1. Weber, Max, 1958, *The Religion of India; The Sociology of Hinduism and Buddhism*, The Free Press.
2. Kapp, William, K., 1963, *Hindu Culture, Economic Development and Economic Planning in India*, New Delhi: Ashish Publishing House.
3. Marx, K., 1906, *Capital*, Chicago.
4. Rostow, W.W., 1960, *The Process of Economic Growth*, 2nd Ed. Oxford Clarendon.
5. Dobb, M., *Some Aspects of Economic Development*.
6. Leibenstain, H., 1957, *Economic Backwardness and Economic Growth*, New York: John Wiley and Sons. Inc.
7. Mclelland, 1961, *The Achieving Society*, Princetor D. Van Nostrand Co., Inc.
8. Harbison, Frederick H and Charles Myers, 1964, *Education Manpower and Economic Growth*, New York: Mc Graw Hill Co.
9. Muthayya, B.C., 1985, Human Development : A prerequisite for Economic Development (ed) S.R. Ramamurthi : *Economic and Social Development*; National Institute of Rural Development Rajendra Nagar, Hyderabad.

Bisht, B.S., 1002, Bahrot: UP Himalayan Kshetra Ki Ek Alpayat Janjati, Manav: Ethnographic and Folk Culture Society, Lucknow.

———, 1992, "Jaunsa Bawa ki Bahupati Vivahi Khasa Janjati mein Shiksha tatha Vyavasaya, Vivah va Pariwar ke Badalte Pratiman", *Manav*: Ethnographic and Folk Culture Society, Lucknow.

———, 1993, "Tharu Janjati mein Samajik Sangathan ke Swaroop avam Unka Arthik Jeevan Par Prabhav" *Manav*: Ethnographic and Folk Culture Society, Lucknow.

10. Bisht, B.S., 1994, Tribal Development : An appraisal: Paper presented in U.P. Sociological Conference, BHU, Varanasi.
11. Tylor, E.B., 1874, *Primitive Culture*, New York.
12. Benedict, Ruth, 1904 *Patterns of Culture*, London: Routledge and Kegan Paul Ltd.
13. Kluckhohn, C. and William Kelly, 1945, *The Concept of Culture*, New York: Columbia University Press.
14. Kroeber, A.L., 1952, *The Nature of Culture*, Chicago: The University of Chicago Press.

Eight

Dilemma of Caste-Tribe and Tribe-Caste Transformation

A.K. KAPOOR

In the broad sphere of Indian society, although the representation of tribes is numerically small but culturally, it is significant and effective. The tribal heritage consists of many valuable ingredients of Indian culture. Hence, a proper identification of these ingredients is essential to explore the real nature of Indian social system and cultural heritage. This may provide a sound base for the study of modernization of Indian society. The caste dominance is a unique characteristic of Indian society. Similarly, the tribals exhibit a variety of customs and traditions typical of their own lifestyles. The sociocultural transformation of tribal societies has occurred more rapidly in recent times. Tribal societies have not remained immune to change. This is mainly because of the break of certain degree of isolation and subsequent growth of cultural contact. The transformation has been generally channelized through the phenomenon of urbanization and by some other processes, such as Sanskritization, acculturation, etc. The marked changes in the tribal communities can be broadly categorized into three stages, from the transformative view point: (1) some tribes have sufficiently changed (modernization stage); (2) some are in transition (adoption stage); and (3) some still remain bogged down within the frame of traditional set-up (latency stage).

It has been observed in the study of Indian civilization that many tribal communities have emulated the elements of caste-Hindus in course of historical development and cultural transformations (Bose, 1941[1]; Sachchiddananda, 1964, 1970[2]; Rao, 1966[3]; Jha, 1983)[4]. There have been instances of individuals and certain tribes being absorbed within the Hindu caste system in

India (Risley, 1951[5]; Sahay, 1962, 1967[6]; Sinha, 1965, Sinha 1980)[7]. Notwithstanding this, some of them have formed socially and culturally distinct communities maintaining their distinct identities in contrast to their neighbouring caste-Hindus (Vidyarthi & Rai, 1985)[8]. It has also been observed that tribes are in continuous contact with the caste-Hindus and vice versa and have been influenced by each other in various socio-economic patterns. It is a fact that Hindus have also been influenced by the tribals in different parts of the country and there is every possibility of tribals as well as Hindu elements coexisting in a given item of culture. Most of the anthropologists have studied caste-tribe and tribe-caste transformation in various parts of India but so far no attempt has been made to study the Himalayan population who have different ethnic history, ecological, socio-economic and cultural life, biological and technological aspect.

In the present study an attempt has been made to study the processes and methods of tribalization and detribalization in three communities, namely, the Harkotiyas, the Barbatiyas and the Rajis of Central Himalayas (UP). What are the forces which compel the caste groups as well as the tribes to come under the influence of the tribals / castes living in the same geographical area and higher stage of civilization? If they come under the influence of modernized societies how are their modes of life modified? What is their present status and condition with reference to socio-economic pattern and welfare measures of the Government of India? With reference to these questions, an attempt has been made in the study to find some answers empirically by analysing the life of the Harkotiyas, the Barbatiyas and the Rajis respectively.

Area of Study

The Hill region of Uttar Pradesh came under the administration of the East India Company in 1851 as a result of the Treaty of Sigauli. This region could not be administered under the regulations meant for other territories under the British company because of regional specialities, difficult geographical conditions and distinct political history, it was administered under non-regulations system.

The geographical conditions of Kumaon and Garhwal region

(two divisions of Uttar Pradesh) are different from plains. These two regions jointly constitute the Uttarakhand zone of the State. The Uttarakhand is populated by different castes namely, Scheduled Tribes, caste groups and ethnic groups. Its mainland is found by the rugged mountainous terrain of Himalayas covered with dense forest and shrubs, while the southern part of the region is constituted by the plain belt of Tarai and Bhabhar which has been stretched from the Western-most part alongwith the foothills of the region. The major part of the region is uneven in altitude and inacessible and abstruse. The region comprises of eight hill districts, namely, Almora, Pithoragarh, Nainital, Tehri, Pauri Garhwal, Chamoli, Uttarkashi and Dehradun. The former three districts form the Kumaon division while the rest five districts constitute Garhwal division. The region has an area of 51,122 sq.km. (Kumaon 21,032 and Garhwal 30,090 sq.km.) The population as per 1991 census comes to 59,26,146 (Kumaon 29,43,199 and Garhwal 29,82,947). About 80 per cent agricultural population possesses approximately 0.5 acre land.

The study is concerned with the ethnic groups (so called caste group) and Scheduled Tribes who live in District Pithoragarh, a small area in northern India adjoining Tibet and Nepal. Its geographical extent lies between 29° and 31°N latitude and 79° and 81°E longitude in the Kumaon Himalaya. The Harkotiyas, the Barbatiyas and the Bhotias (a general reference has been made) to inhabit the Musiari Tahsil whereas the Rajis inhabit the Dharchula, Didihat and Champawat Tahsils of Distt. Pithoragarh.

The region contains not only a diverse ecology with variety of geographical conditions but also the heterogeneous ethnic groups, who represent different cultural traits in the different parts of the region.

Ethnographic Profile and Changing Aspect

Bhotias

The entire Bhotia population of Uttarakhand is scattered over eight main river valleys and some of them derived their names from the name of the valley they dwell in on the basis of which they are subdivided into the main groups, namely, Johari, Jad, Tolcha, Marchha and Rang (Darmi, Byansi and Chaudansi).

Although, these groups are known by different names as above in their territorial boundaries, but in popular parlance they are referred by a common generic term-Bhotia. These Bhotia groups differ culturally, biologically and structurally from each (Kapoor, 1992[9], 1994[10]). These differences are the result of unique historical and ecological factors that affected them in different ways. The detailed account with reference to ecology, biology, demographic structure and socio-economic aspect have been published elsewhere (see Kapoor & Kapoor, 1986[11], Kapoor et al, 1990[12]; Kapoor 1991, 1994, 1997[13]; Aggarwal & Bisht, 1991)[14].

In the present study only the Bhotias of Johar valley of Tahsil Munsiari, have been taken into consideration. The Harkotiyas and the Barbatiyas are also residing in the same Tahsil and share same geographical area. The Bhotias have Mongoloid physical features. Srivastava (1966)[15] studied the tribal caste mobility among the Kumaoni Bhotias with reference to cultural approximation and emphasized that the Johari Bhotias have sought the status equivalence with the Hindu immigrant Rajputs. These Bhotias, therefore, also exercise their superiority over the neighbouring Khasiya-Rajputs on the basis of the cultural approximation which the former have gradually achieved with the immigrant Rajputs. The Bhotias from all the valleys joined together under a new leadership to demand numerous safeguards as a "backward" and special protection of their trade interests. This movement was led by the Johari Bhotias in the main. This new leadership later decided to claim a 'scheduled tribe' status for the Bhotias of Kumaon and Garhwal and they were declared as Scheduled Tribe in 1967, as against the earlier organized efforts to become Rajputs. The Johari Bhotias have a status ranking order in which they place most of the groups they come into contact with. With reference to caste-behaviour with that of the higher castes, Johari Bhotias are more strongly hierarchical in their interaction with other castes. Johari Bhotias rank the people they come into contact with in terms of a broad two-fold division of the caste hierarchy and maintain a Rajput-type social distance. The above details were reported by Srivastava in 1966 and the field work was conducted in 1950's. I started my field work in 1975 and am still continuing in different valleys of Bhotias. It is pertinent to point out here that when

Srivastava in 1950's studied the Bhotias, these groups were in the process of adopting Hinduism and when I studied them in 1975 Johari Bhotias were totally transformed into Hindu caste.

The Johari Bhotia society is a rank stratified society. It is divided into three distinct social classes which are also endogamous. The social classes in Bhotia society are related with a highly differentiated economy and, to some extent, also with the concept of ritual pollution. The economic prosperity of the Johari Bhotias achieved primarily from their Indo-Tibetan Trade in the district of Pithoragarh also resulted in the formation of hierarchical order, based on economic classes.

The Bhotias became the highest among the social classes with their wealth, land and also education. The caste groups of Bhotia region were not only dependent on Bhotias for obtaining certain items imported from Tibet, but also depended on their lands. They started exploiting their lands on share crop basis and in the form of a tenant-landlord relationship. All this helped the Bhotias in building a higher ritual status in the wider Hindu society. However, the secular status system was reinforced gradually by a ritual hierarchy too. This process of ritual status acquirement was facilitated by their superior economic and political position. This resulted in their claiming the status of a Hindu Rajput caste in the caste hierarchy, though they remained endogamous as far as Rajputs of Kumaoni peasant society are concerned. Most of the Bhotia families developed a traditional '*jajmani*' relationship with a certain Brahman family of that region. There are only few deities which are exclusively worshipped by the Bhotias, otherwise most of the deities are also worshipped by their neighbours who are predominantly Hindus. This gives ample testimony that the Johari Bhotias have become highly Hinduized due to the acculturative influence of the neighbouring Hindus.

The casual social relationship has now turned into a perpetual social relationship because of the sedentarization of the migratory Bhotias. Due to this, nowadays, Bhotias are living in a constant company of the Hindu sub-castes and, thus, also are becoming increasingly acculturated and Hinduized but they are maintaining the Scheduled Tribe status for various beneficial measures.

Barbatiyas (Jethras)

The Barbatiyas are an endogamous ethnic group living in Tahsil Munsiari of Pithoragarh Distt. This group is considered the 'autochthons' of the area or 1st settler prior to the Bhotias. They consider themselves as the earliest inhabitants therefore they are also known as Jetharas (Jeth in Kumaoni languages means elder). Very few scholars have discussed about them, e.g. Sherring, 1906[16]; Pant,1935[17]. No anthropological study has been conducted so far on this ethnic group.

They have Mongoloid physical features. They possess skin shades varying from medium yellow to light yellow brown, while the eye colour is observed to be light to dark brown. The hair-form is predominantly cymotrichous with black or brownish tinge. On the beard and moustache the growth of hair is scanty. The epicanthic fold is common. It is interesting to note that the female among the Barbatiyas have comparatively less pronounced Mongoloid characteristics than the males.

They are distributed in twelve villages alongwith their low caste Shilpkars (Domes). They live in twelve (*Barha*) villages and so they are called Barbatiyas (living in twelve villages of their own exclusively). The names of the villages are : Kweri, Jemia, Papari, Barnia, Raskot, Imla, Katalgaon, Josha, Chulkot, Ringu, Tomik and Namik. Their total population is 4,327.

Their villages are situated at the height of 6,000 to 9,500 feet in different geographical areas of Tahsil Munsiari. Each family has a fertile land of its own. Their main occupation is cultivation or agriculture. The subsidiary occupation varies from family to family, i.e. some make floor mats of *ringal*, some of them prepare ghee (oil) and sell in the nearby markets and different local fairs. Most of them keep cows or buffaloes. They exchange potatoes with salt and rice. Bride-price is prevalent in Barbatiyas and few of them also believe in 'Kanyadan' (bestowing of a girl in marriage). The monogamy is generally practised but few cases of polygamy are also witnessed. Junior levirate and sororate are sometimes practised. The surname is taken from the name of the village where they are inhabited. Child marriage is disappearing gradually. The Brahman plays an important role in their various socio-religious ceremonies and functions. Barbatiyas are patrilocal, patrilineal and patripotestal. They worship Hindu gods and goddesses and their own various local deities. The most distinctive element is the prevalance of animal sacrifice during various socio-religious functions.

It has been observed that a variety of acculturative influences are operating in Barbatiyas through a large variety of human agencies. Assimilating their sociocultural and economic factors, tremendous changes in their local culture are predictable. According to the residents and long-time observers, the transition has shown an amazing rate during the last two decades.

They are surrounded by the Bhotias on the one hand and the Khasa Rajput, Brahamans and Shilpkars on the other end. The following order represents their hierachial status in the area.

(i) Brahmans
(ii) Khasa-Rajputs
(iii) Barbatiyas
(iv) Bhotias
(v) Harkotiyas
(vi) Shilpkars (Doms)
(vii) Meerasi

Harkotiyas

According to a personal survey in 1994, the Harkotiyas or Danpurias are a small preliterate community of 1215 persons living in mountainous region of the Danpur *patti* of Almora Distt. (four villages) and in Munsiari Tahsil (One village) of Pithoragarh Distt. in Uttar Pradesh. They are somewhat removed, but not completely out from the general Kumaoni culture since geographically they are located in the midst of the general Khasa culture area on the one hand and on the fringe of the Bhotia culture area on the other.

At one time they were part of the trading Bhotias but now they have settled down and taken up agriculture as a means of subsistence. They domesticate bees (apicary) and sell honey and wax. They have also Mongoloid racial features. Harkotiyas have adopted the Rajput surnames 'Singh' to differentiate themselves from the Domes or low caste *shilpkars* of the area who bear the surname 'Ram'. They take their names from the village and 'ias' is fixed after the name of the village and that becomes the surname of the individual.

The rainfall, flora, fauna, habitational structure, dress and ornaments and the language of the Harkotiyas resembles with the Kumaoni Khasas in general but the marriage and other socio-religious ceremonies are particular to them with a little deviance from Kumaoni culture. They practice marriages among cousins which is absent in other Kumaoni culture as such. The family system is of patrilineal and partilocal type. They maintain friendly relations with other sub-castes but they don't accept the food prepared by Shilpkars. They don't have marriage alliance with the Bhotias but they maintain a good social relationship with the Bhotias and their food habits of sharing the hookah, etc. The structure of the religious system of the Harkotiyas is fairly complex. It consists of an amalgam of animistic beliefs pertaining to a host of ghosts, spirits and a polytheistic pantheon of gods and goddesses, alongside a 'coexisting system' of pan-Hindu polytheism. Within the native system fall the various cults of the local gods, life crisis rites and the family ceremonials in which relevant local gods are propitiated or worshipped. Then there are the ceremonial practices of the coexisting system of the pan-Hindu pantheon of polytheistic gods, in which the village as a whole takes part, such as the annual festivals of the Hindus. The Harkotiyas system can be viewed at three levels, at the level of the individual, the kin group and at the village level.

The Harkotiyas have their own flocks of sheep and cattle. The sheep are allowed to graze in the colder regions bordering the Pindari Glacier so that the wool may grow richer. In this practice the Harkotiyas emulate the Bhotias. The wool sheared off the sheep is used for making blankets and warm clothing much in the manner of the Bhotias.

Rajis

Raji is a small tribal community (declared Scheduled Tribe as well as primitive tribe in 1967) confined in the forest and hilly areas of Dharchula, Didihat and Champawat tahsil of Pithoragarh District in the Kumaon division. The tribe known for its socio-economic distinctiveness, is an example of uniqueness of the district. Rajis, also known as 'Ban-Raut' in the local areas, are the descendants of prehistoric Kiratas, who were comparatively early settlers of 'Uttaranchal' before the Khasas, Nagas, Aryans and the Tibetans. The detailed account on historical and sociocultural perspective have been dealt by Atkinson (1882)[18], Crooke (1886)[19], Majumdar (1944)[20], Bisht (1993)[21], Shah (1994)[22], Kapoor (1997)[23]. In physical appearance Rajis are of wheatish coloured complexion, of average height, straight and scanty hair of slight brownish colour, intermediate headed type with medium nose, round to long face, small eyes with grey pigments (some of them have mongoloid epicanthic fold). They worship the gods, ghosts and demons of the jungle, but they erect no temples in their honour. They have also started worshipping the Hindu gods and goddesses like their Kumaoni neighbours. They were to manufacture crude wooden vessels (still some families make the vessels) which they exchange with the neighbouring people (caste groups) for coarse cloth and grain. They are known locally as invisible traders. They were the food gathers having no permanent settlement. They subsisted on the jungle produce. They are far away from the literacy and the means of communication and transportation and, therefore, deprived from all sorts of inter and intra-tribal relations. In the present day context the sociocultural system of the Rajis has undergone numerous changes. They have got their permanent settlement or residence. They are eking out their maintenance with crude cultivation, jungle produce and as an agricultural labour. The social contact with other caste groups have also brought about some partial structural and organizational changes in their community.

The Dilemma of Transformation

Bhotias

By absorbing numerous traits of Hindu tradition (particularly from immigrant Rajput's cultural tradition which was most observed in Kumaon) in course of the long drawn struggle for Hindu status during which the exercise they had, perhaps, made them loose their own dialect too, the Johari Bhotias had reached a certain stage when their claim for Rajput affiliation was difficult to reject, by the regional Hindus. In several ways they became culturally close to the immigrant Rajputs, who belonged to the aristocracy of the Kumaon. The Johari Bhotias, had surpassed their Khasiya Rajput neighbours in many cultural fields and thus developed a sense of cultural superiority over the latter. The Bhotias got the Scheduled Tribes status in 1967 when they were at varying degree of Hinduization. For the Johari Bhotias the status of 'Scheduled Tribe' is nothing more than a mechanism to acquire facilities thereby ensuring their steady progress. This had nothing to do with their cultural aspirations. They declined to accept that this official status necessitates them to revive their "typical traditional culture" which they had rejected long ago.

In view of this, no significant cultural development, contrary to their Hinduization, has been witnessed.

Barbatiyas

In case of the Barbatiyas who are residing near the Johari Bhotias and have Mongoloid features, some of them maintain their traditional culture. They are considered superior to the Bhotias. They have started emulating the sociocultural system of the Khasa Rajputs and the Bhotias and on the basis of physical features they have also started claiming the status of Scheduled Tribes themselves for reaping benefits. It is predicted that the Barbatiyas will be assimilated with the Bhotias in future and will form a collective Mongoloid population in the area.

Harkotiyas

A general perspective of the historical background of the Harkotiya culture pattern will be relevant to the exposition that follows the Harkotiya claim to have been a part of the Bhotiya group.

The Harkotiya, Bhotiya Association: The Bhotias, who are located in the bordering Johar, Byans, Chaudans and Darma regions of the general Bhot area of Pithoragarh district, were a part of the main trading group with large flocks of sheep and who were engaged in trade and barter with the Tibet (Srivastava, 1957)[24]. The Harkotiyas having broken off from the main Bhotia group sometimes in the past, according to their own testimony, settled in the Danpur area of Almora District in the villages of Chaura, Harkot, Khaljuni and

Mikhila and Harkot in Munsiari tahsil of Pithoragarh District and took up agriculture as a main occupation. The Harkotiyas, however, till now retain their own flocks of sheep and cattle like the Bhotias.

It is perhaps pertinent here to state that in view of the poor technological development and the nature of the rather inhospitable geographical surroundings in which both the Harkotiya and the Bhotias are placed, religion for them becomes considerably involved in both the strictly economical and technological question. Though it may be an over simplification to state that "the more primitive the technology, the more religion is used to bolster man's effort (Yinger, 1957)[25]" and yet the association is not entirely spurious. Radin (1957)[26] believes that the desire to reinforce an inadequate technology is one of the complex of forces that lie at the very roots of religion. According to Malinowski (1953),[27] the Trobrianders had developed an elaborate system of rites around their work in an effort to placate the unknown forces that threatened their success and to rid themselves of the sense of insecurity. This is very true of the Harkotiya activity pattern which at particular points, such as agriculture and schemes of general welfare and in family ceremonies, is largely influenced by rites designed to bring about the intervention of the supernatural element in an effort to achieve the 'life values' which are felt to be threatened.

Thus, the Harkotiya due to their previous association with the Bhotias have a number of local spirits and gods in common, particularly those that are associated with the economic activity. For instance the spiritual personages that look after the welfare of the all important sheep of the Bhotias, namely Sidhwa-Bidhwa, are also the protectors of sheep among the Harkotiyas. However, the Harkotiyas by virtue of the fact of their placement in what is called the Khasa culture area are faced with a particular cultural climate of which they have had to take increasing cognizance. The Khasas are a Hinduized group of agriculturists residing in the villages surrounding those of the Harkotiyas.

The Harkotiya, Khasa Rajput Association: The Khasas have a complicated religious system, consisting in the mainline of Khasa's indigenous gods and goddesses, spirits and spirit beings, with a strong coexisting system of gods of the pan-Hindu panthion. The Harkotiyas have largely adopted the more important gods of the

Khasa pantheon and have also copied the rituals of the Khasa Rajput group. There has been a marked substitution or replacement of the native religious beliefs of the Harkotiyas which as has been noticed, took to some extent of the Bhotia religious systems by the Khasa gods, superimposed by the hierarchy of pan-Hindu polytheism. There are strong compulsions for such a religious infiltration some of which have figured in the caste system.

The Khasas belong to the Hindu caste system, being regarded as a Rajput group. They however, are not the high class Rajput group but are the inferior class of Rajputs. There is also an inferior class of Khasa Brahmins who are significant from the point of view of Khasa ceremonial. The Harkotiyas do not really belong to the caste system, though they have appropriated unto themselves membership of the caste system and regard themselves as Rajputs. The claim of the Harkotiyas is not recognized by the Khasa Rajputs. It is in the light of this somewhat anomalous situation that the compulsions for the religious reorientation by the Harkotiyas are to be viewed. The Harkotiyas, thus, are placed in a fairly intermediate position to the Bhotiyas on the one hand and the Khasa Rajputs and the Khasa Brahmins on the other. Caste, therefore, becomes a living reality for the Harkotiyas because of their placement contiguous to it and they increasingly try to regularize their attempt to enter into the portals of the caste system, even as low Rajputs, in order to derive the social and economic benefits of belonging to the caste structure. Thus, the Harkotiyas attempt to do so by emulating the caste practices of the Khasa Rajputs by taking up the Rajput surname of Singh and particularly by accepting the gods of the Khasa Rajputs and that of the Hindu pantheon as their own through a process of syncretism (Herskovits, 1948: 553-54)[28] and by Sanskritizing (Srinivas, 1962: 42)[29] their own ritual pattern by getting the 'priest' on ceremonial occasions, etc.

It is, therefore, relevant to state that, with the continuing contact of the Harkotiyas with the Khasa Rajputs, who in themselves manifest both the animistic and the Hindu Polytheistic religious pattern, the Harkotiyas have tended to increasingly adopt the religious system of the Khasas because the latter are more prosperous and the Harkotiyas are not so well-off. The argument becomes further debatable when a bad correlation is made by the

Harkotiyas between the Khasa prosperity and the Khasa religious pattern. In the eyes of the Harkotiyas, therefore, the Khasa gods are the more powerful, more "effective" and hence their own belief in their own local spirits is weekened and the "validity" thereof is doubted since these spirits tend to show up somewhat badly in contrast to the powerful Khasa gods in the matter of delivering the goods. Since the effectiveness and validity notions are linked in the Harkotiyas consciousness, the transition through syncretism and substitution between Khasa and Harkotiya pantheons becomes easy. Over and above, the animistic level of religious changes, looms over the highly potent pan-Hindu pantheon, the believers of which are even more prosperous well thought of and powerful. The Khasa Rajputs themselves owe allegiance to the Hindu gods and the Harkotiyas in turn also make great efforts to borrow the gods of the Hindus. There are two principal motives or compulsives involved in the process of borrowing. On the one hand, by this move the Harkotiyas seek to strengthen the spiritual powers of their superempirical world and thereby gain the powerful backing of powerful gods in the fulfilment of their life values and, on the other, by this they hope to become more easily and effectively absorbed into the Hindu caste system and be a part of them, so that they might be socially accepted and freed from the present social discrimination by being forced to stay on the periphery of the caste system. The commanlity of the pantheon and the Sanskritization of the ritual through the participation of the Khasa Brahmin priest in the Harkotiyas ceremonial pattern in considered a desirable goal to strive for. This approximation to the caste system via the religious media is a clear move in the emerging caste pattern of the Harkotiyas.

The animistic beliefs of the Harkotiyas can be taken to be the substratum of their religious pattern, constituting their own indigenous system. This has some common element with the Bhotia indigenous animistic beliefs due to the past association of both the Bhotias and the Harkotiyas. The gods and divine spiritual beings constitute the Harkotiya religious pantheon at the individual, family and village levels. This pantheon has been by and large adopted by the Harkotiyas from Khasa Rajputs and through customary usage in the time dimension has been incorporated into their own religious structure. There is a distinct gradation in this respect. Among Khasa gods like Gol Deota, Haru, Latu, etc, the latter is the more popular god in the adjoining Garhwal region of the Khasa culture area but being absent in the general Kumaoni culture complex, however, enjoys a higher ritual status than do the animistic spirits of the Harkotiya indigenous system. These Harkotiya gods of Khasa origin constitute the pantheons of both the Khasa Rajputs as well as of the Harkotiyas but due to their association with the Khasa Rajputs these gods are considered superior to the Harkotiya animistic spirits. This hierarchical order of the gods and spirits on a superordinate, subordinate scale is reflected also in the social hierarchy of the Harkotiyas and the Khasa Rajputs and the latter are considered superior to the former. At the upper level of the hierarchical order comes the gods of the pan-Hindu pantheon. These gods are regarded with the highest respect in keeping with their sacred character. They are venerated and worshipped in view of their highly potent powers and in the hope of winning their support through rituals and ceremonies in the achievement of the life values. The Harkotiyas, however, received the second-hand Hindu polytheistic pantheon through the Khasa Rajputs since they do not have much sustained direct connection with the Pan-Hindu religious and cultural complex. The Khasa Rajputs, particularly of Danpur, themselves form a fairly distinct cultural and social group, being in a peripheral cultural area to the main Kumaoni Hindu culture area they have had historical connections with the main Chand dynasty in Kumaon. In the due course of time have changed from itinerant herders to settled agriculturists and have imbibed the Hindu polytheistic beliefs in the process. The Harkotiyas, thus, emulate their neighbours - the Khasa Rajputs - in their Hindu polytheistic beliefs.

The Harkotiyas have followed the Hindus in two ways on one hand they have been observing some of the important festivals of the Hindus like the Khasa Rajputs do, and copying the rituals connected therewith, like the Diwali, Holi, Dushehra and Ram Naumi festivals and on the other hand the Harkotiyas have been worshipping the important gods of the Hindus, like Rama, Krishna, Shiva, Hanuman and accepted the sacred images of these gods as elaborated by the Khasa Rajputs. In this process of second-hand adoption, a little dilution has been inevitable and the Harkotiya images of the Hindu pantheon taken over from the Khasa religious structure has become a somewhat pale reflection of the original. Moreover, the quality and quantity of the ritual complex attending the worship of the Hindu gods, has suffered a decline in the Harkotiyas ritual expression so that in effect the Harkotiyas pay little more than lip service to the gods of the Hindu pantheon and practice the rituals of a simplified order, touching upon only the bare essentials.

On an emotive plane also, intense emotional attachment is reflected in respect of their own gods of Khasa origin, rather than towards the adopted gods of the Hindu pantheon. In crisis situations, in times of need, in the hours of travail when succour and comfort is sought, the Harkotiyas turn naturally to their gods of Khasa origin and even to their animistic beings, more than to the gods of the Hindu pantheon. The latter, therefore, are believed out of the necessity of a particular social context and as desirable ornaments to lend prestige and glamour to their own pantheon. This is also regarded as a mechanism for gaining ritual status comparable to that of the Khasa Rajputs in the context of the all important caste hierarchy.

The quandary that the Harkotiyas find themselves in is that, they can neither become acceptable to the Bhotias nor can they become one with the Khasa Rajputs. The paradox of their cultural and social placement between two non-accepting groups and their physical proximity to the Khasa Rajputs, forces upon them the dire necessity to do something to gain social and religious acceptance. This they seek to do through a self-declared adherence to the Khasa and the Hindu polytheistic pantheon. This unilateral action has, however, not been entirely successful, nor has it escaped opposition and criticism by the Khasa Rajputs, but notwithstanding both, the Harkotiyas by individual means in small degree, have persistently made and staked their claim, in the teeth of opposition, to the hegemony of the caste order and the religious structure of the Khasa Rajputs.

It can be gathered that the existing Harkotiyas religious structure is the creation of a number of factors which have cumulatively influenced its expression. First, there is the fact of the historical accident of the Khasa-Bhotia association out of which came the indigenous animistic set-up of the Harkotiyas. Secondly, there is the fact of the subsequent break-up of the Harkotiyas migration and changeover from a trading to an agricultural economy. This necessitated the incorporation of divinities pertaining to the agriculture. The placement of the Harkotiyas in geographical contiguity to the agricultural Khasa Rajputs made it possible for the Harkotiyas to incorporate in their religious structure the gods of the Khasas, particularly those involved in the agricultural complex. The amalgam of the Harkotiyas, the Bhotias and the Khasas religious aspects have thereby emerged. Thirdly, the social climate that the Harkotiyas have found themselves in was permeated by a caste order that was an essential part of the Khasa Rajput cultural and social complex. This has made it imperative for the Harkotiyas to seek entry into the caste hierarchy in order to exist as a vital community with a wide range of social relations. The interpersonal contact pattern being influenced and conditioned by the caste structure surrounding the Harkotiyas made it necessary for them to attempt and become a part of it. The religious media offered a way out of the social impasse and, thus, through a process of caste and religious approximation, the Harkotiyas have succeeded fairly well in getting at least a precarious foothold in the caste complex. Their religious structure had perforce to become an amalgam of the Khasa and Hindu religious order producing the peculiar, complex and to an extent transitional, religious structure to which the Harkotiyas at present owe allegience.

The Rajis

Formerly, when the Rajis inhabited the forests of Chhipula Kot (Kumaon region) they were almost isolated from the rest of the population in the area and nothing new was imbibed from the outside world. Further, cultural contacts were not possible because of their shyness. However, the Rajis today are neither so shy nor are they isolated. They are flanked on the northern side by the Mongoloid Bhotias and on the southern side by the Kumaoni Khasas. Domiciled in the midst of those alien cultures, the Rajis cannot avoid coming in contact with new influences. Originally, they carried out their barter through 'silent trade'. But they could not maintain this isolation for any length of time as their territory was gradually encroached upon by the Kumaoni Khasas. After coming in contact with their Khasa neighbours, the Rajis have gone through a number of changes. It is, needless to say, that they have been influenced entirely by the southern Khasas with whom they have maintained close intimate contacts. The Bhotias being further away from their territory could not influence them much. No missionaries have ever worked among the Rajis. In mundane life, the Rajis take their social superiority over their Khasa neighbours for granted. They have desire for their recognition in the social hierarcy of the Kumaoni Khasa neighbours. They have tried to identify themselves with the Khasa and repudiate any connection with the doms (Shilpkars). Except for casual contact with the village blacksmiths for obtaining axeheads, scythes and adzes, they never encouraged or even maintained any association with them for fear of being relegated to a lower status, in the social set-up of their neighbours. As a consequence, they have managed to secure for themselves a status, which is slightly higher than that of the Doms, but considerably lower than that of the Khasas. The effect of this association has brought about and still continues to bring about, traits in the organization and culture of the Rajis which are characteristically that of the Khasas. The Doms, who are dependent on the Khasas for their existence, are better off materially as compared to the Rajis. This tension between the Rajis and Doms has led to a greater cooperation between the Khasas and the Rajis, as the former have some aversion for the Doms.

In brief, Rajis are emulating various sociocultural and religious patterns of their Khasa neighbours and also started consulting the Brahman for various ceremonies. They have also started copying the names of Khasas and Brahmans for their children. They are trying to become 'Rajput' or 'Khasa' in the eyes of their neighbours, whereas, the Government of India has declared them as Scheduled Tribe and because of poverty, ignorance, suffering and, thus they are not able to adopt various development schemes initiated by the State and the Central Government. They want to enhance their social status in the area but they are not interested in the Constitutional rights.

It has been observed that Barbatiyas and the Harkotiyas first emulated the various lifestyles to come to the caste hierarchy in the local area and after getting the same they are emulating the various benefits for their development. Psychologically the Barbatiyas and the Harkotiyas retain some sort of the latent and manifest attitude and motivation which are considerably different from others. Their emotions and limited world view, indirectly forced them to maintain a separate cultural identity which raises for them a series of interlinked problems in social, economic and cultural adjustment. The Rajis are receiving a constant impetus in a spontaneous manner to modernize their lifestyle by imitating advanced communities residing in their neighbourhood. They are in process of becoming the caste group. Here they are obviously facing serious problems between material wants and the means of achieving it. They try to adopt the lifestyle of the modern society and yet retain the emotions and dark forebodings of the tribal world. When they find these two-half sets as incompatible with one another, they go for overexposure and in the process they exhaust themselves. On the whole, in this transitional phase the Barbatiyas, Harkotiyas and Rajis have aspirations of the modern society but also have emotions of the primitive society which is nothing but a crucial phase which can be best compared with a situation "in the hours of dilemma."

REFERENCES

1. Bose, N.K., 1941, The Hindu method of tribal absorption. *Science and Culture*, 8: 188-194.
2. Sachchidanand, 1964, *Culture Change in Tribal Bihar*, Calcutta: Bookland (P) Ltd.
   ———, 1970, Tribe-caste continuim: A case Study of Gond in Bihar. *Anthropos.*, (2) : 18-31.
3. Rao, V.K.R.V., 1966, Social change and Tribal Society. *J. Social Research*, 9(2): 54-67.
4. Jha, M., 1983, *An Introduction to Anthropological thought*. New Delhi: Vikas Publishing House Pvt. Ltd.
5. Risley, H.H., 1915, *The People of India*, London: Thacker Spink & Co.
6. Sahay, K.N., 1962, Trends of Sanskritisation among the Oraon, *Bulletin of Bihar Tribal Research Institute*, 4(2) : 18-32.

———, 1967, A Study in the process of Transformation from Tribe to Caste : Parahiyas of Lolki : A case study. *J. Social Research*, X(1): 51-62.

7. Sinha, S., 1980, Tribal Indian Civilization: A Perspective. *Man in India*, 60(i): 1-15.
8. Vidyarthi, L.P. and Rai, B.K., 1985, *The Tribal Cultures of India*. New Delhi: Concept Publishing Company.
9. Kapoor, A.K., 1992, *Genetic Diversity among Himalayan Human Populations*. Jammu: Vinod Publishers (P) Ltd.
10. ———, 1994, Ecology and Tribals in Central Himalayas, pp.69-90. In : *Ecology and Man in the Himalayas*. Eds. A.K. Kapoor & S. Kapoor. New Delhi: M.D. Publications.
11. Kapoor, A.K. and Kapoor, S., 1986, The Effects of High Altitude on Age at Menarche and Menopause. *Int. J. Biometeor*, 20: 212-26.
12. Kapoor, A.K., Prasad, R.R. and Tiwari, S.C., 1990, Semi-nomadism and Transhumance in Central Himalayas : A Pragmatic Perspective. *Man in India*, 70 : 47-60.
13. Kapoor, A.K., 1997, *Ecology and culture of Highlanders*.
14. Aggarwal, G.K. and Bisht, B.S. 1991, *Tribes of Uttarakhand*. Agra: Agra Book Store.
15. Srivastava, R.P., 1966, Tribe-caste mobility in India and the case of Kumaon Bhotia. In: C. Furor Haimendolf (Ed.) *Caste and Kin in Nepal, India and Ceylon*. Bombay: Asia Publishing House.
16. Sherring, C.A., 1906, *Western Tibet and the British Borderland*. London.
17. Pant, S.D., 1935, *The Social Economy of the Himalayas*. London: George Allen & Unwin.
18. Atkinson, E.T., 1882, *Himalayan Gazetter*. Vol.I, Part II. Cosmo Publications.
19. Crooke, W., 1886, *Tribes and Castes of the North-West Provinces and Oudh*. Vol.IV, Calcutta.
20. Majumdar, D.N., 1944, *Races and Cultures of India*. Bombay: Asia Publishing House.
21. Bisht, B.S., 1993, *Raji - A Tribe of Indo-Nepal Border of Uttarakhand*. Delhi: Vivek Prakash.
22. Shah, N.C., 1994, Rajis: A Study of their Social, Ethnic, Ethno-Botanical and other relative aspects (pp.91-102). In : *Ecology and Man in the Himalayas*, Eds. A.K. Kapoor & S. Kapoor. New Delhi: M.D. Publications.
23. Kapoor, A.K., 1997b, *Rajis: Primitive Tribe of Uttar Pradesh*.
24. Srivastava, R.P., 1957, Marriage and Divorce among the Eastern Bhotias. *Anthropologist*, 4(1 & 2) : pp.15-29.
25. Yinger, M., 1957, *Religion Society and the Individual*, New York: MacMillan.

26. Radin, 1957
27. Malinowski, B., 1953, *Agronants of the Western Pacific*. George Routleage, London.
28. Herskovits, M.J., 1948, *Man and his Works*. Alfred A. Knopf. New York.
29. Srinivas, M.N., 1962, *Caste in Modern India and other Essays*. Asia Publishing House, Bombay.

Nine

Backward Communities and Conversion

TARACHAND G. MESHRAM

In 1981, Meenakshipuram, a village in Tamil Nadu in Tinnevelly district, made big headlines in leading Indian daily newspapers when thousands of Harijans decided to leave Hinduism and to embrace Islam. This case of mass conversion created a terrible shock among Hindus simply because it threatened to upset the communal balance. The growing awareness of social degradation has led many of these ex-untouchables to convert to Islam.

A small number of Christian Harijans also went over to embrace Islam. Their remark is worth noting 'by becoming Christians, we cannot raise our social status but by becoming Muslims we can'.[1]

In the Hindu-Muslim riots that have taken place all over the country it has been found that: a small number of Muslims can beat the Hindus and beat them badly; it has been proved that the Hindus are beaten not only where they are weak in numbers, but they are beaten by Muslims even where the Hindus preponderate.

Take the example of Sikhs. Sikhism is the only religion in the world where its followers are permitted to keep weapons (Kripan) for their self-defence and protection, including women.

People of other religions would not dare to do injustice to them whether they were alone or in group or in a village. They live like lions in villages.

What about the plight of untouchables? The untouchables even though they are in majority in villages lead miserable life and are at the mercy of the Hindus for their sustenence.

Hindu society is based on the principle of inequality. This

society does not recognize society as the centre nor an individual as centre. It is a class based society with the class of supermen called Brahmins. The purity of the Brahmins is harmoniously linked to the impurity of the untouchables. According to Dick Kooiman (1989), "Hinduism, occupations involving impurity are permanently assigned to specialists like sweepers, tanners, midwives and toddy-tappers. These specialists are considered unfit for social contact."[2]

Dunkin Ferrester in his book *Caste and Christianity* says: "Caste is the Achilles heel of Hinduism. Hence anything that strikes at the heart of caste reaches also a deadly blow to Hinduism; for caste is the chief cornerstone on which the whole Hinduism rests, it is the strong pillar which supports and perpetuates Hindu idolatry of rebirth".[3] Similarly, Dr Laxmi P. Narsu in his *Essence of Buddhism* has observed the relationship of caste and Hindu religion. "The caste distinctions are the chief support of the Hindu religion; when they give away there can be nò doubt that Hinduism will sink to destruction."[4]

Other religions in India teach principles of equality, even though the Hindu religion does not accommodate the principle of equality. Fourester has quoted Fuller as saying : "He argues that the egalitarian aspects of Christianity, as of Islam and Buddhism have had negligible effect on the Hindu way of life.[5] This is the main reason why Hindu religion did not prosper beyond the boundaries of India. Proselytism has never been the practicing creed of the Hindu faith.

Conversion is the means of increasing one's own status

Harold R. Issac in his book *India's Ex-untouchables* quoted Dr Ambedkar and said:

"My self respect cannot assimilate Hinduism. I tell you, religion is for man and man not for religion. If you want to organise, consolidate, and be successful in this world, change this religion. The religion that does not recognize you as a human being or give you water to drink or allow to enter the temples is not worthy to be called a religion. The religion that does not teach its followers to show humanity in dealing with its co-religionists is nothing but a display of a farce. The religion that asks its adherents to suffer the touch of animals but not the touch of human beings is not a religion but a mockery. The religion that compels the ignorant to be ignorant and the poor to be poor is not religion but a visitation".[6]

Dr Ambedkar saw that the stigma of untouchability cannot be removed unless a change in Hindu religion is introduced. He appealed to the Hindus to remove untouchability from their religion. Because he firmly believed that the untouchability is a man-made mechanism. Caste and untouchability is not made by God. It is created by Brahmins for their benefit. Therefore, he thought that the removal of untouchability from Hindu religion is possible. A sufficient opportunity was given to Hindu people for its removal through his experiences and he came to the conclusion to 'reject the religion of caste and accept the religion where caste does not exist.'

Dr Ambedkar's request to remove caste and untouchability from Hindu religion was based on the principle of creating integrity in India for its prosperity. There cannot be a more degrading system of social organization than '*Chaturvarna*'. It is the system which deadens, paralyzes and cripples the people from helpful activity. This is not an exaggeration. History bears ample evidence to this. There is only one period in Indian history, which is a period of freedom, greatness and glory and that is during the period of Mauryan Empire. At all other times the country suffered from defeat and darkness. But during Mauryan dynasty 'Chaturvarna' was completely annihilated, when the Shudras, who constituted the mass, came into their own and became the rulers of the country. The period of defeat and darkness is the period when the 'Chaturvarna' flourished to the damnation of the greater part of the people of the country.

Caste prevents mobilization. Society must mobilize all its resources to one end in order to save itself from a catastrophe like war. Society must mobilize all its resources for militarization. Every one must go for a war. Every one must be a soldier. This is not possible in the theory of caste. Indeed, India had to face defeat several times throughout history due to the caste system. Caste prevented general mobilization or the extent of mobilization was very limited. Only the Kshatriyas were expected to fight. The rest, the Brahmins and the Vaisyas were not armed and the Shudras who formed the large majority of the country were disarmed. The result was that once the small class of Kshatriyas were defeated by the foreign foe, the whole country fell at his feet. It could offer no resistance as it was not capable of offering resistance. Indian wars have been mostly wars of single battles or single campaigns. This was due to the fact that once the Kshatriyas fell everything fell. Why? Simply because there was no general mobilization and the theory deeply imbedded in the psychology of war.

It is the false notion that the Hindu community was among the oldest communities that has withstood the onslaught of many adverse forces, therefore, there must be some native strength and stamina in its culture and civilization as to make it survive. Hindus firmly believe that their community was destined to survive. But, the survival was of many types and not all were weighed equally. One can survive by marching against the enemy and conquering him. Or, one can survive by beating a retreat and hiding oneself in a position of safety. In either case there would be survival. But, certainly the value of two survivals is measured apart. What is important is not the fact of survival but the plan of survival. Survive, the Hindus may, but whether as free men or brave men or slaves or coward is the issue. But the matter seems so hopeless that, granting that they manage to survive as slaves, it does not seem to be altogether certain that they can survive as Hindus. The scope of survival not only narrowed in the physical struggle but they also seem to be narrowed in the cultural struggle. A regular campaign is vigorously conducted by the Muslims and Christians for the spread of Islam and Christianity and by their conversion movement. These two religions have made vast additions to their numerical strength by winning over members of Hindu faith. Fortunately for the Muslims and Christians, there is a large mass of non-descript and marginal population of Scheduled Caste and backward communities, numbering about one-third of India's population, which is classed as Hindus but which has no particular affinity to the Hindu faith and whose position is made so intolerable by that faith that they can be easily induced to embrace any religion, including Islam and Christianity. The Hindus feel that they must save their people from losing their identity and their culture. For this purpose, they propounded the Shuddhi movement, or the movement to reclaim people to the Hindu faith. But the Constitution of Hindu religion does not provide for aliens being made its members and allowed to participate in its social life. While making this, there should not be difference between the individuals born in it and individuals brought into it. It should allow even aliens to enter into its life and, thus, make it possible for him to live and thrive as a member of that society. If there is no such provision on conversion of an alien, the question would at once arise where to place the convert. If there is no place for the converts there can be no invitation for conversion nor can there be an acceptance of it.

There is no place in the Hindu society for a convert to the Hindu faith. Because the Hindu society is constituted of castes and each caste is endogamous in nature and lives in isolation. In other words it only allows individuals born in it, to its membership and does not allow any one from outside being brought into it. Since, the Hindu society being a federation of castes and each caste being self-enclosed there is no place for the converts because no caste will admit him. A caste is incompatible with conversion. This is particularly true in case of mass conversion. The Hindu society could convert and the converts should form a new caste.

The motive behind the 'Shuddhi Movement' is to increase the strength of the Hindu society by increasing its numbers. No society is strong because its members are great in number but because it is solid in its mass. There are many instances where a solid organized band of fanatics have routed a large army of disorganized crusaders. Hindus suffered not from want of numbers but from want of solidarity. To increase solidarity of the Hindu society one must tackle the forces which have brought about its disintegration. If the people whose *shuddhis* have been made and if they are not admitted into the Hindu fold, it will only add one more caste to the existing number. It is an accepted fact that greater the castes, the greater the isolation and the greater the weakness of the Hindu society. If the Hindu society desires to survive, it must think not of adding to its numbers but increasing its solidarity and that means the abolition of caste. If the caste exists it would be harmful to the real *sanghatan* and solidarity of the Hindus.

The backward communities were the real sufferers of the evils of caste system. These communities were denied equality and justice at the hands of upper castes. Backward communities never had much scope to escape from their miserable position of Hindu society. From time to time they joined sects or movements that stressed social equality. The problems of backward communities are not only social but also economic, religious and cultural.

Conversion is not new to India, especially in case of backward communities. Most conversion took place among the lower caste people. Higher castes sometimes showed a refreshing interest in Christian religious discussion and reflection. But, to the utter dismay of the missionaries, they never seriously thought of entering into the Christian fold. Because, for the higher castes, conversion means loosing their ascribed status. The exceptional conversion of Brahmin or Nayar was always celebrated as a main event and a new convert could count upon a most respectable treatment. For the missionaries, the high caste converts were viewed as a quantity whereas the untouchable converts as quantity. According to Hindu philosophy, lower castes are unable to increase their status in the society till their death and even after death.

Through 'sanskritization' process they could enhance their social prestige within their caste only. So the increase of one's own status by way of 'sanskritization' was regarded as positional changes within the caste system. Therefore, if the backward communities wanted to increase their status in society, it becomes necessary for them to change their religion. The change of religion (Hindu) is the only way for increasing their status in India.

Therefore, status conscious people, particularly lower castes, thought of changing their religion. Therefore, the conversion was closely linked to the social aspirations of groups that suffered from discrimination and oppression. The conversion "indicates that the groups involved considered religious identity to be an important factor in their attempts to acquire a better and more dignified place in society."[7]

The people, who were interested in improving their lives in this world, were greatly attracted towards religious conversion. And those who were not, were least bothered about it. Forrester has rightly said : "conversion appealed as at least an apparent escape from caste system for those who despaired of achieving improvement of their lot within the system."[8]

Reasons for Conversion

Conversions have taken place because of various reasons. For some they discard the ascribed status which is based on chance of birth. Because, they feel that the unequal status was given to them in spite of their worth. They observed and experienced that in secular life much importance was given to the achievement process. But religious life is an ascribed process. Therefore, such persons, changed their religion. Forrester has said : "Dignity, self-respect, patrons who will treat one as equal and the ability to choose one's own destiny - all these are powerful incentives to conversion."[9] According to Dr Ambedkar, equality, justice, fraternity, compassion and equal status for women are powerful incentives for conversion. He firmly believed that the route of equality, justice and fraternity is found in love and purity of mind. Therefore, love and purity of mind may lead to the development of humanity. The love and purity of mind is found only in Buddhism and not in other religions. Narsu says "Dogma and miracle are wisdom to the Christians; kismet and fanatism are wisdom to the Muslims; caste and ceremonialism are wisdom to the Brahman; ascetism and nakedness are wisdom to the Jain; mysticism and magic are wisdom to Taoist; formalism and outward piety are wisdom to the Confucian; ancestor worship and loyalty to the Mikado are wisdom to the Shintoist; but love and purity are the first wisdom to the Buddhist.".[10]

Equality is important for the development of one's own personality. Equality without liberty is useless. "Similarly without fraternity, equality and liberty has no meaning. Without equality, liberty would produce the supremacy of the few over many. Equality without liberty will kill individual initiative. Without fraternity, liberty and equality would not become a natural course of things. There is a complete absence of two things in Indian society, one of these is equality."[11] While showing difference between Buddhism and Hinduism, Sunanda Patwardhan quoted Ambedkar in her book : "while Buddhism has its roots in ethics and morality, Hinduism has its own in Karmakanda. The latter is based on hierarchy and differential status between man and man, whereas Buddhism is based on equality."[12]

Louis Dument in his *Homo Hierarchicus* says : "any religious movement which does not accept caste, will not survive in India.".[13]

Accepting this statement one can conclude that the conversion of Dr Ambedkar will get the status of a caste in future and will be known as the new caste. The Hindus would recognize the conversion of Dr Ambedkar as the conversion of Scheduled Castes particularly of Maharas and Chambhar. But this is a false notion about their background developed by the Hindus, Muslims, Christians, Jews, Portuguese in India. They are the people from lower classes. Still these people are not called by Hindus as Scheduled Caste or tribes, but are called Muslims, Christians, Jews, etc. Similarly these new converts to Buddhism, in future, will not be called as Scheduled Caste or Mahars, Chambars, Bhangis but they would be called as Buddhists or Neo-Buddhists.

Forrester in his book quoted Pickett as saying:

What must never be neglected is that conversion movement is like a kind of group identity crisis, in which the group passes through a negative rejection of their lowly place in Hindu society to a positive affirmation of a new social and religious identity. This new identity does not depend on its acceptance and recognition by higher castes; indeed it has been chosen and is sustained despite their refusal to accept it. Only gradually does it lead to significant alterations in behaviour and occupation and sometimes to a recognised enhancement of status.[14]

The previous conversions by the backward communities were mostly personal in nature. In such types of conversions people were materially benefited. These conversions were sometimes known as begging alms conversions. But the conversion of Dr Ambedkar does not fall under such category. This conversion was done for developing dignity and self-respect, sometimes it has ignored the material benefits extended by the Government in the form of preferential treatment.

Forrester pointed out: "But the continuation of group conversions in recent years — Neo-Buddhism is the most spectacular but by no means the only instance — is an interesting and significant phenomena, demonstrating that even at a time when much has been gained for untouchables through political action, the question of religious identity remains real and alive. It is so real that many are willing to sacrifice the protection and advantages which are accrued to Hindu Harijans. There is also probably some disillusionment with the fruits of political action and statutory enactments. They by themselves cannot provide dignity as well as opportunities and material advancement which is sought. Self-respect as missionaries had long before discovered, is more important than charity even if the charity comes from Government."[15]

Accepting the fact that the conversion would promote self-respect, dignity and group identity among the converts; the conversion would not be the final solution for the inhuman, unequal, unjustifiable treatments at the hands of caste Hindus. The new converts should be alert and visible about the injustice done to them. If they are not alert and vigilant, mere conversion would not solve their problem. Therefore, Dr Ambedkar has rightly guided at the youth conference at Pune on 12 and 13th January, 1936, that the conversion alone would not relieve them from their inhuman conditions. They would still be required to fight for liberty and equality.[16]

REFERENCES

1. Dr Ambedkar, B.R., 1989, *Dr Babasaheb Ambedkar writings and speeches*. Vol. 5, 422-25. Education Department of Maharashtra.
2. Kooiman, Dick, 1989, *Conversion and Social Equality in India*, p. 2, New Delhi: Manohar Publications.
   ———, Ibid, p. 2.
3. Forrester, Doken, *Caste and Conversion*, p. 126.
4. Narsu, Laxmi, 1948, *Essence of Buddhism*, p. 153, Bombay: Thaokar and Company.
5. Forrester, Donken, op.cit., p. 103.
6. Issac, Harold, 1965, *India's ex-untouchables*, Bombay: Asia Publishing House.
7. Kooiman, Dick, op. cit., p. 1.
8. Forrester, Dunkan, op.cit., p. 103.
9. Ibid., p. 75.
10. Nasru, Laxmi, P., op. cit., p. 68.

11. Robbin, Jeaneth, 1964, *Dr. Ambedkar and His Movement*, p. 84, Hyderabad.
12. Patwardhan, Sunanda, 1973, *Change Among India's Harijans*. p. 160, New Delhi: Orient Longman.
13. Dument, Louis, *Homo Hierachicus*.
14. Forrester, Dunken, op. cit., p. 77.
15. Ibid, p. 92.
16. Robbin, Jeaneth, op. cit., p. 126.

Ten

Tribal Self-Management and Globalization

G.S. SAUN

At a time when the dominant currents of thinking and practice are sanctimoniously geared towards "globalization" and "liberalization" at a break neck speed, come what may; any attempt to review and reflect on the potentiality and the future prospects of the institutions and values of self-management among the tribal peoples of India may appear tendentious and obsolescent, or at best, of a limited significance for only folkloric exotica. None the less, as the emerging critical scenario unfolds and consequently invigorates the search for a better and more humane alternative, there is a conspicuous and rising trend to locate the substance of human living, managing and reproducing themselves in historical times as well as their contemporary dignified existence in cross-cultural contexts.

When we consider the question of self-management of the tribal communities, it does well to remember the prevalent ethos among them. Western societies have been glorifying the role of the individual more and more. A stage has now been reached when the automized individual finds himself at the centre of the universe around him. He is no longer a part of the holistic societies knit together in kinship, social, economic and hundred other bonds that we in highly differentiated milieu can hardly visualize and appreciate. In non-tribal societies, an individual may be a member of professional groups or clubs where he may find a degree of satisfaction. But, by and large, the smallest viable unit is the nuclear family, which also seems to be cracking up. The powerful western social trends have been making inroads into oriental societies, particularly among the elites. The consequence has been the growing frustration and loneliness of an individual, starkly evident in the homes and related institutions for the old. The tribal societies have, by and large, been able to keep these tendencies in check through the practice of a balance of the interests of the individual and the society. The kin group at the core, regulates the interests and as Clarke and Hindley put it, "the evolution of the integrative social patterns has been regarded as the primitive man's finest achievement just as, some would argue, the failure to maintain them is our worst fault." The tribal societies have created a social network through which the management of their affairs is conducted smoothly and viably. For the purpose, kinship and organizational frameworks have been devised on intricate psycho-social basis. For them, this universe is as important and objective as the physical world. To quote the same authors, "such societies form a framework in which the personality can extend itself and its dialogue with other men and women, not a battlefield for competitive enterprise. Where we exploit 'contacts', the primitive was involved throughout his waking life in personal relationships."

Prerequisites for Tribal Self-Management Systems:

Despite innumerable and conspicuous variations among the tribal peoples of India in terms of organization of production, ecology, demography, external articulations and customary systems of self-management and custodianship, broadly they share certain common principles, values and institutions. The fundamental features of tribal self-management systems are:

(i) both production and social reproduction are based upon communal collective control and institutional regulation of territorial survival resources and individual members' temporal usufructuary rights;

(ii) flexibility and diversity in production subject to the overall condition of balanced interaction with nature and sustainable living in accordance with the historically accumulated knowledge, and of course, with certain limited choices for experimentation or innovation;

(iii) social and/or spatial collectivity based upon the principle of reciprocity and demonstrated by collective responsibility, communal land tenure, cooperative labour, institutionalized community sharing, strong kinship bonds, solidarity and spirituality;

(iv) Substantive corporate autonomy not only over the territorial resources but also with regard to the basic social, economic and cultural functions that guarantee the corporate identity, existence, life, work and the future, which is legitimized by and operated through the internal institutions, values and structure and is so acknowledged by the neighbouring communities and/or regional/national authorities under the broad principle of "live and let live", and,

(v) the power structure largely rooted in the heritage and face to face dialogue and consensual model, wherein authority constitutes only a collective leader(s) to carry out the essential and paramount functions.

Needless to stress that though all the five aforesaid prerequisites are more or less common in the tribal self-management systems, they do not necessarily carry equal significance in all the tribal systems. Nevertheless, the obvious fact is that without group control and its institutionalized autonomy to manage the productive resources and the sociocultural complexes, the self-management systems can hardly survive. Moreover as the above institutions and values are incompatible with the modern State system and capitalist development, it is reasonable to presume that the tribal self-management systems will tend to be irrelevant, redundant and eventually collapse, or at best survive as a "cultural lag".

There are numerous forces which have obstructed the reproduction of an able management system. The sustainability of customary tribal self-management systems are being increasingly threatened or made ineffective by exogenous pressures of State intervention, market intervention, technological expansion as well as internal stresses due to the rising emphasis on integration into the national and global economy, contact with alien and dominant cultures and demographic expansion. It is the exploitative nature of the interests and values of the dominant classes and the global system, internationalization of even the remote tribal economies and direct pressure and hostility from the State and so called development agencies that left little alternative for the tribal people but to gradually abandon their customary management practices. There are two important theories which hold that the tribals cannot have institutions of self-management for their survival resources.

(1) Neo-Malthusian Theory of the Tragedy of Commons; and

(2) Theory of Temporasity and Spatial Flux.

Be that as it may, the viability of the tribal production systems has been radically undermined in the recent decades, not because of their "poverty of management" and lack of future perspective but precisely because of imposition of alien forces in terms of markets, capital, modern technology and the statecraft.

Besides these two perspectives which camouflage the ulterior motives by emphasizing the tribal peoples inability to manage the impersonal landbased endowments, the theories of population dynamics and ironically of poverty, tend to hold that, the poor tribals, expanding their population unmindfully, can hardly be trusted for managing the natural resources of the world. Following the conventional Malthusian approach, it has been argued that demographic expansion leads to over exploitation of natural resources and thus, the management and production become ecologically unsustainable. This oversimplistic assumption diverts attention from more fundamental causes located in the larger political economy and the State policy. There is no simple correlation between population growth and environmental decline and breakdown of the self-management systems. Rather, evidence suggests that at times a decline in population resulted in environmental degradation whereas, elsewhere the growing population has been able to adapt new methods of resource management in a sustainable manner. Of course, when people are deprived of means to adapt its resource management practices, to the changing needs of the community, the resources may tend to be unsustainable.

Amidst the aforesaid bleak scenario, there are several compulsions to hope for reinstitutionalization of self-management systems. The plethora of crises, the tenaciousness of self-management cultures, the recurrent and rising struggles of the tribal peoples and the growth of alternative visions of future, cumulatively indicate that the final verdict on the destruction of tribal self-management system is not yet made; rather there is, considerable scope for their recovery and development. The VIth Schedule of the Indian Constitution provides additional ground for optimism. It is not only a powerful legal instrument towards tribal self-management of ethno-development, but it is applicable to only north/eastern states of India.

Likewise the perception that the widespread poverty destroys the self-management systems and hence, degrades the environment is too simplistic to be analytically useful. It ignores the fact that poverty is essentially a product of a process through which their territorial survival resources are alienated by both the State and the global unequal system. Therefore, any analysis of the impact of poverty on the environment that excludes the national and global unequal structures and disempowerment of the tribal peoples in resource management sphere çannot but conceal the issue. Simultaneously, it must be appreciated that the poor have the highest incentives for managing their resources sustainably for their very subsistence and social reproduction.

Role of State Policies and Global Interventions

Whereas the modernization process, assuming that all pre-industrial forms of economic organization and management must necessarily disappear, has wrecked the tribal cultures of self-management, the mechanisms of nation building has exacerbated the process. In spite of Nehru's Panchsheel, advising to abstain from making the tribals a second rate copy of the majority community and to allow them to develop along the lines of their own genius, in practice, their institutions and values are stigmatized and considered as archaic hangovers. All the sociocultural and political institutions and the principle of consensus in collective decision-making that were responsible for management of their resources, identity, inter-community interactions and futuristic philosophy are relentlessly crushed. The denial of cultural autonomy, control of survival resources and legitimate political self-rule led to the depravation and deprivation of the basis of tribal customary management systems.

In sum, the State policies of individualization, modernization and nation building have seriously eroded the tribal self-management systems and replaced them by a modern market and profit-oriented management system. The articulation of dominant capitalist mode into the tribal matrix created formidable obstacles for the reproduction of customary management practices. Alongwith the State and the local dominant classes and communities, the world capitalism has played a decisive role in the establishment of class and cultural hegemony over the tribal societies.

Much of what is discussed of the State policies is integrally linked with the colonial and neo-colonial orthodoxies and interests. The discussion here is only confined to some of the recent economic and political trends that tend to blighten the tribal survival and indeed the exploitation of natural resources, minerals, timber, marine resources, cash crops, etc, for export has been accelerated and intensified. And as these resources are largely located in the tribal regions, their customary management practices and techniques face the catastrophe.

In the recent past, some US Corporations were granted fishing rights in the Indian territorial waters, which may soon reduce the traditional fisherfolk, including tribals, to penury. The proposed numerous hydropower projects and export based industries will further erode the viability of the customary management practices of the tribal peoples. Even the internationally funded projects for biosphere reserves, game sanctuaries, national parks, etc, have forbidden the tribals to use these customary survival resources, without any alternative provision. So also various social forestry and afforestation programmes funded by USAID, World Bank and others, have despoiled the precious natural forests by single species plantations, aimed at satisfying certain forest-based transactional industries. Examples can be multiplied. But suffice here to state that the interventions of capitalist market, technology, transnational capital and State policies have eroded the basis of tribal self-management systems.

Tribal Struggles

The scenario of tribal movements have sprung up as a formidable force. It may be reiterated that constituting less than eight per cent of the Indian population, they are credited with almost half of the total movements of India against material and cultural domination. Essentially their movements are directed to recuperate their inalienable traditional rights over land and landbased endowments; to defend, maintain and develop their legitimate cultural, social, linguistic, legal and political rights; and to cessation of abuses and subtle forms of discrimination. By and large their struggles for autonomy are essentially democratic, federalistic, anti-imperialist, anti-feudal and anti-bureaucratic. There is an increasing realization of the inbuilt dehumanization and deculturalization of the current welfare policies which tend to deny their self-respect, identity and creativity. Their widespread activism and struggles against mega projects that expropriate and indiscriminately devastate customary corporate resources are increasingly receiving support from diverse environmental, peace, women and human right activists with concerns for equity and sustainability.

Despite the growth of a limited internal structure and class structure, the tribal movements, more or less, unitedly operate outside the formal institutional politics. The tribal peoples have realized that their survival with dignity and creativity rests in their struggles for recognition of collective rights over survival resources and internal self-determination in the legitimate cultural and political spheres as well as a dynamic strategy for sustainable self-development. In fact, they cannot be legally and morally denied the freedom to choose their own path of development and, thus, demand recognition of their own political institutions and cultures to manage their survival resources, life and cultures.

The strategies of divide and rule, distribution of patronage, mediation structure, intimidation, concentration camps, torture, false encounters and brutal mass repressions have either collapsed or become redundant. It is high time to rediscover defend and promote the lifestyles, management practices, technological and knowledge systems of the tribal people who have developed them for centuries for their production of social reproduction and sustainable management of forests, water, seeds and animals.

Unfortunately very little research has been done on the tribal self-management systems as such, and hardly any, on the impact of the world system on the future of their customary management systems. It is important to document how the different self-management institutions and values of tribal peoples in different ecological and socio-economic contexts have responded to the current development process and modified or asserted the management strategies, both individually and collectively. In such a comparative context, the varied potentiality of self-management systems to adopt and remain viable or compatible in the face of pressures from within and without needs to be explored. It is also crucial to record the significance of customary law, corporate rights, gender relations, local political system that sustain the remaining self-management practices, which can further be invigorated. Moreover, the tribal peoples struggles for internal self-determination, for empowerment to continue and develop their self-management practices and maintain sustainability of environment need thorough analysis. So also the significance of the Sixth Schedule in the Indian Constitution for institutionalization of tribal self-management practices require further elaboration.

Eleven

The Cave Dwellers of Kumaun Himalaya Then and Now

B.S. BISHT

Out of various tribal communities of the sub-Himalayan region of the North and North-East India, there are 'Rajis' who are supposed to be the living representatives of the Rajya-Kirat (Atkinson, 1882:365).

The Rajis, denoted by the generic term 'Ban-Raut', are the descendants of prehistoric Kiratas, who were comparatively the early settlers of 'Uttaranchal' before the Khasas, Nagas, Aryans and the Tibetans. As stated by Atkinson: "there is every reason to suppose that the Nagas, Kiratas and Khasas entered India by the same route as the Aryans and that the Kiratas were the first to arrive than the Khasas and Nagas" (1992:365). Referring *Varaha Sanhita*, Atkinson further stated that, "the Rajya-Kirata were spread over Amarvana and China or between Jageswar and Tibet" (1882:365). But by the invasion of different ethnic groups, the Kiratas gradually vanished from Uttaranchal and their descendants remained in Kumaun and Nepal. In Kumaun the descendants of Kiratas were called the Rajis. But the Rajis are not aware with their prehistoric Kirati origin. Hence they claim to be the descendants of one of the princes of Askot. According to Mr Traill, the then Commissioner of Kumaun, "Rajis represent themselves as descendants of one of the aboriginal princes of Kumaon who with his family fled to the jungle to escape the destruction threatened by a usurper (1882:365). William Crooke has linked them with the non-Aryan affinities. Whereas Atkinson has found racial mixture of Tibetans and Khasas in their physical features (1882:366). While D.N. Majumdar has related them with Mongolian affinity. Besides this, Dr Pritchard conjectured that the Rajis resemble the other numerous aboriginal tribes found along the Himalayan borders, all possessing the physical character of the Bhotiyas in general and are very unlike the Doms (1882:366).

Apart from the numerous references of the different scholars, a number of legends connote the affinity of the Rajis with an ancient king of Askot. But the views of different scholars about the origin of the Rajis are not more than just the conjectures or surmises which have been expressed merely on the basis of imaginations. Because there are no particular authentic written records, inscriptions, plates or relics regarding the origin of the Rajis. Though the existence of the Rajya-Kiratas has been referred to in the Puranas, yet no clue of the Kiratas origin or the Rajis are available anywhere. Even the countenance and the physical traits in common do not present any clue of their racial affinity. Today no Mongolian traits can be observed in the physical appearance of the Rajis as the earlier scholars Dr Pritchard and Majumdar had observed. Today the physical appearance and the general countenance of the Rajis are almost wheatish, with average height, straight and scanty hair slight brownish in colour, intermediate headed type with medium nose, round to long face with proportionately small ears and small eyes with grey pigment. Thus, the Rajis are very much like the low Hindu caste in countenance and are unlike the Bhotiyas. It appears that the medly of different ethnic elements for ages has caused the disappearance of the original racial elements among the Rajis.

Thus, it may be concluded that the social scientists are of different opinions about the racial strain of the Rajis. It is, however, incontestable that they, at present, exhibit a mixed racial trait of the Aryo-Dravidians and Mongoloid races are in common.

Socially the Rajis or the 'Ban Rauts' are one of the most backward tribes, therefore, the Government has recognized them as the primitive tribal group in 1965. Rajis numerically a small less-known tribal community confined in the forest and hilly areas of Dharchula and Didihat and Champawat Tahsil of Pithoragarh District in Kumaun region. "They call themselves Hindus by religion. They worship Devi... when any one gets ill, they worship the God, ghosts and demon of the jungle, but they erect no temples in their honour" (Crooke: 1896:212). According to Atkinson, "Rajis themselves are of Hindu origin and are said to have their own peculiar Gods, but they also worship those of the Hindus and like the people of Kumaun and indeed of the entire Himalayas, attribute great power to the local deities, spirits, goblins and defied men (1882:367). According to Crooke (1896:210-211), 'the Rajis observe only three rituals pertaining to birth, betrothal and death.' The whole of the Raji Community has been divided into five 'Dharas'(Bisht : 1982:85). 'Dhara' is an exogamous group which bears the nature of the 'caste', yet nowhere the basis of social stratification exists. Majumdar (1994:148) states that: "They are divided into exogamous clan and are monogamous."

With regard to the economy of the Rajis, Atkinson remarks that: "They manufacture wooden bowls for sale and live under huts frequently moving from place to place amidst the jungle. Their principal subsistence being certain edible roots of wild plants and what game they can catch and they occasionally get presents of cooked food from the village (1882 : 365). According to William Crooke, they live almost altogether on the produce of the jungles and their only industry is that of making crude wooden bowls, which they barter with the people of the plains for scraps of coarse cloth and grain (1982:119). Majumdar has also presented the same views. In his own words : "They are a nomadic people, moving about in search of jungles to clear and virgin soils in which to sow seeds. They also manufacture crude wooden vessels which they exchange with neighbouring people for coarse cloth and grain. They are known locally as invisible traders (1944:150).

Thus, the notes of some prominent scholars prove that about fifty years back the Rajis were in the stage of nomadism. They were food gatherers having no permanent settlement of residence. They subsisted on the jungle produce. Socially they were isolated from the rest of the non-tribal society. They were far away from the literacy and the means of communication, transportation and, therefore, deprived from all sorts of inter and intra-tribal relations. They had their own peculiar traditions which were quite distinct from the neighbouring Kumaun Hindus and the Bhotiyas. But in the present-day context the sociocultural system of the Raji community has undergone numerous changes. Now they have got their permanent settlements. They are eking out their maintenance with crude cultivation, jungle produce and as an agricultural labour. Now they are aware of their tribalism and realize the importance of education, means of transportation and communication for the overall development of their community. The social contacts with sub-groups have also brought about some structural and organizational changes in their community. It appears that the natural process of change has ultimately overcome the prolonged traditional lethargy of the Rajis by dropping a particle of change. Now they have woken up and are anxiously trying to join the flowing stream of change and development.

Habitation and the Demographic Sketch

At present the total population of the Rajis is spread over in nine villages of three tahsils of Pithoragarh district in UP. According to the 1981 census, the total population of the tribe was 371, which now (1996) has grown up to 386. The tahsil and village-wise distribution of the Raji population is presented in Table 11.1.

So far as the question of the habitations of the Rajis are concerned, the survey-based information depicts that the population of the tribe has been scattered in the form of small clusters in different hilly regions which the Government and the people of the contiguous localities have termed as villages. At present Dharchula the interior most tahsil of the district contains four Raji villages namely; Bhoktirwa, Chifaltara, Ganagaun, and Kimkhola. In the forest regions of the Didihat tahsil too there are four Raji villages namely: Aultari, Chaurani, Kantoli and Madanbori while the remaining one Raji village i.e. Khirdwari is located in Champawat tahsil.

Besides the settled habitations, as mentioned above, one more cluster of Rajis with 9 families in total has also been noticed. This cluster, with as much as 29 members in all has still been moving frequently from jungle to jungle in search of the jungle produce and the small game they can catch to meet out their food problems. This cluster of Raji families was seen near the 'Aultari' village in Didihat tahsil. In fact the lack of suitable agro-climatic conditions as well as of the superstitious nature of the tribal people have induced them to follow the nomadic nature of sustenance. Thus, the whole of the Raji community is not in a state of absolute

TABLE - 11.1

TAHSIL AND VILLAGE-WISE BREAK-UP OF RAJI POPULATION IN PITHORAGARH DISTRICT

Name of Tehsil	Name of Village	Nos. of Family	Male				Female				Grand Total
			Unmarried	Married	Widow	Total	Unmarried	Married	Widow	Total	
DHARCHULA											
	Bhokitirwa	04	04	03	—	07	03	03	—	06	13
	Chifaltara	08	12	06	01	19	13	06	—	19	38
	Ganagaun	15	19	11	02	32	11	11	02	24	56
	Kimkhola	14	25	10	01	36	13	11	01	25	61
DIDIHAT											
	Aultari	06	07	07	01	15	06	04	—	10	25
	Chaurani	13	19	11	01	31	18	10	02	30	61
	Kantoli	11	15	10	—	25	14	11	01	26	51
	Madanbori	07	09	05	01	15	11	06	01	18	33
CHAMPAWAT											
	Khirdwari	10	16	08	—	24	13	09	02	24	48
TOTAL:	09	88	126	71	07	204	102	71	09	182	386
PERCENTAGE			66.77	38.80	3.43	100	56.04	39.01	4.95	100	100
PERCENTAGE OF MALE AND FEMALE			52.85				47.15				

settlement so far. Even the census report and the scholarly notes prove this fact that there are certain clusters of Rajis who follow the trans-humane pattern of living and, thus, remain mobile seasonally from one place to another. Sometimes the clusters migrate to the border and forest regions of Nepal on the bank of Kali river. Such nomadic clusters remain busy throughout the day in gathering jungle products, catching small games and trapping fishes and as soon as day breaks and the night falls the clusters take shelter of the caves. Such centuries old routine of moving clusters is still in the way and seems to remain the same in future too unless a practical rather diagnostic solution of the problem is not sorted out.

Social Organization

Rajis are an endogamous group of families. The family, marriage, Dhara system (clan), rituals, Dhara Panchayat and the primitive economy with little modernization altogether constitute the social organization of the Raji tribe. In the community, the traditional sanctions play an important role in determining the individual's behaviour pattern as well as the attitudes and the ideology. There, we can observe the dominance of the superstitions, beliefs and practices, the feeling of sacred and the prophane and the vital attachment with the primitive style of living where the assessment of individual's behaviour, needs, occupations, and the interests is largely oriented towards non-utilitarian and non-pragmatic standards of evaluation. Moreover, the supernatural beings and the metaphysical postulations have an effective, rather determining role in people's day to day life. The informal agencies like the family, Dhara, marriage, kinship and the Dhara Panchayat are the means of social control. The economy of the people is of self-sufficient type. The people collect the jungle products, grow some coarse grain, make their own implements and domestic utensils and this way they subsist on what they could manage by their own efforts. However, they look to the outside world for more requirements like cloth, salt, sugar, kerosene and mustard oil only when they find themselves fit to afford the same. But in general, they use pinewood or torchwood called "Chhula" (in local dialect) in place of kerosene oil and simply have boiled food in the absence of mustard oil or ghee. Thus, the tribal community under study have been confined in the isolation and are little disturbed by the outside world. In other words we can say that the tribal people are still confined within the motherly shelter of the dense forests, hills and valleys. Even today they are subject to the power of nature to their wealth, flora and fauna. They have developed their own code of behaviour patterns, their tools and techniques are those which they can manage well from the materials available and their interest in their environment is that of survival in health and vigour not in the profit and gain which their efforts and application brings forth. Even today they depend on the jungle products for satiating their appetite for the crude type of cultivation which cannot afford much scope for an easy life. Besides this, the pervaded social conditions too have been shaped in accordance with the environment conditions. For instance, the 'Dhara' distribution of the community is absolutely based on the ecological settlements of the region. The small size of the family is also an inevitable result of the natural environment which places some unavoidable impediments on the existence of the joint-family system.

For the Rajis, the family is a 'Kunba' which chiefly consists of a husband, wife and their unmarried children because it is not possible economically to accommodate more than two generations in a family. There are sufficient references to prove the centuries old primitivism of the Raji community because till recently they were in the nomadic stage. Small clusters of the Rajis consist of a group of small families who are constantly moving from one place to another in search of the jungle products. But today the major part of the Raji population has got their permanent settlement amidst the forest land, though, the traditional concept of the 'Kunba' i.e. the small family still exist among them. A newly married couple is separated to set up a new home. The small thatched hutment cannot provide even a temporary shelter to them. The all pervading pauperism is another factor to deprive the two and more generations to live together under a common roof and to have food cooked in a common hearth. However, the small Raji family in some unavoidable circumstances become an alternative social shelter for the widower and unmarried siblings.

The community follows the rules of patriarch and the lineage runs with father's line. In principle, the authority of the father in family is superior, however, the mother predominantly dominates the family in different spheres. She commands a venerable position in the family to such an extent that sometimes an observer may confuse the community as matriarchal. For instance; a wife always behaves with her husband as a mistress. It may, therefore, be assumed that, the Rajis would have been a matriarchal community in remote past. However, some Raji families particularly those who are in close contact with neighbouring Kumaunies have started to impose some socio-religious disabilities on a Raji woman, particularly, when she either undergoes menstruation period or gives birth to an infant. This is the period when she becomes defiled and, therefore, an untouchable even for her own family members. The sense of defilement in the former case lasts three or four days while in the latter case it lasts for nine days. During this period the defiled woman is supposed to maintain a certain physical distance from every person of the family and of the community as well. She is not permitted to touch the hearth, drinking water, worship place and does not share in any ritualistic ceremonies and other religious activities unless the period of defilement ends. Thus, some of the Raji families, particularly those who are in close contact with the Savarn neighbouring Kumauni have started observing the tradition of "familial untouchability." In general all the family members are interrelated in a mechanical solidarity. They have a good organizational as well as cordial and affectionate attachment with one another. But the old age is just a curse for the Rajis, since an aged person neither avails any respect nor any support from the rest of the family members. The same is the position of the step children. In the family none of the members are liable for any particular task, however, the infants are looked after by the parents unless they attain the age of six years because every child of six years and more is supposed to lend one's hands in economic pursuits and, therefore is not needed to be looked after. Parents are not worried at all about the education and proper personality development of their children. The function of every family member remains centralized on the economic pursuits which is one of the basic needs without which an individual cannot live longer. The most striking trait of the Rajis is the absence of the sense of liability of the elders towards their youngsters, since every family member is expected to work according to his own capacity, thus, whatever they produce or glean through collective efforts, is consumed till it comes to an end, afterwards they further make efforts for collecting food. By nature they are lazy, indolent and always remain desirous to manage the foodstuffs as much as is essential to keep the body and soul together. They do not have aspiration for better living yet make efforts for the fulfillment of the minimum needs for food and clothes.

Rajis are an agriculturist, pastorial and food gathering community, being part of the hard and backward economy, where every member of the family, male or female, child or youth, even aged persons are supposed to help in the household works. The children as soon as they attain the age of six years are expected to lend their hands in some small jobs, while the persons more than sixty years of age may have to continue as the working member of the family, provided that aged person are still in a position to function. In the community, the jobs in general are performed by the community members without any differences, yet in order to maintain the balance in between the different routine works, the members are assigned some particular tasks on the basis of age and sex. Thus, the division of labour among the family members is of primitive type.

The whole tribal community has been divided into five major Dharas, namely, the Askoti Pal, Dinsi Pal, Baitara, Baluwakoti, Aeri and Kwaintala. 'Dhara' is a clan group and its members are called 'enbora'. The people follow the rules of Dhara exogamy and also observe certain restrictions pertaining to the marriage and social intercourse. Dhara is not the basis of the hierarchical division of the Raji community, it is rather a vertical division of the community.

People have quite different manners of wedding and acquiring mates. Generally, they follow the rules of community endogamy and the 'Dhara' (clan) and village exogamy. The total population is scattered over in nine villages and every village is predominantly inhabited by the Dhara. Though with the course of time the infiltration of some families from alien clan groups have got their settlement in the villages due to the observance of the tradition of the 'Gharjawain' marriages. However, the rules of village exogamy are strictly observed.

Almost all the 'Dharas' are exogamous, with quite a few examples of violation of the Dhara-exogamy and the village exogamy are found so far. But such cases took place only in some exceptional circumstances.

Rajis are the patriarchal community in principle who follow the rules of patrilocal and patrilineal respectively for ascertaining the residence of the spouses after marriage and the lineage of the offsprings. The Rajis, who claim to be Hindu Rajputs and the descendants of one of the Katur kings in Kumaun, consider the marriage as a contract between the two families but not a sacrament as is observed among the Hindus. As the Rajis assert that the marriage is not more than a get together of male and female in a family life which implies various functional significance for the mates, however, to provide economic assistance to one another the sexual pleasures are given priority. In fact, the economic factor plays an important role at all stages of the settlement of marriage. Hence, a daughter is wedded at an early age, provided the parents are paid a good amount of bride-price.

The marriage among the Rajis is preceded by two formal proceedings, i.e., the "Mang-Jangi" or the proposal for marriage and the 'Tika', i.e., the engagement. The proposal is offered to the girl's parents by the boy's father or the guardian. No mediator is appointed to negotiate the proposal, yet the boy's father with some of his close relatives visits villages getting information about marriageable girls and then approaches the concerned family. On the consent of the girl's father the bride-price is fixed. In general, the matrimonial relationship is established at an early age and sometimes by their parents during the gestation period. In all cases the 'Tika' i.e, the engagement is followed after the mutual consent of both the parties. On this occasion, dresses like saris, blouses and petticoats and nose stud are presented to the girl by the boy's father who is accompanied with some of his relatives. A mark of red vermilion with rice is also applied on the forehead of the girl. The girl's family manages at least a one-time meal for the visitors. Thus, the betrothal (Tika) ceremony gets solemnized.

The betrothal ceremony is followed by the marriage which takes place as soon as the groom's father could manage the bride price. The wedding ceremony is performed at bride's place. Now the Rajis have started to appoint the Brahmin priest for performing the marriage, yet in practice the groom's brother-in-law (sister's husband) or the maternal uncle and the bride's sister-in-law (brother's wife) perform the marriage with mutual collaboration at the bride's place. The groom's side with their relatives and friends visit the bride's place. On the arrival of the marriage procession, the bride is deliberately shunted away towards the jungle, soon after the groom's people are informed about the bride's absconding. At this the groom himself pursues the bride and searches her and stoops to conquer her. The groom's brother-in-law and the bride's sister-in-law who are traditionally entitled to perform the wedding rite ask the groom and the bride to sit on a mat spread-out on the ground floor of the bride's house. A gracious mark of the red vermilion is placed with rice on the forehead of the couple respectively by the brother-in-law and the bride's sister-in-law and then the mates are asked to offer some sweets or 'Gurh' to one another. With this rite, the wedding ceremony is considered to be completed. The invitees and the groom's people (Baratis) then take the dinner. Next morning the groom's relatives and friends are given a light breakfast. The bride and the groom are attired with new garments and the bride is departed to the house of her in-laws. On the arrival of the marriage procession the groom's mother welcomes the newly married couple and applies a mark of vermilion on their foreheads and gives the sweet (Gurh) as a token of an offering. On this occasion a grand feast is given to the villagers. The cooked rice, dal, meat and the wine are offered as the main items of the community dinner. The bride brings water with her affinal lady kin. The water is used for the cooking and drinking and this act is taken as a symbol of acceptance of bride in the kin group. Next day the bride is taken back to her native place by her brothers who come along with the marriage procession to see her off at the groom's residence. The Rajis do not observe any rite like 'Gauna' i.e. the second marriage. Hence, after few days, she comes back to her in-laws house. During first one or two years she keeps on visiting her native place, but these visitations become irregular and long when she gets her first issue.

Besides the formal way, there are still some other socially sanctioned ways of acquiring mates. The love marriage which is the inevitable outcome of the premarital illicit liaison of the mates; marriage by mutual consent and elopement; widow remarriages; divorce remarriages; levirate sororate; polygamy (provided the former wife has no male issue or sometimes the widow of the deceased brother also becomes the wife of the living brother) and the 'Gharjawain' marriages are the common ways of acquiring mates.

Among the Rajis the woman, in principle, holds comparatively a low status because of the patrilineal descent, patrilocal residence and the patriarchal community. Since, in a patriarchal society the position of woman is low, while she enjoys a high status in matriarchal societies as is observed respectively in Todas and Khasis. In general the lineage of the offspring in the Raji community runs with the father's line. The property is inherited only by the sons. A son after marriage is responsible for his wife and the parents as well provided that he does not get separation from his parents. While a daughter after marriage gets the lineage of her husband, she resides at husband's place and shares the property of her husband in common. All these normative conditions bestow a lower position to the Raji-woman in theory. But, in practice she possesses a key status in the socio-economic structure of the Raji community. She is the central pivot around which the whole of the system of the Raji community revolves. She lends her hand in every sphere of community life and performs every tedious toil with the man, to collect the jungle products, to trap the fishes, to dig up the edible roots or the like and, thus brings together the eatables for sustenance so that the body and soul of the family members are kept together. Both the male and female work in the field, or they may attend the kitchen and the cattle, both of them may bring wood from the jungle, they observe no other particular pattern of division of labour in general. Besides this, both the male and female earn their livelihood as daily wagers from the neighbouring villages by rendering their services to them particularly as an agricultural labour. Moreover, she participates in every religious and cultural activity performed on auspicious occasions, namely worship of deities, performance of life cycle rituals and so. Yet she does not join the marriage and funeral procession. Thus, it is observed that the Raji woman, in spite of being the patriarchal community, participates in every sphere of the sociocultural activities of the community. An outstanding nature, which is observed particularly in the normal discourse between the husband and wife is that the wife always addresses here husband with some disdainful pronouns such as '*tu*', and '*tera*' while the husband in response calls his wife with some venerable pronouns like '*tum*' and '*aap*'. This character of the Raji woman shows her venerable position in the community, hence she is respected and honoured by the male. She is never discarded for any offence and misdeed. Even in some adultery cases, only the man who indulges in provoking the woman for seduction is considered to be an offender. Moreover, she has the decision-making power in any family matters. The man as the husband or the son formally asks his wife or mother respectively before commensing any task or to taking decision regarding any family affair whether economical or religious. It is only the mistress of the family who decides whether the suggested task will be done or not and any family matter will be materialized or not. In this way the Raji woman leads every sociocultural activity of the community and, thus, holds practically a dominant position in the community. She does not follow any taboos like protective or preventive or productive as observed in many patriarchal societies in general. No feeling like defilement during her menstruation and child birth makes her unsuited for any socio-religious-ceremonial performances. Yet some Raji women, particularly who are in close contact with the neighbouring Savarana-Hindus and reside in the contiguous regions of Kumauni villages have started following some preventive taboos particularly during menstruation and delivery period. Thus, it may be concluded that Raji women practically holds an important position in the community.

The Rajis call themselves Hindus by religion. There is however, sufficient evidence to prove that the Raji were unaware of the Hindu religion and its beliefs and practices. But in the course of time the impact of Hinduism has motivated them to follow the Hindu lifestyle, subsequently, they begin to observe some of the Hindu beliefs and practices but in a crude and superficial level. Today they also worship some of the Hindu gods or goddesses, and also solemnize some of the ritualistic performances like; birth and death. With the impact of the neighbouring Hindu castes, the tribal people worship the Gods—Malainath, Latainath, Manainath and the Goddess Bhagwati and also some spirits, goblins, ghosts and demons which are generally worshipped by their Hindu neighbours. They offer sacrifices of the goats or hens to appease the deities. Besides this, they have firm faith on their peculiar deities such as; the Jal Devi, Baital, Latbad, Ghanaboobo and Karear Devi, which are the presiding deities of the people. The usages, code of rites, rituals, beliefs and superstitions, as revealed by the deities, are willfully and completely observed by these people in their day to day lifestyle the violation of which may cause harm to them. These people have also the notion that the spirits and even the deities they worship generally forecast about the coming incidents through dreams, echoes, visions of shadows and other natural occurrences, like, untimely death of any of the persons in family or in village, diseases, distress, drought, excessive rain, etc. The poor people having no scientific reasoning about the said occurrences get frightened and therefore worship the spirits and supernatural powers in order to please them. It is observed that the system of beliefs pertaining to the supernatural power, which the tribal people profess is very much identical to the theory of animism propounded by E.B. Tylor to explain the origin of religion.

These people have deep faith on the existence of the evil spirits, goblins and ghosts. All the events, whether good or bad, pertaining to the man's own and even of his community life are supposed to occur due to the effects of the evil spirits. It is their belief that the evil spirit after supernatural being, is the second dominant authority in the area which observes, controls and governs all the aspects of the human life. Even the natural occurrences and the natural calamities overtaking them are due to the influence of the spirits. To them, the soul of deceased person if not reborn, incarnates itself through any one of the living kin of the deceased and, thus, gets recognition as the evil spirit. These people seem to be afraid of the expected harms caused by the displeasure of the spirit, hence they show great reverence towards it and also perform some sort of ritualistic rites so that they might escape from the curse of the spirit. On certain occasions the spirit is also offered sacrifices in order to propitiate and conciliate it. Besides this, the people appear to be afraid of the ghosts, demons and fairies because they often harm them. So, in order to please the various deities, spirits, goblins and the demons, a particular system of worship began and subsequently the beliefs of religious practices came into being.

Apart from the beliefs as cited above, the people have some more superstitions about the evil eye, evil mouth and the 'Ghat' (curse). The superstitions predominantly determine the behaviour patterns of the people in their socio-economic and religious spheres of community life. For instance, during the seventies the people of the Kuta Kanyal village were greatly distressed by mass casualties both among themselves and the children due to landslides. The tribal people finally decided that the evil spirit had taken possession on the village and it should be evacuated. Resultantly the remaining people left the well established village with newly constructed 'pucca' houses by the Government under the rehabilitation scheme and shifted to the contiguous place with their necessary articles, which later on developed as the Madanbori village. These people made temporary shelters for themselves from the grass and the branches of the trees. Even today the people reside there and subsist on the primitive sort of economy, while the former village, i.e., Kutakanyal is still in the state of desolation. Thus, we see how irrational decisions have been taken on account of superstition and the fear of evil spirits. In fact, it is merely the superstition and the fear of evil spirit, which has made these people very conservative and also against any change or innovation on the ground that, any sort of change in the socio-ecological environment which is supposed to be an outcome of the will of the abstract power, will be a violation of its will and, therefore, those who wish to profess any alteration in the former situation will be liable to be punished by the abstract power.

Moreover, the tribals also observe some 'omens' in their social life which bear in common some religious significance as other beliefs have in general. The major 'omens' prevalent in the community are: pulsating of the eyelid, casting an evil eye, sneezing (portending evil) and crossing the way by cat. These people believe that an excellent thing whether organic or inorganic will have to suffer due to the effect of an evil eye. Hence, they are not in favour to keep anything neat and clean as well as healthy and wealthy. Even a beautiful and healthy Raji child is kept as dirty as to escape from the effect of an evil eye. Sometimes, the same child is applied a mark of collyrium on his forehead. Same is the case with the cattle and any other thing like a good house or hut, crop, etc, which is supposed to be ruined due to the effect of the evil eye and, therefore, they are never sincere to make or operate any thing beautifully. In the same way sneezing by any person just at the starting of any auspicious rite or any trip or even routine work is regarded ominous. Besides this, the pulsating of left and right eyes respectively of the male and the female is also considered ominous and a forewarning of some bad event. Moreover, 'cat' is considered as living evil spirit, the appearance of which is regarded ominous making it worst when the cat crosses the way of a wayfarer while beginning his journey. During such incidents the people sometimes suspend even their trip or the work pre-empting its adverse results due to the ominous signs.

The 'Gantuwa' i.e. the traditional prophet plays an important role in superstitions outlook of the people. Whenever a person falls ill, becomes mad or some epidemic breaks out in the community or any person suffers from the effect of an evil eye, or curse, then the 'Gantuwa' is approached. He then makes his own calculation with the help of the abstract power which is supposed to have one's indirect contractions with the prophet. The prophet chants certain hymns, the meaning of which is known only to him, and throws some rice in different directions so as to approach the abstract authorities, and thus finds out the causes of the sufferings and gives out his instruction for its eradication.

Thus, so far as the functions of the superstitious beliefs are concerned, the people have no meaning of the modern techniques of medical treatment or the scientific outlook, because they have a firm belief on the existence of the abstract power which alone is the cause of all sorts of incidents. Hence, they preferably try to find out the solutions even of the sufferings within the limit of the superstitions through traditional operations.

The economy of the Rajis which stands in between the food gleaning and settled agriculture is proved to be inadequate and insufficient to shape well the constituent units of the society and also to provide economic protection to the people, since, the lessening jungle production, the lack of natural resources as well as the implementation of forest laws have altogether deprived the Rajis from their age-old traditional sources of subsistence. On the other hand, the lack of agricultural know-how and the unfavourable agro-climatic conditions have utterly affected the economic lifestyle of the Rajis. Today, they don't have much scope for nomadic or shifting cultivation, because the freeholding of the forest land has strictly been banned by the Government forest policy. Even the unavailability of the timber has adversely affected their centuries old profession of manufacturing wooden utensils and the agricultural equipments. It seems the chapter of prolonged historical nomadism has been closed and the rehabilitation scheme has added a fresh chapter of development in the evolutionary history of the Raji community. Under the rehabilitation scheme, almost all the Raji families have been allotted a piece of land for agricultural purposes. The scheme is of common bilateral importance for both the Raji community and Government. Since, the Government policy objects, firstly, to settle the nomadic Rajis and secondly, to protect the forests from the destruction of illegal cuttings made by the forest-dwellers in general. Thus, the nomadic Rajis have been forced to lead a settled life with no incentives and this state of being presents a living spectre of a backward economy.

REFERENCES

Atkinson, E.T., 1882, *Himalayan Gazzetteer*, Cosmo Publications.

Bisht, B.S., 1982, Social Structure and Organization of Raji Tribe of Kumaun, Ph.D. Dissertation, Kumaun University, Nainital.

———, 1993, Raji : A Tribe of Indo-Nepal Border of Uttarakhand, New Delhi: Vivek Prakashan.

Crooke, William, 1896, *Tribes and Castes of the North West Provinces of Oudh*, Calcutta.

———, 1973, *Races of Northern India*, New Delhi: Cosmo Publications.

Majumdar, D.N., 1944, *Races and Cultures of India*, Bombay: Asia Publishing House.

Twelve

Law and Scheduled Tribes: A Socio-Legal Perspective

A.K. KAPOOR

The study of primitive law, in its widest sense, is perhaps the most general and difficult task of the social anthropologist. Legal institutions take on a fundamentally different form in primitive communities as opposed to modern civilizations; and the law cannot be considered apart from the whole normative system as the body of the moral codes, aesthetic standards, rules of good behaviour and other ethics which institutionalized the methods of legal procedure are but a part, albeit an extremely important part.

This is perhaps the most important fact to be borne in mind considering the primitive law. It was for a long time obscured because the ethnographic observations in the field were confined almost entirely to accounts of crime and punishment and to the procedure adopted in the settlement of disputes. The approach was that of a lawyer rather than that of a scientist. The former who earns his livelihood by correcting the wrongs committed by others, is only interested in the comparatively few instances of breach, as against the overwhelming cases of observance. Like his counterpart in the medical profession, he is only interested when things go wrong, for this is his function in society. But an anthropologist who sets out to study law in its entirety is not merely interested in comparing few instances in which the law is broken; he must also consider the vast majority of cases in which it is kept. He must study all the forces of social conformity, including those positive inducements which ensure that, generally speaking, honesty is the best policy. But, he must not ignore the fact that cases of breach do occur, and that, in such instances, legal mechanisms are brought into play. Law cannot be considered in isolation from other forces of social conformity, but its existence as a specific element in culture must also be recognized.

An approach such as this immediately brings before us an initial difficulty — the problem of definition. In our own society law is highly institutionalized. It has its own special personnel judges, advocates and police; legal business is transacted in special places, is subject to highly codified rules and correlated with a specialized terminology. But, in many primitive societies there is nothing corresponding to this elaborate body of legal institutions, with their complex and highly differentiated organization. For this reason no purely formal definition of law, as operative in our own society, is applicable to primitive communities. The definition of primitive law is to be found ultimately in an empirical description of the way in which primitive communities cope with situations comparable to those which arise in our own courts of law.

The scientific study of primitive law and custom — the normative systems of primitive people — is fraught with many difficulties, which have in the past produced many misleading interpretations. The first impression was that epitomized in the word "savage". Early travellers were shocked, horrified or disgusted by the ways in which primitive types of behaviour differ from our own. Thus, arose the figment of primitive conditions marked by anarchy and internecine hostility, by constant war against each other, by dominance of the instinct of self-preservation with "an insatiable appetite for power leading each individual to pursue his own aggrandizement at the cost of any loss or suffering to the rest".

At the other extreme there was the diametrically opposite view of the "Golden Age", of the primitive man as an essentially kind, unselfish and law abiding being. This view was strengthened by field-workers who studied more closely, though by no means, thoroughly, the social life of primitive communities. Their observations revealed, instead of anarchy and chaos, a well-ordered social system in which tradition, taboo and the "cake of custom" laid-down certain rules which the members of the community invariably obeyed or said they did. Hence, arose the artificial conception of the savage "automatically" obeying the traditional rules of his society, either from his own goodness of heart or because of some almost mystical quality or primitive social behaviour such as "group consciousness" or communistic organization.

"Regulations bearing upon the conduct of life, which the western culture might be deemed to come within the province of Government, were automatically controlled by established customs. Customs indicate appropriate procedure under the various circumstances which face the individual or the community. Children, by observing their elders or by parental instruction, are taught the correct procedure and no other mode of action occurs to them in life. Customs act automatically, and there is no need for Government control. What constituted right and wrong conduct had been defined by the custom. Custom was obeyed without any thought of opposition, and there was little need of courts of law with police to hale male-factors to justice. Prohibitions by tapus were observed out of fear and ingrained obedience". (Radclife-Brown, 1933: Hoebel, 1954).

Both the contrasting views of primitive anarchy on the one hand and of "automatic conformity" on the other - have been shown by modern field work as exaggeration. Primitive societies are governed by laws and moral rules, but these are by no means obeyed invariably and certainly not automatically. The study of these forces induce people to conform to the vast majority of cases and to the procedures adopted in cases of evasions and breaches of normative standards.

A modern welfare State presents a picture where some form of legal regulations has infiltrated into almost every conceivable aspect of man's social, economic, ecological, biological and political affairs. Thus, the vast expansion of government functions which has occurred as a result of both growing complexity of modern life and of the minimum postulates of social justice which are now a part of the established public philosophy in all civilized countries. The concept of modern welfare State, has thus, become an interplay between law and society. The use of law as a tool of directed social change is widespread in all contemporary societies whether underdeveloped or post-industrial, democratic or totalitarian. But, our systematic knowledge both on how to use law effectively and efficiently in order to achieve more of our goals and our practical state-of-the-art of doing so is approximately zero.

Anthropologists, sociologists and the legal scientists have devoted their efforts to the study of law and social change and have made important contributions to many aspects of the subjects in western countries. But, in India, social scientists have not given much attention on this aspect of knowledge. In India, the role of law has not simply remained as one of the agencies of social control but it has played / and is playing a role of directed social change. The growing complexity of Indian life and welfare programmes of the government need a comprehensive policy-oriented theory of law as a tool of directed social change.

The basic difficulties of studying and improving the use of law as a tool of directed social change results from the fact that law by itself is the only component of a large set of policy instruments and usually cannot and is not used by itself. (Friedmann, 1970; Lloyd, 1970). The perspective and policy-oriented aspect of law as an instrument of social direction needs the attention of social scientists. The study of law as a tool of directed social change can be taken in two ways :-

(i) As a sub-component of the study of social policy instruments and;
(ii) As a sub-component of normative policy analysis.

The use of law as a tool of directed social change within an adequate framework of social policy instruments involves consideration of law within the legal system. Each component of legal system-substantive law, procedural law, personal law, organizations, resources, decision rules and decision habits - is a potential policy instrument. It is essential in each case to examine carefully the interdependencies between various components of the relevant legal systems, the interrelations between these components and the target phenomena, and the feasibility and costs, including political feasibility and costs of changing those components of the legal system which are more salient for the target phenomena (Nader, 1965).

The legal system being a subsystem of society and a consideration of legal policy instruments from other social policy instrument is misleading. The use of law as a tool of directed social change must be considered within a broader series of policy instruments such as economic, education, ecological, political and technological ones. Thus, it requires a new methodology for designing and identifying preferable combinations of multiplicity of policy instrument settings. Policy analysis constitutes an extension of system analysis to complex policy issues which cannot be quantified and represented by exercizable models. Thus, there is a need to evolve a policy analysis methodology.

When law produces social change, there has been a basic restructuring of how people in a society relate to each other with regard to basic human interaction activities. Not all legal changes, however, result in social change, since many rules and decisions affect very few people. Likewise, not all social changes result in legal change, since some aspects of human interactions in many societies are not covered by formal legal rules, although social change being more fundamental is, more likely to produce legal change than vice versa. Legal changes as a force promoting social change, thus, can be viewed in two ways. (1) Perspective is value free, simply, concerned with describing the effects of law on behaviour and attitudes and, (2) The other perspective is goal-oriented and takes certain goals, as given and then describes what policies will optimize or satisfy the goals. Both approaches are objective in the sense that personal values do not influence the perspective. Policy evaluations aim only in terms of empirically tested means and ends statements.

The last five decades in India have, if anything reinforced the crucial importance of natural reflections on the interrelation between social and legal change. In practically all the welfare-oriented policies, most of the changes have been brought about through legislation. The application of various laws to these scheduled areas without any machinery will look into their possible consequences on the tribals and how non-tribals have reacted to such legislations which have remained untouched by the social scientists. Thus, there is a need to study the role of law a tool of directed social change with special reference to the tribals and in wider national context, if it is to fulfill its function as a paramount instrument of social order. Referring to such priorities in research on Scheduled Tribes "Report of the Scheduled areas and Scheduled Tribes Commission (1961)" made certain recommendations that:

(a) At the State-level, a section should be created in the legal department to undertake a study of the central and State laws relating to

(i) Social matters;

(ii) Right in land, including tenancy laws;

(iii) Allotment of land and setting apart land for village purposes; and

(iv) Private money lending and village management, including establishment of village Panchayats, and to suggest modifications to protect the rights of the tribals in regard to these matters.

This should be undertaken without any further loss of time.

(b) A survey should be undertaken in each State with a view to ascertain to what extent the interests of the tribals have suffered, which require restoration or retrospective legislative assistance.

Upto this time only a few studies have been undertaken on some legislations but a serious attention of social scientists is needed to understand the role of law as a tool of directed social change. As we are aware, all major social roles in tribal life have changed substantially in recent years and, these changes in roles have helped generate changes in some laws which in turn have produced important social changes. Tribal participation in the political, economic and cultural process of the country has produced change and also the problem of adjustment of the Scheduled Tribes to the new social environment. The very function of law as a social institution demands that changes should be managed, law must be approached as a purposive goal-oriented system and it may be understood that behaviour of the legal actors is designed to achieve adjustment to new social environment, to achieve effective social engineering. Thus, there is a need to understand:

(i) what impact the legal changes have had on this changing role of tribals and,

(ii) what impact changing roles of tribals have had on the changes in law? How legal changes have played a large part in social change and vice versa. The problems of adjustment of the

Scheduled Tribes have come up with the changes of social roles of an average tribal. The role of a tribal as a family member, consumer, producer, citizen, employee, landowner and ethnic group member, etc, have changed tremendously and these changes need to be studied keeping in view the impact of legal changes. On the other hand studies of law in tribal society should be given priority in order to find out the customary methods of dispute settlement and the structure of the basic social institutions that govern the system. For what purposes do the tribals make use of the legal system of the country? How tribals have been brought under the jurisdiction of Indian legal system? To what extent and for what purpose the non-tribals have made use of the law against tribals and vice-versa? All these questions should thus be studied in detail. Thus, the tribals participation with the law of the land would uncover structural preconditions which in other areas remain tacit and less readily observable.

This important area which has been left untouched by social anthropologists, sociologists and legal scientists thus needs attention. Tribal contact with the legal system of the country will further uncover the tribal values and social structure at a particular time and place. A study of Nyaya Panchayat in a tribal area has revealed the basic interest and institutions of the tribals and, the nature of relationship between tribals and non-tribals. A general observation revealed the frustration of non-tribals regarding various legislations introduced to protect tribals from social injustice and exploitation of all kinds. These legislations have widely affected the nature of contacts and communication between tribals and non-tribals (Swaroop, 1990). Under Article 19(5) of the Constitution of India the imposition of reasonable restrictions in the interests of general public or for the protection of the interests of any Scheduled Tribes, has alienated the non-tribals to acquire property or practice any trade in the tribal areas. On the other hand the concept of tribal area has attached the tribals to a limited physical boundary and raised a feeling of separatism leading to unrest, due to previous exploitation by the non-tribals. The concept of the tribal areas has been further exploited by some political parties and by the emerging leadership among the tribals, who are seeking their new identities. In the similar manner the economic restrictions on non-tribals to do trade or business in tribal areas has further isolated the tribals. Legislations have further affected the social mobility and restricted the tribals integration with the mainstream of national life. In such a situation there is a need to study the impact of law on tribals and non-tribals and, how both have expressed their attitudes and opinions about various legislations.

The problem is of status of the tribals, which cannot be fixed by legislation but it will be determined by their participation with non-tribals in economic, political and cultural processes of the country. The increasing contact and communication with non-tribals will help to evolve a national culture. Those who plea for the preservation of tribal culture should preserve it in books not in action. As we know that with growing complexities and with the growth of industrial complexes, liberalization, globalization and popular participation in political life of the country, a new culture has emerged in the country. In order to evolve a secular, democratic and socialist culture every cultural group has sacrificed and will sacrifice his own culture, thus, the studies of cultural contact and fusion may have theoretical relevance but for policy programmes we have to study the spread of secular, democratic and socialist culture among the tribals and non-tribals both.

The role of the law as a secular, democratic and socialist tool has become very important to shape a national culture, which needs the attention of social scientists.

REFERENCES

Friedmann.W., 1970, *Law in Changing Society* (Indian Print).

Hoebel, E. Adamson, 1954, *The Law of Primitive Man: A study in comparative legal dynamics*. Cambridge: Harvard University Press.

Lloyd, Bennis, 1970, The Idea of Law, Nader, L. 1965. The Ethnography of Law. *Amer Anthropol*. 67: 118-125.

Radcliffe-Brown, A.R., 1933, Law: Primitive Social Sanctions. In: *Encyclopaedia of the Social Sciences*.

Swaroop, B.B., 1990, Nyaya Panchayat - as an indicator of Tribal situation pp.516-518. In : *The Tribal Situation in India*, Ed. K.S. Singh. Indian Institute of Advanced Study, Simla, (Second Reprint).

Thirteen

Tribal Situation in Bihar: A Demographic Profile

B.K. SINGH *and* **N. KUMAR**

Bihar has a rich tribal heritage. The population of this State as per 1981 census was 6,99,14,734 and as per figures of the 1991 census is 86,37,4465. Thus, population-wise Bihar is the second largest State of the country. The tribal population of this State as per 1981 census was 58,10,867 which becomes the third largest State in the country in tribal population. The Scheduled Tribes population constitute 8.31 per cent of the total population of the State. As per 1991 census, Scheduled Caste population is 12,57,1700 and Scheduled Tribe population is 66,16,914. The percentage of Scheduled Caste and Scheduled Tribe population is 14.55 and 7.66 respectively (R.P. Singh, 1993 : 13).[1]

Thus, it is evident that Bihar has a substantial tribal population. Most of the areas, where the tribal people are concentrated traditionally, are the hill and forested areas of the Chotanagpur Plateau although over the years some have migrated to the districts north of the Ganga, especially Purnia and Katihar. The tribals have an economy and sociocultural system that is quite distinct from the rest of the population of Bihar. Most of the areas that the tribals live in are poor in their infrastructure and development.

The seventy-four blocks of Bihar which had higher tribal population than non-tribal population in 1981 are shown in Table 13.1.

It may be mentioned here that Barwadih (Palamau), Lohardaga, Adhaura (Rohtas) and Namkum (Ranchi) changed its status between 1971 and 1981. In this period, the first three blocks witnessed a fall in the proportion of tribal population from 52.85%,

50.53% and 61% in 1971 to 47.38%, 47.73% and 49% respectively in 1981. Nankum, however, showed remarkable rise in the tribal population in the same decade. In 1971, it had 38%, tribal population as compared to 67% in 1981, and thus, qualified as a tribal block.

TABLE - 13.1

BLOCKS WITH A MAJORITY OF TRIBAL POPULATION

Year	*1971*	*1981*
No. of Blocks with tribal population >50% of Block population.	76	74
No. of Blocks with tribal population <50% of Block population	511	513
Total No. of Blocks	587	587

Tables 13.2 and 13.3 give a general idea of the distribution of tribal population in the blocks of Bihar.

TABLE - 13.2

DISTRIBUTION OF SCHEDULED TRIBES IN BLOCKS 1981

Number of STs	*Number of Blocks*
Greater than 10,000	164
5,000 to 10,000	35
Less than 5,000	388
Total	587

TABLE 13.3

PERCENTAGE DISTRIBUTION OF SCHEDULED TRIBE IN BLOCKS 1981

Per cent S.T. out of Total Block Population	*Total Number of Blocks*
Less than 1 per cent	327
1 to 25 per cent	144
25 to 50 per cent	42
50 to 100 per cent	74
Total	587

On the basis of population projections from the 1981 census, only two of the thirty-nine districts of Bihar in 1989 had a tribal, that is Scheduled Tribe (ST) population, greater than the non-tribal population. These were Gumla and Lohardaga. It should be noted that in 1981, had undivided Ranchi been considered (i.e. including the present-day districts of Gumla and Lohardaga) then it would feature as the only district having a predominantly tribal population in Bihar.

Table 13.4 shows all districts with a significant proportion of tribal population in descending order of the proportion of tribal population in the district (1981).

TABLE - 13.4
PERCENTAGE OF SCHEDULED TRIBE IN THE DISTRICTS OF BIHAR 1981

District	*Per cent*	*District*	*Per cent*
Lohardaga	73.55	Giridih	12.99
Gumla	58.68	Dhanbad	9.16
Dumka	47.25	Hazaribagh	9.05
Ranchi	46.25	Katihar	6.15
Singhbhum	44.11	Bhagalpur	3.52
Sahebganj	44.03	Purnea	3.15
Godda	29.37	Munger	2.38
Palamau	18.34	Rohtas	1.63
Deoghar	15.29	W.Champaran	1.36

Table 13.5 shows summary figures for blocks which have less than 50 per cent of their total population from the STs. Of these blocks those who have more than 5,000 STs form the tribal pockets of the State. It may be mentioned here that 74 blocks have more than 50 per cent of their total population from the Scheduled Tribe, 229 blocks have less than 50% of their total population from the Scheduled Tribe and 284 blocks have no tribal population.

According to list of Scheduled Tribes of Bihar as notified under the Government of India, Ministry of Home Affairs notification No. SRO - 2477 - dated 29th October, 1954 issued under Articles 341 (1) and 342(1) of the Constitution, thirty tribes have been recognized as Scheduled Tribes in the State of Bihar.

Individuals who were reported as 'Adivasi' at the time of census were grouped as unspecified.

Table 13.6 reveals the population of different tribes in Bihar in 1991. It is worth mentioning here that out of 30 tribes, those which have been identified as the most primitive, applying various indicators of backwardness and their present precarious social existence are: Asur, Birhor, Birjia, Korwa, Mal Paharia, Paharia, Sauria Paharia and Savar. R.P. Singh (1993:17).

TABLE - 13.5
SUMMARY FIGURES FOR BLOCKS WITH TRIBAL POPULATION LESS THAN HALF THE TOTAL POPULATION

District	*No.of blocks with <50% Tribals*	*No.of Blocks with >10,000 Tribals*	*No.of Blocks with 5,000 - 10,000 Tribals*	*No.of Blocks with <5,000 Tribals*
Purnea	27	3	6	18
Katihar	11	4	3	4
Dumka	8	8	0	0
Sahebganj	5	4	1	0
Godda	5	4	1	0
Ranchi	6	6	0	0
Lohardaga	1	1	0	0
Singhbhum	13	13	0	0
Palamau	22	11	7	4
Hazaribagh	24	5	5	14
Girdih	18	12	1	5
Dhanbad	10	8	2	0
Rohtas	22	1	1	20
Bhagalpur	21	4	3	14
Munger	20	0	3	17
West Champaran	16	1	0	15
Total	229	85	33	111

These tribes of Bihar are mostly confined in the plateau of Chotanagpur and Santhal Parganas. The Bihar tribals have a distinct culture and social organization different from the dominant community. Each tribe uses its own dialect for intra-tribal communication as these tribals have in their small autonomous villages from the very beginning.

TABLE 13.6
POPULATION OF DIFFERENT TRIBES IN BIHAR - 1991 CENSUS

Sl. No.	*Tribes*	*Population*	*% of population*
1.	Asur	7783	0.13
2.	Baiga	3553	0.06
3.	Banjara	412	Neg.
4.	Bathudi	1595	0.03
5.	Bedia	60445	1.04
6.	Binjhia	10009	0.17
7.	Birhor	4377	0.07
8.	Birjia	4057	0.07
9.	Chero	52210	0.90
10.	Chick Baraik	40339	0.69
11.	Gond	96574	1.66
12.	Gorait	5206	0.09
13.	Ho	536524	9.23
14.	Karmali	38652	0.66
15.	Kharia	141771	2.44
16.	Kharwar	222758	3.83
17.	Khond	1263	0.02
18.	Kisan	23420	0.40
19.	Kora	33951	0.58
20.	Korwa	21940	0.38
21.	Lohra	169090	2.91
22.	Mahli	91865	1.59
23.	Mal Paharia	79322	1.37
24.	Munda	845887	14.56
25.	Oraon	1048064	18.05
26.	Paharia	24012	0.41
27.	Santhal	2060732	35.47
28.	Sauriya Pahariya	39269	0.68
29.	Savar	3014	0.05
30.	Bhumij	136110	2.35
31.	Unspecified	6660	0.1
		58,10,867	100.00

Since 1947, several efforts have been made to improve the status of the indigenous people of Chotanagpur and Santhal

Parganas. The Government of India and Bihar have been trying to help the indigenous people, going ahead with her development programmes to sustain the Constitutional safeguards given to them. It is well-known that the strategy for integrated development led to the launching of the tribal sub-plan concept in the Fifth Plan period. Since then many development plans have been executed for these indigenous people. But in the appraisal of tribal development and in the experience of a few decades, it has become evident that the desired results could not be achieved and our objectives to uplift the indigenous people have suffered at many levels (Oraon, 1993:1).[2]

To bring the tribals into the mainstream of development, the Fifth Five Year Plan of the Government of India outlined the tribal sub-Plan for areas with a majority of tribal population. The Seventh Plan Document states : that the tribal sub-plan (TSP) strategy adopted comprises of identification in a State of Community Development Blocks where tribal population is in a majority and their constitution into Integrated Tribal Development Projects with a view to adopting them in an integrated and project-based approach for development. Thus, all blocks with a tribal population of over 50 per cent of the total population are qualified for the special grants and Integrated Tribal Development Projects. In the Sixth Five Year Plan other pockets of tribal population, where tribals formed clusters of at least 10,000 (later changed to 5,000) were also included (Lahiri 1992 : 84).[3]

I.B. Singh,[4] a prominent psychologist from Bihar has analysed the psychological dimensions of 'Santhal' youths in Bihar. It may be mentioned here that the 'Santhals, are the most important and numerically the largest tribe of the Santhal Parganas of Bihar. They have a distinct and unique sociocultural background and a remarkable patriotic zeal and fervour reflected in their significant role in the first work of Indian independence. He observes: Santhals have been subjected to exploitation through generations. It has affected them adversely and they have started to feel themselves socially isolated, frustrated and deprived. They have not yet been able to develop a concrete shape of their self image and sense of self-identity. But the winds of change blowing across the country have not left them untouched, though for lack of acclimatization with the changes and innovations, they are finding themselves under severe stress and strain in the face of this fast changing situation (I.B. Singh, 1988: Preface).

Indeed, Dr Singh has presented an unseen aspect of tribal situation in Bihar. This study, an offshoot of intense researches made on Santhal students, deals with some of their personality characteristics and academic achievements. The results obtained in this study reveal that the Santhal students are significantly higher in anxiety, lower in intelligence achievement motivation and academic achievement than their 'non-Santhal' counterparts.

H.R. Noamani,[5] Dy. Director, Bihar Tribal Welfare Research Institute, Ranchi, has analysed the various aspects of the tribal development goals (Nomani, 1993). According to his study, the tribals have to be brought from the subsistence level of economy to become settled agricultural operators. For this, increasing of income and strengthening of the material aspect of tribal culture is very essential. Better utilization of the environmental resources such as forests, minerals, flora and fauna, agriculture, animal husbandary and industrial potential are very important improvement of existing levels of nutrition which have to be considered on priority basis. Education is the significant area for deriving the economic goals.

REFERENCES

1. Singh, R.P., 1993, *Bihar and its Scheduled Tribes*, Ranchi.
2. Oraon, P.C., 1993, *Action Plans for the Development of Indigenous People under the Changing Scenario of Chotanagpur*, Ranchi.
3. Lahiri, Manosi, 1992, *The Bihar Geographic Information System*, Bombay.
4. Singh, I.B., 1988, *Santhal Youths: An Unseen Talent*, New Delhi.
5. Noamani, H.R., 1993, The Tribal Development Goals, Bulletin of Bihar Tribal Welfare Research Institute, Ranchi.

Fourteen

The Anwal: Quest for Social Identity

B.S. BISHT

Anwal, the socially and geographically isolated lesser known community of Uttarakhand Himalaya, have been confined to the Himalayan ranges, located at an elevation of 5,000ft. to 10,000 ft. from the sea-level since long. The social identity of the Anwal community, their historical background, socio-economic and cultural organization are still beyond socio-anthropological experiences.

Etymologically the term, 'Anwal' and the legends associated with this appellation, no doubt may be helpful to sketch out their self image and identity. Yet the historical account about the moorings of its origin and social affinity is the quest to be carried out scientifically.

Having no socially sanctioned position, the Anwal community is cut off from the mainstream of the society. In spite of being socio-economically backward, it is not categorized as 'backward'. The community is geographically isolated and bears in common the traits generally found among the Indian tribes, yet not classified as the tribals. The community as a whole has been treated as the untouchables by the traditional twice-born neighbouring Hindus, yet not enlisted within the category of the Scheduled Castes.

As such the Anwal community has no place socially as well as Constitutionally in the broad spectrum of Indian social stratification so far.

The prevalent legend connotes that the Anwal people are the offsprings of the eloped pairs who absconded from Gharwal and Kumaun Hills to the dense forests of Himalaya valleys in order to hide themselves from the calumination resulted due to the violation of the family incest regulations in remote past.

In the due course of time they took shelter in the aboriginal tribe, namely, the Bhotiyas of Uttarakhand Himalaya. According to a legend, the term 'Anwal' is a corrupted form of 'Ounwal' i.e., the person earning one's livelihood by splitting wool from tamed sheep. The other legend describes that the term 'Anwal' is a corrupted form of 'Anna-wala', i.e., the porter carrying the food grain to the far flung areas of Himalayas through goats and mules. Thus, etymologically the appellation i.e., 'Anwal' deals with the 'work agent class' dependent on the Bhotiyas of Uttarakhand Himalaya which later on emerged as the serf. Today they have land ownership, however, known as the serfs.

The available first-hand information gathered through participant observation method depicts that the Anwal community bears the following characteristics in general.

Geographically, Anwal is an isolated group mainly concentrated in the valleys of Darma, Vyans and Chaundas of Dharchula Tahsil in Pithoragarh District. The Anwal community has not been included into the traditional Hindu caste hierarchy. The social status of this community in pre-acculturated stage was like that of the untouchables, particularly for the neighbouring twice-born Hindus. The Anwal community entertains almost all common beliefs customary law and practices and in true sense, the community still adheres/ professes animism. Anwal people speak common dialect with frequent use of the word of Ran (Bhotiya) and Kumauni dialects. The people of Anwal Community consider themselves as the members of a small unit with the feeling of belongingness to that unit. Economically they are underdeveloped with a backward economy. The community follows common occupational practices, which include sheep and goat rearing. Crude type of cultivation, wage-earning through physical labour, collection of jungle products of various kinds. Today they have land ownership, yet the acute poverty has reduced them to perpetuated serfdom. They used to have their own community Panchayat which has now transformed into the democratic pattern. However, the status quo of the elderly people is maintained. They are more effective in their decision making about the community matters. They do not have common ancestoral origin. Anwal is an endogamous group, the elopement (Urhal) is a prevalent way of acquiring mates.

Though the social scientists are not consensual on criteria of the 'tribe'. However, if we take reference of the prominent anthropologists like Prof. D.N. Majumdar (1944), Gillin and Gillin (1950), Prof.. Ehrenfels, etc., we come to the conclusion that the 'Anwal community' bearing in common the characteristics as mentioned above, may be classified as 'tribals'.

REFERENCES

Gillin and Gillin, 1950, *Cultural Sociology*, The Macmillan Co., New York.

Majumdar, D.N., 1944, *Races and Cultures of India*, Asia Publishing House, Bombay.

Fifteen

State Measures for Rural Development of SCs

J.K. PUNDIR

In India several States have initiated various welfare measures for the development of the weaker sections like the Scheduled Castes, the Scheduled Tribes and others. In fact, under the Constitution the State is obliged to take up special measures to promote the economic and educational interests of these backward, weaker sections in particular, thereby protecting these sections from social injustice and all forms of exploitation. Since independence various measures have gone into the welfare of these sections. The large, masses 73 per cent of India live in rural areas and Scheduled Castes largely living in rural areas comprising 16.73 per cent constitute a significant segment of the rural society. Thus, the State owes a greater responsibility towards this segment of the society. Thereby the State welfare measures have been initiated from the very outset of the planned efforts of development for the rural society in general and these weaker sections in particular. These welfare measures for rural populace have come to be commonly known as rural development programmes. The present study focuses in this background upon three main issues with special reference to the Scheduled Castes. These issues are:

(i) What has been the focus of the rural development programmes?
(ii) What changes have been brought about in these programme? and
(iii) What have been the consequences of these rural development programmes?

These questions and issues have been explored by tracing the rural development programmes implemented since the very beginning of the First Five Year Plan in 1952. Later changes and shifts introduced, especially focusing upon the weaker sections, are noted to understand the nature and focus of the new welfare measures. The evidence on the consequences of all these welfare measures is indicated from earlier studies, from some recent ones and from our own observations and ongoing studies. Particular focus of the recent evidence is limited to parts of northern India. This evidence is not exhaustive but selective and illustrative so as to indicate the nature and direction of consequences.

State Welfare Measures

The enactment of the Constitution provided for in the Article 38 is as follows:

"State to secure a social order for the promotion of welfare of the people

(i) the State shall strive to promote the welfare of the people by securing and protecting as effectively as it may a social order in which justice, social, economic and political shall inform all the institutions of the national life.

(ii) The State shall, in particular strive to minimize the inequalities in income and endeavour to eliminate inequalities in status, facilities and opportunities, not only amongst individuals but also amongst groups of people residing in different areas or engaged in different vocations."

Further the Article 46 more legibly indicates:

"The State shall promote with special care the educational and economic interests of the weaker sections of the people, and in particular, of the Scheduled Castes and the Scheduled Tribes, and shall protect them from social injustice and all forms of exploitation."

Thus, all the measures initiated by the State for welfare of people at large or for welfare of particular deprived backward sections of society like the Scheduled Castes and Scheduled Tribes are to be considered as welfare measures. We have a two-tier Government in the country—the Union Government and the Government of the provinces, the State Government. Any measures initiated by the Union Government for the country as a whole and by the State for the people of the State, are taken together as State welfare measures. Since Independence and especially since the implementation of the First Five-Year Plan in 1952 our society has experienced such welfare measures as planned programmes. If necessary the State has also gone into passing the legislations at either of the two levels aimed at the welfare of these sections.

Broadly speaking and also as a matter of convenience, these programmes (welfare measures) and legislations may by divided into four categories:

(i) Measures aimed at removing social disabilities (injustice) like the legislations for removing untouchability and to ensure its enforcement;

(ii) Measures like land reforms policies and programmes, including abolition of Zamindari system, consolidation of landholdings, ceiling on land, allotment and distribution of custodian lands, wastelands, surplus village Panchayat lands, and of surplus land made available by ceiling;

(iii) The measures of equality like Universal Adult Franchise for electing representatives of people for Central and State legislatures, for village and local democratic institutions and reservations of Scheduled Castes, Scheduled Tribes and women, etc., in these democratic institutions at all levels and of seats and posts in education and services; and

(iv) The measures as programmes of rural development, which manifestly appear to aim at economic development of people at large with and special preference or provisions for the socio-economically and educationally weaker sections like the Scheduled Castes and the Scheduled Tribes.

In the specific framework of this study, looking at the majority i.e. 73 per cent of the population living in the rural areas and majority of Scheduled Castes still living in this context, we focus especially on the analysis of rural development programmes as welfare measures.

In Independent India more than 50 plus such programmes

have been implemented till now aiming at overall development of the community and other developments - specially of the down-trodden sections.

The first programme of rural development, named as Community Development Programme, was launched in 1952 in some selected blocks and later on it was extended to the whole nation. Aiming at the development of the community as a whole, it specifically aimed at development of the area with a minimum of all round progress, self help, development of the community as a whole with special preference to the weaker and under privileged sections, agricultural improvement, increase in food production, rural health-sanitation, construction of roads and nutritional improvement.

The later programmes also aimed at augmenting food production, economic development, improvement of nutritional status of women. Intensive Agriculture Development Programmes (1960) was introduced with an aim to meet Indian food crises. High yielding variety programme (1965) aimed at increasing production with massive use of new seeds, fertilizers and irrigation and technology. Small farmers development agencies aimed at improving the lot of small and marginal farmers, increasing production and diversifying rural economy. During drought conditions, some of the programmes provided assistance in eliminating scarcity of water.

Several programmes in the 1970's were initiated to generate employment for the masses in the rural areas like Crash Scheme for Rural Employment (1971). Employment Guarantee Scheme (1974), etc. These entailed improvement and construction of roads, development of wasteland, minor irrigation, etc., and thus to generate employment. Minimum Needs Programme (1974) included facilities of education, nutritive diet for children and drinking water facilities, etc.

There came a well publicised programme known as the Twenty-point programme in 1975 which incorporated much of the total included so far. It aimed at the upliftment of the rural poor and raise their economic institutions from a stage of stagnation to a more dynamic stage towards higher level of living and better quality of life. Priorities were laid down for Scheduled Castes and

Tribes and other weaker sections and to take care of their economic, educational and social interests and save them from exploitation. Priorities were fixed for their development by involving public sector financial institutions for the first time. The development bureaucracy and the public sector banks were involved to provide financial assistance, subsidies and loans for various self-employment schemes for the rural poor for the first time.

Then came the programmes like Food For Work Programmes (1977), Desert Area Development Programme (1977-78), Command Area Development, etc, aimed at generating additional employment in rural areas and create durable community assets which would strengthen infrastructure. Payment for work came in the form of food grains and cash together. The Antyodaya programme which was introduced along with the above, apparently aimed at the upliftment of the poorest of man.

In the light of the experiences of these earlier programmes the State came out with a new programme in the name of IRDP (1978). It also aimed at alleviating poverty by augmenting the income of the poorest families in the rural areas by engaging them in gainful occupations. The eligible beneficiaries would be assisted in the income generating schemes covering agriculture and allied activities. At least 30 per cent of the beneficiaries would be from Scheduled Castes and the Tribes. It included other appendices of programmes like NREP and TRYSEM (1980) to generate additional gainful employment, train the rural youth and create durable infrastructure.

Special programmes for women and children and for educated rural youth (1983) focused upon different groups to engage different categories of population in gainful employment. The landless employment guarantee programme aimed to provide work to atleast one person in every landless family.

The Jawahar Rozgar Yojna was launched by the State in a bigway in 1989 with the merger of several existing programmes. It aimed at involving the elected village Panchayat in a big way and supplying resources largely for the village development. It included land development, reform of land sterility, plantation, social forestry, road, village school, 'Panchayat ghar' construction, construction of wells, repair of drainage and house construction of weaker sections. Later on, this house construction came to be known as Indira Awas Yojna. It aimed at generating resources, employment through self-employment especially for the Scheduled Castes, Scheduled Tribes and other weaker sections and, thus, an all round development.

Other programmes included like construction of million wells scheme, village small industries, landless employment, insurance, tools and kits programmes, biogas development, improved hearth, Scheduled Castes and Tribes drinking water programme, etc.

One of the latest programmes is the Ambedkar Rural Development Scheme (1991) for the villages where Scheduled Caste and Scheduled Tribes population is more than 50 per cent. The aims are to provide basic amenities like link roads, training the youth under several other programmes like TRYSEM, electrification, drinking water, primary health services, primary schools' buildings, etc.

All these programmes have been aimed at the welfare of the people in the rural area at large in which development of the weaker sections was imperative. The emphasis of the programmes can be observed in terms of providing infrastructural facilities for the rural people, involving them for self help, improvement of resources like land, facilities of irrigation, technology, roads, etc. They include the component of generating employment for the rural unemployed and the landless, various facilities for the poor to start the self employment and new occupations, etc. Thus, the rural development programmes, as welfare measures, from the very beginning got initiated in the manner to promote the development of the people at large, as well as that of the weaker sections like the Scheduled Castes and the Scheduled Tribes, etc. Some special components for these sections were included within those and also separate provisions were made.

We may look at the special provisions which were made for these sections in those programmes. These are briefly listed here.

1. From the very beginning the State welfare measures like the Community Development Programme (1952) were aimed at welfare of the rural community as a whole but some preference to the backward and weaker sections like the Scheduled Castes was implied in it;

2. The special provisions for the reservation of seats in the Panchayat were made for these backward and weaker sections to ensure their participation in the democratic processes and sharing of power (e.g. Panchayati Raj Legislation 1959);
3. Their special case was considered in economic development, education, housing etc. (e.g. twenty-point programme, 1975; Indira Awas Yojna);
4. Reservation of 30 per cent of beneficiaries from among the Scheduled Castes and other weaker sections in the financial assistance from public sector banks (e.g. I.R.D.P., 1978);
5. Earmarking of 10 per cent of the resources for the welfare of weaker sections like the Scheduled Castes and the Tribes (e.g. NREP, 1980);
6. Integrated services for children, training to women in handicraft etc. (Women and Children Programme);
7. House building through Indira Awas Yojna and other works for the downtrodden sections (e.g. Jawahar Rozgar Yojna, 1989);
8. Tubewells for small and marginal farmers especially included the beneficiaries from these downtrodden;
9. Improved hearth scheme included 30 per cent share of Scheduled Castes (1992), drinking water facilities especially meant for them; and
10. Other welfare measures included electricity and roads to their colonies and localities, training for youth under TRYSEM, pre-primary health care, school facilities for welfare of these backward weaker sections.

Observable Shifts in the Welfare Measures

Several measures for the welfare of the rural people have been initiated since independence which have aimed at improving the lifestyle of the people as a whole. Largely the programmes, started earlier, were aimed at the welfare and development of the village community as a whole. Assumption behind all of them was that during the process of overall development the weaker sections like the Scheduled Castes and the Scheduled Tribes, etc, will develop.

By the end of the Fourth Five Year Plan feedback was coming through the evaluation studies that all these programmes which aimed at the development of the community as a whole, were not taking care of the welfare of these backward weaker sections. A separate programme was required from them and henceforth it was decided at the highest policy planning level that special components and measures were required for the welfare of these sections.

Thus, after the Fourth Five Year Plan, special measures were envisaged for these sections. The "trickle down approach" was considered to be befitting for their welfare. This trickle down approach aimed at hitting the crux where it was supposed to take care of the welfare of these weaker sections directly by special programmes. Though the very first programme, C.D.P., of rural development included as one of its aims, the "development of the whole community with special preference to weaker and under privileged in the rural area."

When the Fifth Five Year Plan was in progress, 21 point programme, initiated in the mid 1970's especially aimed at improving the social conditions of these weaker sections. It is during this period that the public sector banks entered rural areas in a big way and especially started sponsoring the self employment schemes and occupational change schemes of these weaker sections for the first time. It was the then political will that especially had gone ahead for the new welfare measures for these weaker sections.

Later on the improved versions of these programmes got consolidated into Integrated Rural Development Programme. Initiated in 1978 this programme was aimed at alleviation of poverty by augmenting the income of the poorest families in rural areas by engaging them in gainful occupations. It envisaged at least 30 per cent beneficiaries from among the Scheduled Castes and the Scheduled Tribes. This also included training of the rural youth for self employment as a part of it.

Later on the National Rural Employment Programme which aimed at generating gainful employment upto 300 days a year, for poor men and women was also introduced. It also encouraged to create community assets for strengthening the rural infrastructure.

Special programmes were also implemented for women and children, Jawahar Rozgar Yojna, Million Wells Scheme, drinking water facilities programme and latest among all these the Ambedkar Rural Development Schemes especially aim at the welfare of these backward sections.

Thus, we observe a shift in the later programmes of rural development. The earlier welfare measures included within them the provisions for these sections while the measures were for the community as a whole. But after the Fourth Five Year Plan the trickle down approach was followed. Special components were envisaged in all welfare measures or special measures were initiated for the welfare of these weaker sections. The latest welfare measures have been planned and initiated for Scheduled Caste majority villages, etc, separately. Thus, the changes and shifts in favour of these weaker sections have come through.

We may now look at the consequences of these welfare measures.

Consequences of the Welfare Measures

The shifts in various welfare measures and introduction of the newer measures indicate by implication that these measures were not succeeding to the extent and in the direction they were supposed to. In addition to these measures other concomitant factors and progress have also contributed to the welfare and upliftment of these sections or acted contrary to the desired goals. Therefore, the consequences have to be understood in wider frame in which the welfare measures have contributed.

A survey research study on Scheduled Castes with special reference to change till 1970s has indicated that in addition to other processes like westernization, sanskritization and reform movements, the State action in the form of welfare measures have also introduced desired changes in the life of the Scheduled Castes (Sachchidanand, 1974: 296). The earlier studies considered State action as very much favourable special treatment for these depressed classes of India (Dushkin: 1957). State action initiated some possibilities for advancement and change to these lowest castes. It was also found that the provisions like removal of untouchability were disregarded at a large-scale (Galanter : 1969). Later on, this Constitutional measure invited further measures (a legislation) for its enforcement. These welfare measures and reports against not following them, meant that the Scheduled Castes were becoming more vigilant about their rights. Various groups of Harijans show a differential degree of development and a differential capacity to utilize these welfare measures (Patwardhan: 1972)

In participation and power sharing at the local level they were not coming up effectively in some areas despite reservation and their numerical strength (M.Ali Khan : 1980). It was also observed that their leaders played a crucial role in bringing about social change but they were playing a somewhat cosmopolitan role (Sachchidananda : 1977).

Later and recent studies indicate a mixed trend of success and limited success. In eastern Uttar Pradesh, in rural situation, less effective participation in making use of the welfare measures of rural development programmes is observed. The sharing of power despite numerical strength is still weak (Upadhyaya: 1992). In the initial stages of taking benefits of the facilities of the public sector banks under the twenty-point programme, a segment of the Scheduled Castes got benefited. But these benefits remained limited to fewer families. The village elite of the higher castes played an important role in materializing the benefits and, thus, the benefits were differentially distributed. This section of Scheduled Castes was not the poorest among the poor (Pundhir, 1991: 221-22).

A progressive trend in attaining economic and educational status has been observed. According to some the stigma of untouchability and other social disabilities still continue. These measures have had less significant impact. It has also been observed that the State measures have also introduced changes like reducing social distance in the rural area and economic dependence upon the higher castes is getting considerably reduced (Pundir: 1990). In Terai villages it has been noted that some mobile families of Scheduled Castes are going ahead in education, new occupations, lifestyle and in political participation at local level, the economic dependency upon higher castes is becoming lesser (Sisaudia: 1987).

Some other recent evidence indicate that the State welfare measures are succeeding in bringing change and upliftment of Scheduled Castes in some cases atleast. Their own voluntary organizations have started mediating between the State machinery and the poor Scheduled Caste beneficiaries (Kumar, 1995).

These changes, which are coming as a consequence of the State welfare measures and other factors and processes, are observable in four dimensions, namely, economic, social, political and cultural. More changes are observable in the transformation, upgradation and diversification of their traditional occupations and adoptions of new occupations.

The adoption of new occupations, clean and prestigious, has been facilitated largely by State welfare measures. On the social dimension lessening of social distance, increasing intercourse in daily activities indicate a qualitative change. Change in political dimension is indicated by the facts like increasing participation in democratic processes frequently, achieving positions in the community power structure as a consequence of state measures like that of reservation of seats. The cultural changes are marked by adopting the clean occupations by making use of reservations, transforming and modernizing technologically, updating and changing occupations, following lifestyles of the upper castes, etc.

Thus, various changes as a consequence of the Constitutional provisions and welfare measures clubbed with other processes are observable among the Scheduled Castes in north India. But it is not stated that the Scheduled Castes as a whole have changed or the same changes are occurring in all the regions.

Conclusion

Three main questions posed in the beginning of this study were: What has been the focus of the various rural development programmes, as welfare measures?, What changes have been brought about in these programmes? and What have been the consequences of these programmes?

On the issues raised in the above questions we find that several programmes have been initiated by the State for the welfare of the backward communities like the Scheduled Castes. The very first programme introduced for the development of the village community, namely, the C.D.P. focussed upon the participation of people in development and special preference was laid upon the development of the underprivileged weaker sections. It was aimed at all round development of the village community.

The later programmes aimed at their participation in

community affairs and power structure, improvement of the lot of landless and the small land owners, employment generation, self employment, afforestation, drinking and irrigation water, programmes for women and children, training and employment of youth, biogas and hearth, housing and development of the infrastructure for village community where large number of the backward community of Scheduled Castes are living. Lastly, special measures have been initiated for Scheduled Caste in majority of villages.

All these programmes included special provisions and portions to focus upon these communities, highlighting the upliftment of these communities.

Looking at the second issue of changes in these programmes we find that, on the basis of the feedback, new measures, focussing upon these communities have been taken up. After the Fourth Five Year Plan the trickle down approach was adopted and thereby all these measures focussed upon their various needs like occupation, income, health and housing. Thus, we observe an entire shift in the focus of the welfare measures taken up for these backward communities. These shifts in the focus have been necessitated as the earlier measures could not bring about the desired changes to the extent they were expected to do, and in the desired direction.

On the third issue, the consequences of these State welfare measures as rural development programmes, we observe that if not everywhere atleast in some situations, the desired changes are observable in economic, social, political and cultural life of the people of these backward communities. These changes are manifestly visible in better occupations, modernizing of traditional occupations, somewhat lesser dependency upon higher castes in employment, better ways of life and housing, better intercourse in daily life though not without strains, participation in local power structure, and decision making, in material aspects of life and culture.

It should be noted here that all such changes are coming up as consequences of the State welfare measures and also alongwith other concomitant factors and processes. Secondly, these changes are neither observable among all members of the Scheduled Castes nor in all parts even of north India. There are variations in respect of different castes within the Scheduled Castes and they vary in degrees even in the same region. These few changes in situations may only provide as model illustrations for their brethren and for others. In a large amount they are yet to come up in larger parts of the country.

The State welfare measures have limitations in the social contexts where these institutional arrangements need to be acted upon. Thus, changes have to be explained in terms of the social structural variations of the respective social milieu. In this way, it is enough that these positive illustrative evidences are there to indicate the trend and not the universal reality. New linkages are also emerging in all these processes of the implementation of the State welfare measures and these linkages have no single basis or single criteria.

Lastly, it is hoped that some such consequences may follow other situations as well as some structural conditions may emerge which are conducive to the development of the backward communities like the Scheduled Castes.

REFERENCES

Dushkin, L., 1957, "The Policy of Indian National Congress Towards the Depressed Classes" (Unpublished Dissertation), quoted by Sachchidanand, 1974 (ibid, below).

Galanter, 1969, "Untouchability And the Law", *Economic and Political Weekly*, Annual Numbers, 131-170.

Khan, Mumtaz Ali, 1980, *Scheduled Castes and their Status in India*, New Delhi: Uppal Publishing House.

Kumar, Anoop, 1995, "Rural Development Programmes and Scheduled Castes in Kishtwar" Unpublished dissertation, C.C.S. University, Meerut.

Maurya, R.L., 1991, "Changing Status of the Scheduled Castes". In R.S. Tripathi and P.D. Tiwari (eds.) *Dimensions of Scheduled Caste Development in India*, pp. 106-21, New Delhi: Uppal.

Patwardhan, Sunanda, 1972, *Change Among India's Harijans*, New Delhi: Orient Longman.

Pundir, J.K., 1980, "Law and Weaker Sections". In I. N. Tiwary et. al. (eds.); *Challenges and Alternatives*, U.P. Pol. Sc. Association, pp: 64-68.

———, 1991, Differentiation Consequences of Rural Development of Weaker Section". In R.S. Tripathi and P.D. Tiwari (eds.); ibid. pp: 206-224.

———, 1995, "Social Change Among Scheduled Castes in North India", *Social Change*, Vol. 25, No. 4, pp: 109-120.

Sachchidanand, 1974, "Research on Scheduled Castes with Special Reference to Change", *A Survey of Research in Sociology and Social Anthropology* (ICSSR), Vol. 1, Bombay: Popular, 276-310.

———, 1977, *The Harijan Elite*, Faridabad: Thompson Press.

Upadhyaya, Arun Kumar, 1992, "Scheduled Caste Leaders in A Rural Setting in Eastern U.P.", Unpublished Project Report, Meerut, Meerut University.

Sixteen

The Buxas of Uttarakhand: Habitat, Society, Economy and Transformation

SAROJINI DEVI BISHT

Origin

The origin of the Bhukasas or Buxas is based on some legends concocted by different people in different manners. Even the etymology of the Bhukasas or Buxas leads to a number of stories to prove the adequacy of the appellation used for the Buxa community. For instance, some Buxas of Bijnor area are of the opinion that their ancestors had the long beard quite resembling the 'Bok' a 'he goat' found in the adjoining hill provinces of their settlement and therefore they were called the Bokasas or Buxas. While some Buxas relate the etymology of their name with the English word 'Bogus'. Amir Hasan stated that : "the word Buxa is a corrupted form of the Persian word 'eksa' which means uniformity. Such a name might have been given by the Mughals, who were struck by the fact that unlike most of other Indian communities, this tribe has no caste or sub-caste differences among its members." But the etymological explanation of the name Bhukasas or the Buxas is not more than a surmise presented as a 'derivation' by the Buxas themselves and the scholars in general. There are some other views which asserted that the term 'Bhokasa' is rather a corrupted form of the Hindi term, 'Sarva Bhaksi' or the 'Bhakosane Wala' means the 'Omnivorous'. This notion of etymological explanation has been supported by a number of aged Buxas of the Nainital Tarai who as early as their settlement in the Tarai used to devour everything to keep their body and soul together and, thus, called to be a 'Bhaksi' and gradually as 'Bhukas' by the neighbouring communities. With the passage of time this nomadic tribe has also adhered to the appellation 'Bhuksa' and simultaneously claimed their 'Rajput' origin. In the district Gazetteer of Nainital, we look upon the Bhukasas and their neighbours i.e. the Thaurs as the kindred races. Both of them claim royal blood from the female side. A prevalent Tharu legend describes that the king of Tarai was once defeated by an invader in the remote past. The women of the royal palace fled to a jungle alongwith their servants i.e.. The 'Chamars' and 'Sais' of the palace. From them sprang the two indigenous races of Tharus and Buxas, the former being descendants of 'Chamars' and the latter from the 'Sais'. While Henry Eliot has said:

> They claim to be Panwar Rajputs and assert that their chief, Udayjit, was driven from home because of quarrel that he had with his brother Jagat Deo, the Raja of Dharanagar. Udayjit had come with a few dependents at Banbasa on the Sarda. Udayjit had not been there long, before his aid was solicited by the Raja of Kumaun whose territories required defence against some of the neighbouring powers. Success attended the efforts of the Panwar and the gratitude of the Raja induced him to offer his defenders asylum in his territories. Upon this, they left Banbasa and have taken up their residence in their present abodes. Even today the Buxas claim that they belong to Panwar clan of Dhara Nagar.

In this regard another study goes to prove that, Buxas were descendents of Raja Jagat Deo, a great warrior of Rajasthan. According to Crooke: Jagat Deo was a worshipper of Goddess Durga and offered his head to her. The Buxas claim to have brought the deity Durga (now known as Kashipur Devi) to Tarai. The 'Narial" (Palmnut) is offered to the deity as symbolic of his head. Some Buxas say that Raja Jagat Deo had two sons-Chittaur and Nandhaur, while Tharus are the descendants of the former one and Buxas are stated to have descended from the latter. Crooke further mentions that, many Buxas say that: "they came from the Dakkhin, others from Delhi, but they were expelled from the Dakkhin by the Marathas". It is obvious that the historical facts presented by earlier scholars depict a frequent contradiction in regard to the origin of the Buxas. In fact the Buxas are not of the Rajput origin but in the absence of any historical clue, a number of legends prove their Rajput ancestory. The aged Buxas too admitted that at the time of their migration to Tarai and Bhabar area, every one was not the descendant of the Rajputs. There were the people belonging to different castes who managed to come under one community due to some adverse geo-social circumstances dispensing with all their previous caste and class barriers. They later on emerged as the Buxa community. It is, however, more authentic to mention that the so-called Buxas are of the non-Aryan origin, who at the end of their nomadic lifestyle got settled in the isolated and quite uninhabited provinces of Tarai Bhabar of Nainital and Dehradun districts. With the passage of time the medley of different ethnic groups in Uttaranchal and the frequent contact of Hindus inspired them to concoct the legends to prove their ancestry with Rajput origin so that they may have a social position in the broad spectrum of Hindu caste hierarchy. This fact is self evident by the countenance, physical traits of the Buxas and the mores, beliefs and rituals they have observed ever since.

Racial Traits

Anthropologists traced the origin of the Buxas with Mongolian racial groups. By appearance an average Buxa possesses an average height ranging 5'4" to 5'11" in the case of male and 5'4" to 5'8" in the case of female, with stout built. Both the male and female are wheatish or dark complexioned with broad face, oblique eyes, flat nose, thick lips and black hair. The beard and moustaches of a Buxa is very scanty. Such a countenance and the physical features gave no clue to any specific racial region. It is rather a sketch of a mixed racial trait which came into existence as an outcome of the mixture of different racial elements occurred due to the medley of the different ethnic groups in Uttaranchal, in the remote past. Stewart, as referred by William Crooke, has stated that the Buxas are of stout stature not differing much from the general peasantry of the area. Their eyes are small, the opening of eyelids being narrow, linear and horizontal (the inner angle not inclining downwards, so far as observed): the face is very broad, the cheek bones and their nose is depressed, thus, increasing the general fitness as of the face. The jaw is prominent and the lower lip thick and the moustache and beard scanty. The features of the women are also similar to those of the men.

Habitat

Since long the Buxas are known as the original owners of the Tarai and Bhabar plains of Uttarakhand, including Pilibhit and Bijnor districts of Uttar Pradesh. Atkinson has stated that, the Buxas, a tribe somewhat similar to the Tharus are found in the Tarai and Bhabar from the Pilibhit district on the east to Chandpur on the Ganges on the west and few scattered colonies also occur in Deharadun. At present the population of Buxa tribe is spread over in the Tarai plains of Dehradun, Paurhi and Udham Singh Nagar districts of Uttarakhand and also in Bijnor district of UP. According to Singh and Shukla (1990: 83) the Buxa population is spread over in 17 villages of Sirmaur district in Himachal Pradesh. In Udham Singh Nagar district the Buxa population is spread mainly in Bajpur, Kashipur, Gadarpur and Ram Nagar Development Blocks. The place of their habitation is known as Buxar. In Dehradun district, there are only two development blocks, namely, Doiwala and Sahaspur where the Buxa population is residing, while in Paurhi Garhwal only one development block, i.e. Dogadda is there which is inhabited by this tribe. According to the census survey, the total population of Buxa, mainly in Uttarakhand, is dwelling in 173 villages. (Bisht, 1996 : 163)

The Buxas live generally in self-made huts, called 'Chhappar.' The hut, built in rectangular shape is made up of upright wooden logs on which rest the horizontally fixed logs or *ballies* with thatched rods called 'Dabna' and 'Bharai' found in jungles or by 'Jhau' found by the sides of the rivulets. The huts are single storied with a verandah. All the familial tasks pertaining to kitchen, sleeping, storing food grains, etc, are performed within the huts itself. The grain bins which are quite large in size and are made with the mixture of viscous soil (found in river or ponds) and the husks are generally installed with the huts in such a way that they make partition of hut by dividing it into two parts. The walls of the hut are made up of wooden frames plastered by cow dung and husk mixed mud. The front portion of the hut wall is decorated with different sorts of drawings and paintings which symbolically present not only their inherent talents but also their beliefs and practices. Some well-off families bring-out these drawings and paintings with different colours as to make them more and more impressive, attractive as well as meaningful. The realistic sort of drawing and painting sketched on the hut-walls and carved into wooden works of Buxa huts indicate the speciality of the Buxa culture. In one corner of the hut, the clan deity is installed. In Buxar area, the Buxa huts are made sequentially in a line facing east. Correspondingly they possess a large and combined courtyard, but the family uses only a portion of the courtyard. But during festivity the whole of the courtyard is used according to ones requirement. On the end of the courtyard the huts are made parallel to the former ones facing west. Adjoining the huts, the people have their cattle shades called 'Sar' which are also made with wooden logs horizontally fixed on the upright wooden logs and thatched over by grass. A single hut has only one door. There is no provision for ventilation. Today most of the Buxa villages are electrified, however, most of the huts have no electric connections. They generally use kerosene lamps. But some economically well-off Buxas have pucca houses with electric connections.

Populace and its Nature

The total population of Buxas is 25,536 out of which 22,378 is spread over in Dehradun, Paurhi Garhwal and Udham Singh Nagar districts of Uttarakhand Himalaya while 3158 population resides in Bijnor, an adjoining district of Uttarakhand. District and blockwise distribution of Buxa tribe is presented in Table 16.1 where the Buxas constitute 13.62% of the total Scheduled Tribe population of the region.

TABLE - 16.1
DISTRICT AND BLOCKWISE DISTRIBUTION OF BUXA POPULATION

District	*Block*	*Population*
1. Udham Singh Nagar	Bajpur	7307
	Gadarpur	7867
	Kashipur	121
	Ramnagar	969
2. Dehradun	Doiwala	1053
	Sahaspur	4168
3. Paurhi Garhwal	Dogadda	893
4. Bijnor	Kotwali	3158
	Afjalgarh	
Total : 04	09	25,536

Social Organization

Buxa is an endogamous group which is divided into various clans named after their sub-castes and the place of habitations called 'Khera'. Each clan is an exogamous group. Like the Hindus, the Buxas do not find affinity to the origin of their clan with any mythological ancestor rather they are known with the surname or sub-caste names like Tomar, Chauhan, etc, while some others name their clan with 'khera' i.e. the original place of their residence, namely, the Buxas living in Jogipur Khera have Jogipuriya clan; Polgarh Khera have Polgarhiya clan and Chanakpur Khera have Chankpuriya clan. H.M. Elliot has mentioned 15 *gotras* of which 12 are superior and three are inferior. The *gotras* are : the Bargujar, Tabari, Barahniya, Jalwar, Aadhoi, Dugugiya, Rathaur, Nagariya, Jalal, Upadhyay, Chauhan, Dunwariya (Superior), Dimer Rathaur (Descended from a Teli Woman), Dhangra (from a hill woman), Goli (from a barbar woman). While Shukla (1974) has stated that Buxas have 56 *gotras* named after their 'Kheras'. Infact there are number of *gotras* who indicate and confirm this view that the name of these *gotras* have originated from the Hindu sub-castes of the same name. But in spite of being divided in a number of *gotras* there is no social hierarchy and the difference of higher and lower status among the *gotras*, though the Buxas, having some affinity with the Kshatriyas in terms of their origin, possess a feeling of superiority over others. Same is the case of those *gotras* representing higher Hindu castes. However, in practice there is no bar on inter-*gotra*-marriages as well as in commensal relations among different clan groups. Today, most of the Buxas have no knowledge about their *gotra* origin, in such cases a number of marriages have taken place within the members of the same *gotras* living in different villages. It is, thus, observed that the growing Buxa population is unable to stand upto the mark in maintaining their *gotra* identity.

So far as the kinship relations are concerned, we observe that both types of kinship terms i.e. the classified and the particular are used by the people to denote different types of similarities related respectively with affinal and consanguineous kinship categories. The people are observed to follow a particular system of kinship usages consisting of the avoidance, joking and teknonymy relations.

Marriage and Rituals

Originally, Buxas do not have any particular pattern of life cycle rituals. However, with the influence and acquaintence of neighbouring twice-born Hindus they have started observing the Chhati Karm, namakaran, marriage and death and cremation rituals. The formal marriage, which takes place with due negotiation between both the parties after the proposal made by girls parents and relatives, is generally followed by a number of ceremonies like : Mangani, Ganna, Ratjaga, Haldi, Chheie Katna, worship of Gamkheri Devi, Nauta, Bhatlagana, Fere, Pachalerhi, Vidai and Gauna. Apart from the formal marriage there still are some other prevalent forms of marriages or the ways of acquiring mates among the Buxas. These are: love marriages, marriage by abduction, Gharjawain marriage, widow re-marriage, levirate, sororate, levirate senior, exchange marriage, mutual consent and elopement. Premarital sex relations are not permitted and socially sanctioned. However, the youths sometimes indulge themselves in such illicit sex liaison. This act of amorous relations are defamed and the parties involved are punished, only when, the virgin gets conceived. This act resulted either in elopement or in court marriage. For Buxas, a virgin in particular is blamed for having conceived before marriage and is entrusted to any needy and desirous man ready to accept such a woman. But such couples are generally looked down upon in the Buxa community. The Buxas also observe some prohibition like incest taboo, *gotra* and Khera exogamy and community endogamy. Cross-cousin marriages are prohibited atleast for three generations.

Buxa is a patriarchal, patrilocal and patrilineal community. The male members theoretically wield greater influence over womenfolk. Both, the joint and nuclear type of families exist in the community but the recent study shows that nuclear families are on the rise (1994 : 124). Both type of families bear in common the traditional characters. The father or the aged male members of the family hold the status of the head of the family and his advice continues to be sought in family matters. Sometimes the aging father hands over his authority as well as the familial liabilities to his eldest son or the eldest male member of the family and continues to be the nominal head of the family. It is, however, observed sometimes that the nominal head avoids any such situation which can put his position in jeopardy and therefore, decisions mainly rely on the eldest male member in the family. In connection with the right of property ownership the Buxas follow the rules of 'Dayabhag'. The father is the sole owner of his property during his life time unless he himself does not agree principally to share the property with his sons. Hence the father and the sons make every possible efforts to live together under the common roof. In fact, the father, to avoid any such complications and the libellous situation at community level tolerates every hardship of the family but does not divide the land and the property because it is considered to be humiliating and disgraceful in the community particularly when the father is alive. This act indeed makes the position of the father ludicrous in the community and also invites the misfortune, sufferings and perplexities in his life. However, the situations arising out of the quarrels between the mother-in-law and daughter-in-law, strained relations among the daughter-in-law regarding the division of labour and sharing the responsibilities of the family and estrangement among brothers over property have ultimately been bringing about the disorientation of the joint family system and the emergence of nuclear family system among the Buxas. Today most of the nuclear families among the Buxas are the outcome of the familial dispute. The peace loving Buxas, therefore, separate their sons as soon as they are married so that the possibilities of the familial disputes are curtailed and cordiality among the separating nuclear families can be maintained. Generally an average Buxa nuclear family consists of a husband, a wife, unmarried children and sometimes the widow mother, widower father and the unmarried siblings of the husband. The interpersonal relations among the family members are authoritarian. An elder person holds respectively a higher position, power and privilege to order the youngsters. The youngsters are supposed to obey their elders and also to pay due respect and veneration to them in the family.

The status of a Buxa woman is highly venerable. In practice the aged woman in family possesses equal status to that of the male head. Mostly the familial matters are decided with the mutual consent of the head as well as of the aged woman of the family.

Because of the royal origin in female line, the Buxa woman holds superior position and plays an important role in family matters and decision making. It is her privilege to perform all the domestic tasks. She cooks food and feeds all the family members. She never takes the meal touched by the male members in the family. In practice she pushes the dish of meal by her toe to the husband who humbly takes it and eats. This instance also exhibits the female dominance over male and the disdainful status of the male as compared to the female in the community. In agricultural field the woman also lends her hand particularly in transplanting, weeding, reaping the crops, threshing paddy and husking the corn with motor. Besides this she traps fishes and goes to market to sell the agricultural produce with her husband.

Buxas are basically an agriculturist tribal community with a low agricultural pattern and socio-economic standard. By nature, Buxas are introverted. They have no liking for modernization, education and better living. They wish to procure only as much as is necessary to keep the body and soul together. The community still observes the primitive way of the division of labour based on sex dichotomy. Since the Buxa woman comparatively wields a privileged status in practice and, therefore, confines herself to the easier household jobs such as rearing and caring the children, cooking food and managing all the household matters. She commands greater respect over the menfolk and assigns their duties. The males are supposed to obey the female and perform all the tedious tasks assigned to them. He is also liable to manage the essential provisions for the subsistence of the family by any means. However, the major agricultural jobs are performed simultaneously by the males and the females. The ploughing goes to male members of the family only. The children also lend their hands in every sort of economic pursuits side by side with the elder members of the family. Though the tendency for schooling is growing among the Buxa children. However, the main concentration always remains on the economic gains. The children as soon they attain the age of six years, are supposed to be an integral part of the Buxa economy. Hence, they are attached preferably to any jobs having direct or indirect concern with economic gain rather than schooling.

Most of the Buxas are the followers of Hindu religion. They

also claim to be of Hindu origin in their beliefs, practices and caste structure. They themselves belong to the different Hindu castes and sub-castes from Kshatriyas to Sudras. However, they still have deep faith in their original tribal religion i.e. animism and spiritism. At the same time, there are Buxas, in considerable number, who have faith in Islam and Sikhism. Some Buxas are followers of Muslim saints and worship Muslim 'Pirs' while some show their deep reverence for Guru Nanak Dev too. It seems that the Buxas are in the process of Hinduization while the impact of Sikhism and Islam is decreasing day by day. Amir Hasan has, therefore, aptly remarked that the Buxas are one of the most Hinduized tribes of India (1979 : 25). However, there are Buxas who used to consider Guru Nanak as a great religious leader and preacher and worship him. They are also known as Guruware. While the Buxas worshipping Devi known as Deviware. These were the two sects of Buxas. But, since the Sikh community has emerged in the Tarai as land grabbers and exploiters, the popularity of Guru Nanak among Buxas is decreasing day by day because they associate Guru Nanak with their exploiters and, therefore, they now prefer to be known as Deviware rather than Guruware. Besides this, the impact of Muslim thinkers and saints has also been observed among the Buxas.

It is said that the Buxas have been in contact of Muslims for more than four hundred years. The existence of Muswani *gotra* among the Buxas, particularly in Dehradun district proves this fact. According to a legend the 'Muswani' were originally 'Muwans' or 'Musalmans' who served Rajput Ranis (queens) and migrated to the Tarai plain with them and with the passage of time merged with the composite community sprung after the merger of various castes and creeds to which the 'ranis' and their humble guards belonged (1979 : 27). Even Crooke (1896 : Vol. II) has stated that two Muslim saints; Sarwar Lakhi and Kalu Sayyed are worshipped by the Buxas. Zahir Aulya Pir is quite popular among the Buxas of Baijpur who maintain that the 'Pir' was originally a Kshatriya, who later embraced Islam. He is also offered flowers and Matka (earthen pots) during worship (1979: 28). Hasan mentions about the impact of Christianity on the Buxas with the effect of the functioning of Catholic mission at Bajpur and Catholic farm at Bajpur and Dhamola.

But, today we hardly trace out any impact of Christianity on the Buxas. However, the impact of Sikh culture may be observed on the behaviour patterns of those Buxas who have dwelling near to that of the Sikhs. But they have no faith and trust on Guru Nanak's tenets as it concerns with the community of those who have been responsible for the land alienation and indebtedness among the Buxas. The Buxas, particularly living in Bajpur, Bijnor and Pauri area still have faith on Islamic beliefs and practices. But, today the Islamic faiths have been merged into their religious life and, thus, they seem to be their own.

Despite this, the majority of the Buxa population worship and revere most of the Hindu Gods like; Shiv-Parvati, Krishna, Ram, etc. They have a number of local deities to worship. The Kashipur Devi, the Atariya Devi, the Ilawas Devi, the Basundari Devi, the Sundari Devi, the Gamkheri Devi, etc., are some of them. Besides this, the Bhumsen, the Bhumia, the Sankariya, etc., are the Buxa deities worshipped by them in different occasions. Buxas also believe in spirits and goblins. Some of the spirits worshipped in Bajpur, Gadarpur, Ramnagar and Kashipur area are the Mani-Ram-Thokedar, the Kothan Padhan, the Dalpuriya and the Buxaro Padhan. Amir Hasan has rightly observed that the Buxa religious structure mainly consists of popular Hinduism, heavily coated with tribal religion and admixtured with Guru Nanak's worship and a light sprinkling of Muslim thought and ideas as spread by the Muslim Fakirs and Sufis (1979: 28).

Buxas also believe in magical practices. The 'Bharare' exercise some of the magical practices for the treatment of the illness by reciting 'Mantras'. Different kinds of diseases have different methods to eradicate with different requisites. But today, with the introduction of medical facilities, the functional importance magical practices in Buxar area are decreasing day by day. However, the sufferer disappointed by the modern medical treatment, as well as the sufferer deprived from medical facility ultimately takes the shelter of the magical expert. Only, a Bharare, honestly devoted to one's cause and profession has been able to maintain functional influence over the common mass while there are Bharare who have imperfect magical knowledge. This state of being has led to despair among the masses and caused distrust towards the magical practices. Today a common notion about the Bharare is prevalent that while a man has become liar and false, how can the magical practices remain effective. Infact the faith on magical practices seems to be shaken due to the imperfect knowledge of magic. The people (Buxas) have begun to state it as the 'Thaga Vidhya' which means science of swindling.

Buxas are also very fond of fairs and festivals. They lavishly spend and make extravagance on these occasions.

REFERENCES

Bisht, B.S., 1994, *Tribes of India, Nepal, Tibet Border Land,* New Delhi: Gyan Publishing House.

———, 1996, Uttarakhand Ki Janjatiyan; In *Uttarakhand Today* (ed) K.S. Vaidiya, Shree Almora Book Depot, The Mall, Almora, (U.P.).

Crooke W., 1896, *Tribes and Castes of the North-West Provinces and Oudh,* Delhi: Cosmo Publications.

Hasan, Amir, 1979, *The Buxas of Tarai,* Delhi: B.R. Publishing Corporations.

Singh, U.P. and Shukla, B.K., 1990, Buxa Janjati Mai Jeevan Sathi Ka Chayan; In: *Manar*; Year - 18, Volume -3, 1990, Ethnographic and Folk Culture Society, Lucknow.

Shukla R., 1974, Uttar Bharat Ki Buxa Janjati; Ph.D. Thesis, Kashi Vidhyapith, Varanasi, U.P.

Seventeen

Inter-Societal Tension; Feeling of Insecurity and Ingroup Identity among Muslims

MOHAMMAD GHUFRAN

Ingroup and outgroup formations are the most important aspects of social interaction. The group with which we identify ourselves is the 'ingroup' formation wherein the members of the family, caste, religion, nation, etc, are perceived as like forces and identified with readily. The persons forming other groups are outgroups and are looked upon with fear, suspicion or dislike and they are perceived as antagonistic to the progress and welfare of the ingroup. This perception causes hostility and is bolstered by ingroup solidarity and a greater awareness of ingroup identity on the part of the members of the ingroup. The greater awareness of ingroup identity which results in the 'tightness' of the ingroup boundaries has been labelled as ethnocentrism (Lindgren, 1979). James Drever (1968) in *A Dictionary of Psychology* has defined ethnocentrism as "exaggerated tendency to think the characteristics of ones' own group or rate superior to those of other groups or race." McDavid and Harari (1986) stated that certain individuals are particularly inclined to express tendencies to centre their attitude within their own social groups and exaggerated prejudice against alien groups. These groups are said to be ethnocentric or centred in their own ethos. Thus, ethnocentric induces in an individual a tendency to prefer his own group over other groups. That is why Mohsin (1976) operationally defined ethnocentric in terms of preponderance of good over bad qualities attributed to the ingroup.

Taylor and Jaggi (1974), in their study of ethnocentric and casual attribution found that subjects made internal attributes when ingroup members performed socially desirable acts and external attributes for undesirable acts. The converse was observed when the same behaviour was performed by the outgroups. Singh (1985) has described the development of religious and ethnic identities as the development of ethnocentrism in Indian context. On the basis of researches conducted by Mona Jabbi (1982), Lipi Chatterjee (1983) and Khalique (1985), Singh has concluded that ethnic identities emerge very early in childhood. They crystalize and become fully blown in early adolescence.

It has been observed that the affiliation with any group is strengthened only if one derives strength or power in any form as a result of his affiliation. This inferred power is termed as 'identity'. The evolution of identity is based upon the inherent need of human beings to feel that he or she belongs to a particular group.

When an individual finds himself belonging to a particular group, at that time the processes of social comparison occurs at the intergroup level and to a great extent belongingness with a group contributes to his sense of positive social identity and an individual will remain a member of that group. If the group fails to satisfy these requirements, the individuals may (I) try to change the structure of the group; (II) seek a new dimension of comparison to enhance a sense of positive social identity; and (III) leave the group and distance himself from it. However, individuals who are members of a group that suffer inferior social status develop weaker identity. Members of ethnic minorities usually find themselves in complex network of social relationship within which they try to define their social identity (Tajfel, 1984).

Feeling of insecurity has been regarded as the major factor contributing to the development of ethnocentrism. Two well known publications, *Nature of Conflict* (UNESCO, 1957) and *Nature of Prejudice* (Allport, 1955) give a penetrating analysis of the factors which ultimately lead to group violence and ethnocentricism. Among them, feeling of insecurity is one of the most important factors. According to Maslow, human desires are arranged in ascending hierarchy of needs. As soon as ones needs are satisfied, the next need in the hierarchy is activated. The needs are basically physiological, safety or security, belongingness and love, self-esteem and lastly self-actualization for personal fulfilment. The primary motivating force of security need is to ensure a reasonable degree of certainty, order, structure and predictablity in one's own environment. Barel conceptualizes security as an inherent striving for reducing environmental situations to cause and effect relationships, thus, enabling the individual to predict and have control over his environment.

Security is the opposite of insecurity. For Maslow (1954) insecurity refers to a feeling of rejection, of being unloved, isolated, a constant feeling of anxiety, tension and danger.

After independence certain sections of the majority community nourished feelings of resentment against Muslims for supporting the partition of the country. The Muslims felt insecure and helpless and the horrifying tales of uprooting the families, bloodshed, rapes, arsons and loot on both sides of the artificially created borders, in refugee camps and trains, in cities and countrysides resulting from communal riots, made them all the more unsafe and insecure, particularly in northern Indian cities and villages. Political activists and *goonda* elements took advantages of the deteriorating law and order situation. Members of the majority community in different areas, particularly in communally sensitive localities became more assertive and Muslims, finding themselves helpless, developed a fear psychosis. Muslim League leadership migrated to Pakistan and there was no leadership except the nationalist Muslims who they could trust or rely upon. But the seed of bitterness and enimity sown between Muslim masses and nationalist leaders by the Muslim League leadership added to their feelings of helplessness and insecurity. They started shrinking to the narrow shell and preferred isolation within protective ghetto-like areas of their own choice. The ingroup feeling that developed cut them from the mainstream of national life in the post-Partition days. In the name of religion and imaginary threats to the security of the nation, the extremist elements among the majority community organized themselves in various forms. With Jan Sangh (now Bhartiya Janta Party) as its political wing, R.S.S. established its *shakhas* at district and town levels and started their drillings in schools and other public places in defence of their religion. They also tried to propagate the view that Hindus represent the mainstream of national culture and they alone can preserve and safeguard the national interests and territorial integrity of the country. In order to achieve this goal, they firmly believed that all minorities should merge their identities and assimilate their culture through the process of Indianization into what they call Indian culture and which in their way of thinking, is essentially the Hindu culture. Accordingly, maintaining separate cultural identities on the part of various minority groups is dangerous to the very existence of the nation State. Persistence of such a demand by extremist organizations of the majority community generates a feeling of insecurity, fear and hostility among the members of minority communities, particularly, among Muslims, who constitute the largest national minority.

Muslims in India are economically and educationally backward. The reasons for their backwardness are many and varied. For example, Muslim community experiences economic hardship due to the rigid adherence to the family trades and business. Their sociocultural constraints are also responsible for their economic backwardness. But Muslims, in general, believe that their economic and educational backwardness is due to discrimination practised against them. Moreover, communal riots mostly occurred in places where Muslims have established their trade and business and have established educational institutions. Recurrence of communal riots in these places gives an impression that there is a planned conspiracy to keep the Muslims economically and educationally backward. On the other hand, extremists among the members of majority community regard concentration of Muslims in such areas a breeding ground for communal and sectarian tendencies fueling Islamic ingroup solidarity and revivalism of Islamic fundamentalism. These suspicions increase the already existing gulf between the two communities and further generate a feeling of insecurity among the Muslims.

The most important empirical works in the field of inter-group tension, especially on communal tensions has been done by a team of six researchers headed by Gardener Murphy (1953). Taking into account the historical background of Hindu-Muslim relations and using the interview schedules, they were able to delineate a number of factors which lead to communal strife. The feeling of insecurity prevailing among the Muslims was considered by them as one of the important causes of Hindu-Muslim tension. On the other hand Chatterjee et.al (1967), in their ex-post-facto research in Rourkela, did not find any permanent social insecurity or deep rooted communal mistrust among Muslims for non-Muslims. Mohsin (1976), in his study of attitude formation and change, observed a high correlation between the feeling of insecurity and ethnic prejudice. He also found a strong negative attitude of the two major ethnic groups towards each other which was consistent with the realistic group conflict theory developed by Campbell. It may be pointed out that Campbell (1966) had maintained that a real threat causes hostility towards the source of the threat. Thus, real threat increases prejudice and ethnocentricism. Conflicts among members of different castes and religious groups are an important force in the development of ethnocentricism. Dodd (1935) mentioned on the basis of his findings that a substantial amount of hostility shown by different groups towards each other was closely related with the amount of recent group conflict. Dudycha (1942), Seago (1947) and Buchanan (1951) also obtained the same results. The experimental studies carried out by Sherif et.al (1961) also showed that inter-group conflict and competition led to the development of hostile feelings and tensions between the groups. Not only the social distance between the groups increased but, in addition, the members of one group developed and applied highly negative stereotypes to the members of the other group.

From the above discussion the importance of studying the ingroup identity in Muslims in the context of their feeling of insecurity and communal conflict became self explanatory. The present investigation is planned to study the ethnocentricism in Muslim subjects in relation to feeling of insecurity and social tension.

Methodology

Sample

Social tension is one of the variables of this study, so the first step of sampling was to identify high and low social tension prevailing cities, where the study was to be conducted. The two cities from where the sample was drawn were Mau Nath Bhanjan - a city where several communal riots have taken place and regarded as a high tension prevailing city and Azamgarh - a city free from communal riots and regarded a low tension city. It should also be noted that the Muslim population of Mau Nath Bhanjan belongs to Momin Ansar caste of Muslim community which is constitutionally recognized as backward caste.

Initially, 130 male adult subjects belonging to backward Muslim community with ages ranging from 28 to 40 years were taken. Half of the sample, i.e. 65 subjects were selected from Mau Nath Bhanjan and remaining half were from Azamgarh. The short form of Maslow Security - Insecurity Inventory (Developed by Srivastava, 1976) was administered separately to identify subjects of high and low insecurity feeling groups. These groups were identified on the basis of a median. (The median was computed separately for each group of subjects). In the process of identifying subjects of high and low insecurity feelings some of the subjects falling at median point had to be dropped. In order to equate groups in terms of size, some cases had again to be dropped, so final sample comprised of 120 subjects divided in four groups in equal numbers.

Tools

(1) Short form of Maslow Security-Insecurity Inventory developed by Srivastava (1976) was used to identify subjects of high and low insecurity feelings.

(2) Mohsin's (1976) measure of ethnic attitude was used to study ethnocentricism. It is comprised of 50 traits descriptive adjectives, 50 per cent desirable and 50 per cent undesirable. A score of one is given for each adjective ticked by the subjects. Ethnocentric score is obtained by totalling the good qualities ticked by the subjects to the ingroup and subtracting from it the bad qualities assigned to the ingroup and adding to it 10, a constant.

Results

The present study consists of two variables, namely, social tension and insecurity feeling and each variables are varied in two ways. Thus, using a 2 x 2 factorial design, the scores obtained by four groups of subjects were analyzed with a view to study separate, as well as, interactional effects of social tension and insecurity feeling.

TABLE - 17.1
SHOWING MEAN ETHNOCENTRISM SCORES OBTAINED BY 4 GROUPS OF SUBJECTS

Groups	*High Social Tension*	*Low Social Tension*	*Mean*
High insecurity Feeling	25.38	20.56	22.97
Low insecurity Feeling	23.50	16.27	19.89
Mean	24.44	18.42	21.43

TABLE - 17.2
SUMMARY OF ANALYSIS OF VARIANCE BASED ON ETHNOCENTRISM SCORES

Source of Variation	*Sum of Squares*	*df*	*Mean*	*F*
Social Tension (A)	296.43	1	296.43	8.19*
Insecurity feeling (B)	338.65	1	338.65	9.35*
Social Tension × Insecurity feeling (A × B)	192.58	1	192.58	5.32*
Error	419.20	116	36.20	

*Significant at .01 level

Results of ANOVA presented in Table 17.1 reveals that F-ratio for the main effect of social tension is 8.19 which is significant at .01 level of confidence. The mean score of subjects residing in high social tension area is 24.44 and for those of low tension area is 18.42. This result indicates that subjects residing in high social tension are more ethnocentric than subjects belonging to low social tension area.

The F-ratio for the main effect of insecurity feeling is 9.35 which is significant at .01 level. As evident from the means of educated and uneducated (Table 17.2), subjects having high insecurity feeling are more ethnocentric as compared to subjects having less insecurity feeling.

The F-ratio for interaction between the social tension and insecurity feeling is 5.32 which is statistically significant at .01 level of confidence. This result shows that social tension and insecurity feeling interact in a significant way to give rise to ethnocentrism.

Discussion

The higher mean score of Muslim subjects, belonging to high social tension prevailing city on ethnocentrism, indicates that social tension generates ingroup feeling and sectarian tendencies. Muslims living in such areas, where communal riot occur frequently, are more prone to develop ingroup identity which is often termed as Islamic identity. People living in communally sensitive areas think more in terms of their own community and tend to ignore the good qualities of other communities. The people living in the areas where communal riots do not take place frequently are more tolerant and appreciative towards other communities. Moreover, people residing in high tension areas do not seem to interact positively with the members of other community. Thus, communal riots and conflicts compel the members of minority community to take shelter into their own narrow shell and become more sensitive on the question of their ingroup identity. Although, there is no specific study on the effects of social tension or ethnocentrism. Nonetheless, studies conducted by Dodd (1935), Dudycha (1942), Seago (1947) and Buchanan (1951) show that intergroup conflict and tension lead to the development of unfavourable attitudes towards the members of other groups.

The higher mean score is of subjects having high insecurity feeling than subjects who are low in the feeling of insecurity. This suggests that subjects having high insecurity feeling are more ethnocentric and are more conscious about their identity. Thus, a feeling of insecurity emerges out as the important factor in developing ingroup feeling and identity. The higher ethnocentrism score of Muslim subjects having high insecurity feeling indicates that insecure Muslims are more prone to develop sectarian tendencies. Such people started to think more about the welfare of their own community and become more conscious about the positive qualities, whether real or imaginary, of their own community and, in turn, might have started to shrink into their narrow shell and, hence, developed more ingroup identity and ethnocentrism. This result is in consonance with earlier findings of Allport (1955), Murphy(1953) and Mohsin(1976). These investigators have also observed that feeling of insecurity is one of the major contributing factors in developing of ethnocentrism and prejudice.

The significant interactional effect of social tension and insecurity feeling indicates that the two variables interact in a significant way to influence the ethnocentrism of the Muslim subjects. This finding leads us to suggest that high insecurity feeling among subjects of high social tension prevailing areas may further add to the increment of their ethnocentrism. One possible explanation of this finding may be that due to frequent occurrence of communal riots and economic hardship experienced by them due to rigid adherence of traditional values and also of family trades and business, the already insecure Muslim subjects might have started to think more about the positive qualities and welfare of their own community. Thus, they become more conscious about their ingroup identity.

It may be noted here that communal riots and conflicts are a manifestation of frustration, expression of anger, weakness and overcoming of failures. They are a mean to achieve goals through foul means. Moreover, communal riots and its continuity for a longer period of time bring the victims at the point of revolt and agression or alienation, insecurity and withdrawls because of their sufferings. The minorities, poor and weaker have been the worst sufferers of the communal carnage. The need of the hour is to stop these monstrous and barbaric practices in society. For this the basic principles of discouraging the exploitation of emotion, stopping the division of the society, giving fair treatment to all, recognizing the individual worth, improving social communication, cultivating scientific attitude and bringing the minorities and downtrodden to the mainstream will be a step in the direction of achieving the goal. Moreover, politics of opportunism, appeasement, communalism and discrimination have to be tackled with honesty and justice.

REFERENCES

Allport, G.W., 1955, The Nature of Prejudice: Harvard University 'Boston', Massachusetts.

Buchanan, W., 1961, Stereotypes and tensions as revealed by the UNESCO international Poll. International Social Bulletin, 3, 515-528.

Campbell, A.A., 1947, Factors Associated with Attitudes Towards Jews. In T.M. New Comb and E.L. Hartley (eds.) *Reading in Social Psychology*, pp. 518-627, New York: Holt.

Chatterjee, B.B., Singh, P.N. and Rao, G.R.S., 1967, *Riots in Rourkela: A Psychological Study*, New Delhi: Popular Book Services.

Chatterjee, L., 1983, Development of Religious Identity and Prejudice in Hindu Children, Ph.D. Thesis Ranchi University.

Dodd, S.C., 1935, A Social Distance Test in the Near East American *Journal of Psychology*, 41, 194-204.

Dudycha, G.K., 1942, The attitudes of college students towards war and the Germans before and during the Second World War. *Journal of Social Psychology*, 15: 317-324.

Jabbi, M., 1982, Development of Religious Identity and Prejudice in Sikh Children. *Social Change*, 12, (4): 20-27.

James, Drever, 1968, *A Dictionary of Psychology*. The English Language Book Society and Penguin Books.

Khalique, A., 1985, Development of Religious Identity and Prejudice in Muslim Children. Proceedings of the 72nd session of Indian Science Congress.

Lindgren, H.C., 1993, *An Introduction to Social Psychology*. Wiley Eastern Limited.

Maslow, A.H., 1943, A Theory of Human Motivation. *Psychological Review*, 50, 570-396.

McDavid, J.W. and Harari, H., 1986, *Psychology and Social Behaviour*, New York: Harper.

Mohsin, S.M., 1976, Reinterpretations of dynamics of Attitude Formation and Change. *Indian Journal of Psychology*, 51 (1), 1-60.

Murphy, G., 1953, *In the Minds of Men. The Study of Human Behaviour and Social Tensions in India*. Basic Books Inc. Publishers.

Seago, D.W., 1947, Stereotypes : Before Pearl Harbour and After. *Journal of Psychology*, 83: 55-63.

Sherif, M., 1961, *Intergroup Conflict and Cooperation: The Robbers Cave Experiment*. Norman Okla, University of Oklahama. Institute of Group Relations.

Singh, A.K., 1985, Development of secularism and national integration in India. Presidential address. 72nd Session of Indian Science Congress.

Tajfel, H., 1982, *Social Identity and Intergroup Relations*. P. Maison desk Society de L' Homme Cambridge Paris and Cambridge University Press.

Taylor, D.M. and Jaggi, V., 1974, Ethnocentrism and Casual Attribution in South Indian context. *Journal of Cross-Cultural Psychology*, 5(2): 162-170.

Eighteen

Social Transformation and the Tribes of Orissa

P.K. KAR

India, after Africa, has the second largest concentration of tribal people in the world. Orissa is one of the most fascinating ethnographic States of India which has been the house of as many as 62 different tribal stocks. According to 1971 census, the tribal population was nearly 38.02 lakh which rose to 59.15 lakh in 1981 and further increased to 70.32 lakh in 1991. One among every 4.5 persons in Orissa is tribal. Though a small State, Orissa has comparatively more tribal population than many other States and union territories in India and accounts for 23.11% of the tribal population. The tribes caste a dragging trend on the State's economy because of their low level of per capita income in a State where the per capita income is probably the lowest among the major states of India.

Tribes, in general, prefer to inhabit the forests and foothills and depend largely on the jungle. Traditionally, tribal economy as well as society is so closely associated with forests that the tribals can not visualize a life without forests which not only provide food, fodder and fruits to them but also satisfy their deeprooted sentiments and sociocultural needs (Jha and Sen, 1991) The Economic Survey of Orissa reveals that forests cover nearly 79 per cent of the area of inland region which roughly comprises nine undivided districts namely, Koraput, Mayurbhanj, Sundargarh, Sambalpur, Keonjhar, Kalahandi, Phulbani, Bolangir and Dhenkanal. The mountainous and forest inland region of Orissa has been ideally suited to the tribal inhabitations for centuries. According to 1991 census, the inland region of Orissa covers 74 per cent area and nearly 89 per cent of tribal population of the State.

Distribution

It is quite natural that Orissa's tribal people are very uneven in their distribution and they tend to be concentrated in the areas where they find congenial environment for their livelihood. Since they prefer to inhabit the rural and jungle, areas and on the fringe and largely depend on jungle, they are distributed in almost all the districts including those in the coastal belt. The analysis of census data shows that the tribes such as Juang, Godaba, Poroja, Banda, Koya, etc, live in compact area, while the Saora, Kondh, Gond and Bhuinya have a wide distribution in different districts. Most of them practise shifting cultivation on the hillslopes and hence few of them take to sedentary peasant cultivation in the narrow valleys of the eastern Ghats. Thus there is no wonder that the undivided district of Koraput with 1.63 million tribal people has got the largest tribal population in the State of Orissa. It is followed by Mayurbhanj and Sundargarh with 1.09 million and 0.79 million tribal population respectively. The coastal district of Puri accounts for the lowest percentage of tribal population. It is preceded by Cuttack and Balasore. Seven undivided districts of Orissa, out of thirteen, have higher concentration of tribal population. In comparison with the State's average, all these seven undivided districts, forming the tribal belt of Orissa, have higher percentage of tribal population. The core of tribal population in Orissa is formed in three patches : Koraput in the South-west, Mayurbhanj in the North-west and Sundargarh in the North of Orissa. Koraput, the second largest district in India with a tribal population of more than 50 per cent has been one of the most backward districts of India. Till today road communication is hazardous and strained. Many areas are still cut-off from the reach of Modern civilization.

Apart from Koraput, in other core areas also the population exceeds 50 per cent of the total at the district level. The core tribal area has its connection with 'high density' tribal areas. Such as Sundargarh in the north and Mayurbhanj and Keonjhar in the north-east. Boudh-Khandamal and Kalahandi districts constitute the northern and north-eastern ring of Koraput core-tribal region where the tribal population exceeds 29 per cent of the total population. It is noteworthy that in the State of Orissa more than

50 per cent of the total tribal population is found in three districts namely Koraput, Sundargarh and Mayurbhanj. Of the total Scheduled Tribe population, males constitute 49.70 per cent and females 50.30 per cent (1981 census). According to the 1991 census, the inland region of Orissa covers 74 per cent area and nearly 89 per cent of tribal population of the State.

Tribewise Distribution

The Kondh or the Kui as they call themselves, top the list in numerical preponderance numbering over one million. They inhabit most of Phulbani district and continue eastward into Ganjam. Westward, they spread into Kalahandi and Balangir Districts also north-eastward into Dhenkanal. Southwards, 400,000 Kuvi speaking Kondhs occupy the northern half of Koraput district. Considering the levels of economic development the Kondh are divided into several sub-sections such as Kutia Kondh, Dongaria Kondh, Jharia Kondh and Desias Kondh, etc. Apart from the districts already mentioned, the Kondhs are found more or less everywhere. However, they are mostly found in the hilly tracts of the Eastern Ghats to the South-west of Mahanadi valley.

Their hill-tracts are bounded on the east by the precipitous slopes where the Eastern Ghats drop to the coastal plains. The floor of their high plateau varies from 2,000 ft. in the north to 3,000 feet in the South, dropping to approximately 1,500 ft in the narrower river valleys of the South-west and west. High peaks are plentiful, rising in the south above 4,500 ft. and in the Niyamgiri range in Koraput almost to 5,000 ft. The plateau region streches from west Ganjam through most of Phulbani and Koraput into eastern Kalahandi. Its rocks are all of igneous and metamorphic type. They are the oldest in the Indian subcontinent being Archaean gneisses and schists together with intrusive bands of charnockite and Khondalite gneissose granite. Cappings of high-level horizontal laterite upto 200 ft. thick are common at about 4,000 ft. In Tumudibandh area of Phulbani district, graphite is found.

The Kondh as a whole were widely known for their earlier practice of human sacrifice and female infanticide. Mr Rusell's reports show how the British Government stopped the practise not by force but by moral influence and conciliatory measures.

Other steps taken by the British officers for reclaiming the Kondh from the savage practices were the establishment of friendship with them through direct contact and by strictly interdicting the army and camp followers from entering their villages and meddling in any way with them or with their domesticated animals such as fowls, goats, etc. Fairs and market centres which were discontinued for some reason or the other were revived and articles such as salt, salt-fish, brass utensils, red blankets and all but the coarsest kind of cotton clothes which the Kondh were excessively fond of were made available on sale to them at these places at most reasonable rates.

Family is mostly of nuclear type among the Kondhs, consisting of parents and their unmarried children. The total extended families having the married son or sons and their children living with the father and mother are comparatively less and still less are the number of joint families run by married brothers and their spouses after the death of parents. Such heterogeneous families comprising of the spouses of adopted son-in-law, widow sister and the like are grouped in separate category. The Kondhs are a patrilocal and patrilineal tribe. There are a few families having their son-in-law living with them as Ghar-Jamai but such families are an exception. Membership in the family is acquired by birth, though girls leave their parental families for good after marriage. Descent is carried through the male spouses. Even in case of adoption of son-in-law the male spouses retain descent through their father only. The size of Kondh families is usually small consisting of 4 to 6 persons. Economic cooperation, common residence, common cooking are other general features of Kondh family. All the members of a family cooperate in economic pursuits and contribute for the maintenance of the family. Common cooking is the main feature of family solidarity and separate cooking leads to breakdown of joint families. Quarrel between family members, economic disparity of earning members and excessive growth of family size to accommodate all in a common residence lead to the formation of new families. It is usual for the sons of a father or the brothers, to establish their independent households soon after their marriage so that there may not be scope for growing misunderstanding between the newcomers leading to quarrels and conflicts. The kin tie between blood relatives like father and son and between the brothers is conceptually strong, but cases of full brothers living in separate families and in separate villages and father and sons living in separate families are quite numerous. A lineage among the Kondhs is composed of a number of families, and the members of a lineage consider themselves to be the descendents of a common ancestor. In case of minor lineages the relation of its members can be traced out genealogically, but in some major lineages such common ancestory is difficult to be traced out. The members of minor lineage consider themselves to be closer kin to each other and there is more kin obligation among themselves than with the members of major lineages. The following rites are marked between the families belonging to a single minor lineage :

(a) All the families of a minor lineage throw away their used earthen cooking pots and earthen vessels in cases of death of any lineage member.

(b) All mourn for any death within the lineage and observe food taboos like eating vegetarian diet, till the funerary rites are performed.

(c) The families of a minor lineage contribute liquor for purificatory rites in cases of death.

(d) A widow may be remarried to her deceased husband's younger brother who has a claim over her, but in case the deceased ceases to have any younger brother, the widow may preferably be remarried, to a member of her deceased husband's lineage who stands her as husband's younger brother in classificatory sense. For such marriage, no bride-price need be paid to the widow's parents, as once she is brought by marriage she becomes the property of the lineage at large.

(e) Greater economic cooperation is expected from the members of a lineage who tend to help each other in various economic pursuits.

(f) In connection with birth ceremony, the lineage-members bring contributions of money, chicken, grains, etc, for the newborn which may be used as a saving for the future life for the child.

(g) In marriage, the lineage members exhibit greater co-operation to make the occasion a success and are fed more frequently than the villagers.

(h) In case of girl's marriage, one cattle from the bride-wealth paid by the groom goes to the lineage. The cattle is sold and the money is utilized for holding a communal feast.

(i) Shares of food and cakes are distributed among the families of a lineage on festive or ceremonial occasions.

When some members of major lineages are taken together they form barrage. The members of which consider themselves to be agnates to each other descending from a common ancestor. One such clan is the Maghi, Dalpat and Pradhan. They consider themselves as brothers of the same clan and distinguish themselves from other Kandhas of this area. The Bhuanpara Kandhas belong to this clan. The clan cult is Pat Khandha as acquired from Kandhamal. The clan group is then identified with the name of the area where its members inhabit having a clan of their own. The second clan is Masu Kandha or Mausia Kandha who inhabit the Masia Chaka or area with their clan cult Sulia. The third one is known as Kudurkia and/or Turkia Chak with their cult Bhim Boiri and Paha Sulia. The fourth one is Sika Kandhas of Sika Chak with their cult Barubhai Nad. The fifth one is Kadanungia Chak or Khadangu Chak inhabited by Kadanungia Kandhas with their cult Sikerpat or Sikelpat. All these clans are exogamous and should not bring brides from kin clans. There is however, an exception as regards Mulingia Kandhas. These Kandhas, although inhabit the Khadanga Chak do not come under the clan of Kadanungia Kandhas. They call themselves brother of Majhi clan. A reference may be made here of the migration of Majhi clan from Kandhal. The other social divisions of Kandhas like Bachha Timkia and Binjhalka have come into origin with the Majhi Kondhs on their arrival in this area with communities of their own as well as untouchable castes. When a Kondhs takes a wife from other communities he is allowed to form another section of Kondhs instead of being excommunicated. The original Kondhs established marriage relationship with such a new section as mentioned above.

There is another section called Ganka Kondha who inhabit Belgaon and Titlagarh areas. All the sections mentioned above can bring brides from that section. The Kondhs of this area say that the Ganka Kondhs have no brother clan in this area. The Kondhs have been so much diversified socially that on the eve of marriage negotiations the elders take immense trouble to trace out the clan ancestry so as to decide whether negotiation and ties could be possible. Kandhas of this area trace their descent through their father line. The organization of family is same as other local castes with the father becoming the head of family till he becomes very old when the eldest brother assumes the position of head of the family with regard to family affairs. But soon after marriage, sons build separate houses to live separately. Thus the nuclear type of family still continues although brothers unite to cultivate the family agricultural land and share the produce equally.

Marriage

The Orissa Kondhs have also responded to change with regard to various social institutions. The institution of marriage has undergone the process of transformation with its underlying system of belief. Important among this is the change in the traditional system of payment of bride-price to the bride's father. Today the bride's father is no more in advantageous position to enjoy the bride-price. He has to present his daughter and son-in-law equal amount of gift to tally with the bride-price. If the bride's father only receives and never spends in presents to couple, he is socially decried. This is on a par with the local Hindu custom of presenting dowry to son-in-law and daughter. Introduction of this new trait of status consciousness following Hindu social custom has resulted in another problem. Many young Kondh boys are unable to marry as a result of the strict principles that are being followed with regard to payment of bride-price. The father of a bride does not show any inclination to relax the payment of bride-price which amounts to as much as seven heads of cattle, new clothes for the parents and maternal uncle of the bride, one goat or sheep for feast, 2 pots of liquor and one *puti* of rice. Besides, the groom has to spend to entertain bride's party on the day of marriage. Kondhs say that the father of the bride could relax the payment of bride-price, in consideration of the paying capacity of the groom. But during these days they are insisting upon the full payment as a result of which many young men cannot marry which again reflects on the marriageable girls who cannot marry in absence of wealthy grooms. The rituals in the ceremony of marriage have also changed in accordance with the pattern of Hindu customs like playing of "arecanuts" by the couple, sending of Jalingia (in the pattern of Bardhara), to bring the bride to the groom's village on the day of marriage. The ceremony of Nirbandha or ceremonial fixing up of marriage has been introduced which was not there previously.

The forms of marriage have however, not changed much. The most common form of marriage is known as Biha which has been described above and is done after negotiations between the grooms father and bride's father. The next form is the system of capturing the bride by force. If the girl, however, gives her consent her parents are paid bride-price which is less than the amount paid in marriages by negotiation. In another form of marriage the girl forceably comes to the house of the groom and her parents in this case depend upon the mercy of the groom as to the payment of bride-price. The groom may give whatever he likes, which is nominal.

Although the religious institution of the Kondhs during these days essentially remain primitive the influence of Hinduism is found to be conspicuous. It may be perceived that some of the tribal cults are in the process of achieving the status of Hindu Gods whereas some others are still in the transitional phase. There are certain others who are still worshipped in the primitive manner. By observing Laxmipuja, Ditia Osa and Raksha-bandhan Kondhs have taken a further step towards Hinduism so far as their religion is concerned. Yet most of the deities are associated either with agricultural activities or with diseases, especially those that break out in epidemic form. So they are required to be appeased annually and occasionally. The spirits responsible for diseases are generally worshipped during that period while the agricultural deities receive their share of offerings at the beginning or end of those particular operations over which they preside. The religious performances are mostly communal in nature. All Kondh households of the village jointly worship the deities and all contribute their share. The collection of subscription and the management of the whole affair together with the actual preference of the ritual rest with the Jhankar (village-priest). In spite of this, the villagers cannot remain at home or follow their daily pursuits undisturbed as they are required to participate in the performances as observers. It is interesting to note that excepting the Jhankar or Dehuri no other Kondh household sacrifices animals themselves. The religion of Kondhs is mainly based on the belief in the cult of two Gods, namely Patkhanda and Sikerpat or Sikelpat. Kondhs who worship 'Sikerpat' live in a hilly and forested area whereas the 'Patkhanda' worshippers live in comparatively plain, and open areas. Thus the Kandhas worshipping the 'Sikerpat' cult are more tradition directed with regard to their religious practices.

The 'Patkhanda' is worshipped in the month of 'Dushehra'. It begins with the 9th day of Aswina during dark fortnight and continues for 16 days till the 'Dushehra' day (10th day of bright fortnight). Prior to this festival, the 'Jhankar' collects subscription of Re. 1 and 1/2 seer of rice from all the households to purchase puja articles and sacrificial animals (at least 8 to 10 numbers of he-goats). On the first day of the festival, the Dehuri visits each household in the night to get Bandana (ceremonial welcome). The owner of the house washes his feet and welcomes him by circumbulating a lamp in a winnowing fan and throwing some *arua* (raw) rice. He observes fasting throughout the day. On the second day at dawn the Dehuri takes bath and proceeds to Patkhanda Shrine accompanied by the Jhankar and the drum-beaters. Sometimes, females also join the procession to blow conch shells. The deity is brought to the village in a procession by Dehuri, Jhankar and Pujari. Dehuri gets possessed and practically rolls on the ground. He is carried to the shrine where he forecastes about the health and wealth of the people. Those afflicted by illness, approach him one after another and the Dehuri prescribes medicine. Hindu castes also approach the Dehuri with sacrificial animals seeking fire. The state of trance and return to normal continues alternately till evening. In the evening he becomes senseless. Then the Jhankar starts the rituals and the Pujari kills the animals one after the other. Gradually the Dehuri comes to senses and joins the worship of Patkhanda. The sacrificed animals are then cooked with rice and eaten by all male members. The heads of the sacrificed animals are shared by Dehuri, Jhankar and Pujari. The drum-beaters get only remuneration in cash.

The ceremony continues till the day when the Patkhanda is taken back to the original seat in the jungle from where it is brought to the village for worship. Patkhanda is worshipped and propitiated in order to bring good harvest and ensure general well-being. However, it is believed that sterile women by propitiating this God can bear children. The priest who is possessed by the God foretells about the child bearing capacity. The couple are asked to lie before the altar and the priest puts his feet on their belly as well as back. The ceremonial bringing of the God from jungle to Desh for the ceremony may be said to indicate the onward movement of a tribal cult to the plains inhabited by caste Hindus. The original seat of the God in the jungle symbolizes the primaeval abode of tribals and its carriage to Desh symbolizes its acceptance by Hindus living in plains. Although the Sikerpat is the clan deity of the Khadange Chak Kondhs it is at present worshipped by the local Hindus. The original seat of God which is believed to be on the top of the hill of Sikerpat at an altitude of 2,000 ft. is no more visited by Konds. The Kondhs relate a legend regarding the deity's desire to be worshipped in a site near village. The ceremony is observed twice in a year. Once on the 2nd day of Ashar and the other on the 5th or 10th day in the month of *Pus*. There are certain restrictions observed by the participants as well as onlookers. Nobody should wear a shoe or shirt while going to see or take part in the ceremony. No female is allowed to witness the ceremony. Even the wife of the priest is not allowed to come near the sacred spot on the eve of the ceremony. No *dhoti* should be worn in the manner of clean caste Hindus. Dhoti worn should rest on or above knees. No cycle or any vehicle is allowed to be ridden by the visitors. Nobody who has drunk liquor is allowed to enter the area. No umbrella is allowed to be carried to the sacred site. These are certain taboos which are observed by all going to observe the ceremony or to offer worship. The priest who is a Kondha is never allowed to cross river Tel. He may go in any other direction except crossing the river Tel. The Gonds constitute the second popular tribal stock in Orissa. They are mostly concentrated in the district of Kalahandi, Sambalpur and Sundargarh. They are sparsely found in the district of Balasore, Koraput, Keonjhar, Mayurbhanj, Dhenkanal, Phulbani and Bolangir. The Gond is the most predominant tribal community of India inhabiting the mountainous tracts of central and southern India popularly known as Gondwana land. The country of Gondwana includes the Satpura plateau and a section of the Nagpur plain and Narmada Valley to the south and the west. Professor Haimendorf considered the Koyas as Telugu speaking Gonds. As the Gonds speak a common language, they have common name and habitation and a contiguous territory, their cultural diversity did not come in the way of considering them as belonging to a common tribe.

In Orissa State, the Gonds inhabiting the Raigarh Block adjoining Bastar and Raipur districts have still retained their language though under considerable influence by Hindi and Halbani, they call themselves Gond while another section of Gonds living in the plains call themselves Gonds and consider themselves superior to other Gonds. The Gonds inhabiting the Kalahandi and Bolangir districts have completely lost their language and speak Oriya and call themselves Oriya Gonds.

The generic term 'Gond' encompasses several endogamous and linguistically distinct groups. The Gonds are neither racially, nor culturally nor linguistically a homogenous group. The cultural material and physical differences are so great that one wonders why they should not be grouped under the same tribe. The Gonds are segmented either on territorial or hierarchical grounds. Thus the Gonds of Bastar (M.P) are the Muriz Gonds and Mariz Gonds, while the Chhatisgarh Gonds are segmented as Amat Gonds, Ghur Gonds, Oriya Gonds, etc.

In the Rayagada area of Orissa, the Gonds cultivate millet for food and maize as cash crop. The soils of Bastar and Orissa are not suitable for cotton cultivation. Maize is introduced recently and is becoming popular in Dandakaranya region. Maize alongwith red gram or field beans form the staple food, while in Orissa, Ragee, Kodi or Italian millet form the staple diet. Rice is grown as a rain-fed dry crop in Orissa.

The Gonds descent system is based on structural principles

of unity and indivisibility and that makes it categorically distinct from the Indian caste system. However, structurally Gond Kinship system is a part of wide Hindu system. The Gonds see themselves as totally separate. Prof Haimendorf observed that Gond society is conceptually a total system and no segment of it can contract out of basic framework of Phratries and clans. On the contrary, Hindu caste system have an inbuilt tendency to split up into endogamous sub-sets of varying social status. However, the Phratry system among the Gonds is not so strong in Orissa. The Gonds all over India are polytheistic. All deities are thought of in anthromorphic terms. The Orissa Gonds worship a supreme being called Badiyel pen. The belief in witchcraft and magic is strong among Gonds. In the recent past the Gonds used to sacrifice cows. It was also recorded that the Gonds had the custom of offering human sacrifice. Mr Hislop is of the view that human sacrifices were offered until well into 19th century. This practice is not in vogue now and has been given up completely. However, it was reported by the officials that in the Jalanpura village of Raigarh block a case of human sacrifice was traced around 1978. The Gond festivals are associated with the first eating and sowing of the new crops. In the month of Chait (March) Chaitra festival is celebrated. A pig or fowl is offered to the village Gods and the new beans and Jowar or other foods are offered uncooked. After dancing and singing for the whole night they start eating the new foods. Before sowing new millet a sacrifice for the mother goddess and a sacrifice for the village deities are performed to ensure the successful germination of the seeds. Some grains, fowls, and a pig are sacrificed to the deity and blood of the sacrificed animal is sprinkled over the seeds offered to the god then distributed to all the villagers who sow it in their fields for luck.

The Santhals, one of the largest tribes of India are spread over a wide area in Bihar, Orissa, West Bengal, Tripura, Assam and also in Bangladesh. A majority of them live in Bihar and West Bengal. In Orissa, the Santhals constitute the third largest tribal group and are found in the hilly tracts to the south of Chhotanagpur plateau which forms the catchment area of Budhabalanga river. 85 per cent of the tribal population in Mayurbhanj district comprises of Santhals. They are also found in the Keonjhar plateau and

Nilgiri Hills of Balasore district. Nearly 10 per cent of the total Scheduled Tribe population of India belongs to Santhal community. In Orissa the Santhals constitute little over 2 per cent of the total population.

The Santhals are very conscious of their identity and heritage. They have been able to build up a sense of solidarity amongst themselves. Their internal solidarity is often based on a shared cultural characteristic which binds them together. At the same time, their existence has been threatened by certain external forces. The moneylenders, contractors, political infiltrators and such other exploiters, otherwise known as 'Dikus' constitute the external force posing threats to the Santhals. The myth regarding the origin of the Santhals is accepted and shared by the Mundas. Hos and other neighbouring tribes also help in the formation of regional solidarity. There is a close linguistic relation among the Santhals, Hos, Mundas and Bhumijs which contributes to this solidarity. Seasonal migration plays a dominant role in the socio-economic life of Santhals. Landless Santhal labourers from Mayurbhanj area of Orissa come to Hooghly, Howrah, Burdwan and Murshidabad districts of the neighbouring West Bengal to work in the agriculture and brick fields. The Santhal immigrants are generally looked upon as sturdy/and dependable workers and find ready employment among the non-tribals of the district. The seasonal migration of the Santhals appears to be functional in a couple of ways. First, it curbs the boundaries of separation between the Santhals and rural peasantry, because they work in close economic relationship to a considerable extent. Secondly, migration also helps to refresh and reinvigorate their distinctive cultural tracts and retain their identity in spite of small numbers in the districts, as the Santhal labourers can come in close contact with those of the Santhals of Santhal Parganas.

The Santhals call themselves 'Hor Hopon' or 'Sons of Man'. Although they possess distinctive social and religious characteristics, they may be classified into two major territorial groups: the Santhals inhabiting in the north of the Damodar river and the Santhals of Southern fringe of Bihar, northern fringe of Orissa and south-western fringe of West Bengal lying south of the river Damodar. The Orissan Santhals are called by the Northerners as 'Bugri Hor' meaning people who don't use chaste form of language.

In spite of being a dominant tribal population in the Eastern India, the Santhals have a lower achievement, in the field of education, in comparison with Mongoloid and other small tribal groups. In case of female literacy only Orissa could not put a mark above the line of progress.

The Santhals were formerly engaged in collection of forest produce, hunting, fishing and cultivation on hill slopes. At present they are not only engaged in cultivation, but mainly in the capacity of share croppers, agricultural labourers and small farmers. The Santhals make beautiful houses and decorate their walls with different colours, figures of human beings, flowers, animals or birds. The typical way of dressing of the Santhals distinguishes them from the local non-tribals. The men wear rough *dhoti* or 'Gamcha' and women wear green, blue check print sarees made by local weavers. Nowadays mill made clothes are also used. The use of petticoats and blouses has become a common fashion for young women.

In earlier days Indian corn was their staple food but gradually they came to depend more on rice, though they cultivate other cereals also. Vegetables, dryfish or pulses are taken as the side dishes. The Santhals depend upon rivers, streams, wells, etc, for getting their drinking water. In summer when the wells dry up the Santhal women collect water from the holes dug on the sand bed of the river. Handia or the rice beer continues to be the traditional drink of the Santhals. That apart, they also take toddy and *mahua-*liquor. The Santhals offer Handia to the ancestral spirits on ceremonial occasions. It is also consumed when friends and relatives gather at festivals to start ceremonies of birth, betrothal, marriage and funerals.

The Santhals are prone to various types of diseases like malaria, influenza, scabies, itches, etc. Incidents of leprosy, T.B. and yaws appears to be negligible. It is believed that stomach trouble and scabies are common due to scarcity of safe drinking water especially, during hot days.

The Santhal tradition relates that the first human couple Pilchu Haram and Pilchu Buri divided them into twelve ancestral clans one of which has been lost. These clans are totemic in nature and exogamic in character. Clans are subdivided into sub-clans, such as: Hasdak, Murmu, Kishu, Hembram, Soren, Nandi, Tudru, Baske, Besra, Paurih, Ceral and Bedes. The first eleven ancestral clans exist today but the last clan has been lost. The Santhals consider the violation of tribal endogamy and clan exogamy as the greatest offences. The violation of such rules attract expulsion from Santhal society. The Santhals are a partriarchal people and follow patrilineal descent. The strong community fellowship feeling of the Santhal is demonstrated in the few important and crucial stages in the life of the individual. They perform certain rites in which the whole village population participates. Such ceremonies include ceremonial cleaning after birth, ceremony performed for giving full social rights, marriage ceremony, death and funeral ceremony. Adult marriage or 'Bapla' is the norm among the Santhals. The essential features of marriage are *Sundur dan* and serving marriage feast. Thereafter the wife joins her husband's family.

The Saora with nearly four lakhs population constitute the fourth largest tribal stock of Orissa. They are mostly confined to the South Western Orissa, consisting of undivided Ganjam and Koraput districts. That apart, they are also found in small number in other parts of the State. They are mostly found in the high altitude of the eastern Ghats of Ganjam and Koraput districts. Agriculturally they lag far behind the Kondh. They are dependant upon hill cultivation for their livelihood. The Saoras do not classify themselves into a totemic clan. The extended unit consisting of a number of families called 'Berundar' is important like a lineage for the Saoras. Similarly, a Saora woman belongs to the 'berundar' of her family of orientation, throughout her life and marriage does not alter the lineage. A village consists of the combination of a number of lineages which are united in terms of sociocultural life. The next higher unit is occupational and territorial in nature and the tribe is divided into 17 such endogamous groups. These endogamous groups may be compared with the sub-tribes of the Savaras. They are shifting cultivators. Lamba Lanjias, Jodhs, brass worker, Manes Raikas, Bamboo-basket makers, Kindals, Arsis, Palm-cutter, Jauris, Archer Kanchers, Kurma Savars, Sudha Savarns, Telugu-speaking Kampoes, potter Kumbits, metal worker

Gonturas, Blacksmith Luhars, Sardas and Jaras. The Saora Society is also stratified mainly into two strata and form the Saora society, such as, Saora aristocrat and the Buyya. The Saora aristocrats comprise of the Gamangs as secular head who is assisted by Dol-Behera and Mondal. The Buyya is the religious head. Those who are not covered within these two groups are called Ryats (Elwin,1995: 50). Thus they make spheres like tribe-sub-tribe-Moiety-local group-village group-lineage-family-individual, village studies. (Panda, 1965) reveal that the Saora's are in the process of transformation due to their contact with Hindu Society, administrative machinery and Christianity. However, these three forces are not mutually exclusive in bringing about changes in the Saora culture. Some Saoras have started migrating to the nearby Hindu villages to work in the farm as agricultural labourers. In the process the migrant Saoras participate in the village factions as individuals rather than as members of a specific community. All their secular relationships are not confined to the village alone, but cut across village boundaries and spread to nearby villages. The migrant Saoras, in matters relating to their tribal custom and religion refer to Gamang and Buya or their parent villages.

The Munda with nearly 3.5 lakh population are the fifth highest tribe in Orissa. They are an autochthonous community living mainly in Chotanagpur plateau and in other adjoining places. Once they lived in the Sylvan jungles, having agriculture as their main economy, supplemented, at times, by hunting and other pursuits. Earlier accounts of Dalton (1872), Risley (1891) and later works of Roy (1912) throw some light on their manners and customs and these accounts may be considered as the baseline of their cultural patterns. They also noticed at that time, some sort of cross-groups, having commensal and connubial relations with other neighbouring communities. This has resulted in the birth of hybrid stocks like Munda-Kharia, Munda-Lohar, Munda-Mahali Munda-Manjhi, Munda-Urao, etc. It indicates that the community under compelling circumstances must have assimilated and absorbed the local cultural traits. These persisting forces are at play even at present which are easily observable and have contributed largely towards their gradual Hinduization. In Orissa the Mundas are confined to the North and North Eastern hills which form the southern boundary of the Chotnagpur plateau. The Mundas are almost fully confined, like the Santhals to the districts of Mayurbhanj and Keonjhar. They are found in small number in the district of Sundargarh. Although both the tribes, Santhals as well as the Mundas, inhabit almost the same region, the former dominate in the north-east and Mundas in the north.

The Munda speak a distinctive dialect of their own. which indirectly helped keeping intact their tribal traits, so far. Agriculture is the main economy of the Mundas and the people of these two villages are found to be mostly engaged in agricultural operations, sometimes in their own fields and sometimes in the fields of others. Due to their employment as seasonal or wholesome domestic servants, mainly performing agricultural works and other domestic chores, many a time, the Mundas frequently come in contact with the neighbouring Hindu. A good number of Mundas are found landless. Such Mundas are found to cultivate agricultural fields, the owners of which are generally people of caste Hindu groups. As a result, the Mundas depend on the cooperation of their Hindu neighbours. Sometimes, a few money-lending communities of the village or of the locality, advance loans of cash money or paddy to them, for which the debtors have to pay interest and the whole of the amount is to be repaid after the harvest. The Mundas ceremonially organize a hunting excursion on the Chaitra Sankranti day. Prior to this expedition, the village priest (Dehuri) worships Baram or the tutelary deity, when the hunting implements are dumped together and placed on the floor of the shrine. Games killed during the hunting excursion are brought to the village 'Akhra' and distributed amongst the participants. During the month of Vaisak (April-May) two such hunting expeditions are generally organized. The Mundas also observe a few festivals connected with agriculture. "Ashari-Festival" is held before the first transplantation commences. The Mundas believe that the performance of this festival ensures trouble-free cultivation and profuse crops. The Mundas worship "Dhulia-Baram" during the month of Vaisak (April-May). This ensures better agricultural operations. "Ashari-Festival" is held communally at the same place, where a fowl is sacrificed. After this festival the ceremonial transplantation commences. The

Mundas think that this festival will protect the villagers from unforeseen dangers, in general and from snake-bite in particular. "Karam" festival is associated with agriculture in which a few sprouting grains or seeds are required at the time of performance. Cattle caressing is done in "Soharai" festival.

As regards the social structure of the Mundas, it has been observed that quite a number of clans are included in it. Each clan has a distinctive totem. The clan members owe a deep sense of regard to their totems and never kill or injure these. The Mundas affiliate themselves with some patrilineal lineages (Banshas) through a sub-lineage of Bansha. Sub-lineage exogamy is strictly followed among the Mundas. In respect of the size of the family amongst Mundas it has been found that the small sized families predominate. Marriage by mutual consent or love marriage is also in vogue in the Munda Society. Widow remarriage or marriage with a divorced man is not uncommon. Dissolution of marriage is not difficult. After obtaining the report with regard to the intention of divorce, the village Panchayat formally approves divorce.

A Munda's life cycle comprises of a good number of rituals and observances. They observe a number of taboos and restrictions at the time of pregnancy and at the time of delivery of the baby. Name giving ceremony takes place on the 10th day of the child's birth. The ceremonial boring of the ears of the baby is done by a relative who is invited to do this. Rice cakes are prepared and distributed to the villagers on this occasion. The wedding ceremony of the Mundas is full of rituals. The whole of nuptial cycle has got a few phases like: (a) preliminary enquiries, (b) ceremonial paying of bride-price or betrothal, (c) ceremony proper and (d) Post-nuptial ceremonies. The Mundas attribute death to natural causes as well as to the malice of other spirits. They practise both cremation and burial. In case of fully-grown adult, cremation is performed. Before cremation takes place, the dead body is washed and turmeric paste is applied on it. Then it is taken to the cremation ground by the male members.

The Mundas believe that their destiny is controlled by many deities and minor spirits. The spirit hover over their habitations. Therefore, the Mundas try to appease these spirits with prayers. offerings and sacrifices. They worship 'Sitala' in the month of

Magh (February-March); 'Ulian' during Falgun (March-April); Dhulia Baram in Vaishak (April-May); 'Kusna' in the last day of Ashar (June-July) and 'Manasha' in Sravan (July-August). The 'Karama' festival is held in the month of Bhadra (Aug-September). The Mundas worship 'Dasai' in the month of Aswin (September-October); Gotbonga worship is performed during the month of Kartik (October-November). The 'Tusu' Festival is observed in the last day of Paush (December-January).

On the cultural front during the last couple of centuries or so it appears that the Munda culture has been influenced by Hinduism and Christianity. Vaisnavism may be construed to have been one of the earliest factors to bring about this change. It is said that the great Vaisnava reformer Chaitanya passed through the region inhabited by the Mundas. Although large-scale conversion never took place among the Mundas, indirectly however, early Vaisnavism left an impression on the Munda culture. Roy observes that "even among the unconverted, Vaisnavism has left its mark on songs and religious festivals. The `Karama' festival with its Lahusa songs can be clearly traced to Vaïsnava influence. Besides the Vaisnava influence, the early Munda culture appears to have been partially acculturated by the surrounding Hindu population. Roy gives a succinct account of the result of this prolonged Hindu-Munda cultural interaction in the following words. "Although the bulk of the Mundas have hitherto rejected Hinduism, clear trace of their social influence are observable in many of their social ceremonies and religious festivals. Thus the "Sindur dan" or besmearing of vermilion on the foreheads of the bride and bride-groom by each other, the use of `Sasang' or turmeric in marriages, the fasts and ceremonial ablutions practised in Munda religious festivals, besides some other practices are evidently borrowed from the Hindus. Christianity is another element that has influenced the pattern of Munda culture during the last hundred years or so. The first mission to begin its activities was the Gossuer Evangelical Lutheran Mission in 1845. It was soon followed by other missions i.e. Society for the Propagation of Gospel and Roman Catholic Mission. After an initial failure, the number of Christian converts increased. It has been said that the motives in joining the mission, except few cases, were not purely spiritual but secular.

The people hoped that the missions would be able to check the malpractices of the landlords and redress their grievances. As a matter of fact, the missionary activities inserted an eloquent element into the agrarian situation. The converts become more conscious, organized and defiant. In the social sphere, apart from injecting a new religious rein in the traditional Munda culture, Christianity was instrumental in bringing modern education among these people. Though Christianity discouraged drinking and dancing, it allowed the converts to live in harmony with their non-Christian brethren. Instead of forming an isolated class of their own, these converts continued to maintain the basic elements of their social system.

These five tribes taken together thus constitute more than 50 per cent of the entire tribal population of Orissa. Apart from these five tribal stocks some other major tribal group include Bhottade Bhuyan, Kolha, etc, with a population of nearly three lakhs. Bhottada or Bhotada mainly concentrates in Kalahandi and Koraput districts of Orissa. They are divided into two endogamous divisions i.e. Bodo and Sona who are further subdivided into various totemic clans. In the like manner the Bhuiya tribe of Orissa, with more than 2 lakh population, are initially divided into two clans i.e. Hill or Pauri or Desh Bhuiyas and plains Bhuyans or Sem. The plain Bhuiyas are having five sub-divisions i.e. Khandist or Paik Bhuiyan, militias of the former state; Rajkot or Rartaci, mainly agriculturists Powanbans and Rikhiagan Mahatwar and lastly the plain Bhuiyas. The last sub-group i.e. the plain Bhuiyas have adopted the names of Hindu *gotras* like Kachhap, Naga, Gaja, etc. However, the adoption of the same *gotra* by two or more families doesn't impose any restriction on inter-marriage. Although the *gotras* appear to be endogamous, actually they have a lineage type of organization Sangya whose members presume that they all belong to the same ancestor. Marriages are allowed within the same Sangya. In the like manner the Pauri Bhuiyas are also divided into endogamous *Kutumbs*. The members of a *Kutumb* who inhabit the same village presumably belong to a common ancestry.

Among the tribal groups having less than one lakh population, the Godabas of Koraput, are often taken as a single stock. But in real terms, it covers within itself a number of small tribal groups such as the Bondo Paraja, Bodo Gadaba, Poya Godaba, etc. All these sub-tribes have been divided into a number of patrilineal totemic and exogamous clans. The clans are further sub-divided into sub-clans called '*Kutamba*', often indicating their local origins. The *Kutumbas* may also be linked with their special traditional occupation. The 'Sibs' are further sub-divisions of *Kutumbas*. Members belonging to the same 'sib' cannot inter-marry but maintain close friendly relationship among them called as Panjabhai, making up the panchayat and Moitur, derived from the Sanskrit term *mitra* meaning friend.

The Juangs of Keonjhar region, with less than half a lakh of population, are divided into two sub-groups—Thaniya and Bhagudiya. Their territorial units are scattered over the hills of Jharkhand, Satkhand, Rebena and Kathua. The entire Juang population is further sub-divided into a number of clans known as Gutra or bok or Baor Sainga. The sub-clans of the Juang consist of a dual organization of Bandhu and Bhai. Marriage is permitted among the Bandhus but not among the Bhais.

The Bhunjias constitute a minor tribal group in Orissa and are mostly found in Kalahandi district. Their social design looks like: Tribe-Moiety-Territorial; Group-clan-lineage-family-individual. In the Moiety of Routs mainly four territorial divisions are found such as Chakatia, Khalasia, Nuagarhia and Sharia. The Chakatia is further divided into two groups namely Netam and Markam. Whereas the Netam comprises of ten *barag* or clans the Markam consists of nine *barags*. Each *barag* is an exogamous group comprising of several lineages and a tutelary deity.

Process of Transformation

The advent of the British marked the beginning of an infiltration by plainsmen into tribal regions. With the expansion of British dominion across the hills and development of means of communication, people from the plain areas who were afraid of the unhealthy conditions of the dense forests and hills did not hesitate to migrate there. Thereafter developed the process of cultural contact with the tribals. The relationship of tribals with the non-tribals in their vicinity gradually grew up in various directions. However, such a cultural contact had both positive as well as negative effects. Positively speaking, the untouchable caste of Pano and Dom who may be construed as the first non-tribal people to settle down on the hills, live in intimate relationship with the Saoras and Kondhs of southern part of Orissa. In the like manner, the oilmen and milkmen along-with some other castes settle amicably with the Paudi Bhuiyas and Juangs of North Orissa. The findings of the surveys and studies conducted by the Tribal Research Bureau reveal some of the negative effects. The non-tribal migrants, after settling down on the hills have been instrumental in exploiting and draining the life and blood of the tribals, so much so that at the articulation level of the Jharkhand movement was based on a strong antipathy towards the outsiders or the "Dikus". The meaning of the term Diku has changed from time to time. Originally it meant the Zamindar and his employees who were non-tribals; at the time of the Jharkhand movement it meant non-tribals of the upper class; at present it refers to the people of north Bihar. One of the Jharkhand slogans for the election was "*jharkhand abua daku diku senoa*" (Jharkhand is ours, the dacoit dikus will go)" and we shall take Jharkhand". Jaipal Singh, the leader of the movement had negotiations with the Congress leaders of Orissa for inclusion of Jharkhand region in the province. This proposal was put forth by the Adivasis before the British Government, soon after the formation of the province of Bihar and Orissa in 1912. However, the then Congress Government of Orissa did not accept the proposal on a couple of pleas; first inclusion of Jharkhand region in the province would have reduced the Oriya speaking population to an effective minority and secondly, it would have been in negation of the fundamental governing principle for creation of new provinces on the basis of language.

Adivasi uprising sponsored by the Jharkhand leaders in support of merger of two ex-states in Bihar thereby retaliating the steps taken by the provincial Government Orissa resulted in violence, involving 14 deaths, according to official estimate, but non-official statement puts number to several thousands.

The studies of the Tribal Research Bureau also reveal that notwithstanding all these persuasions and acrimonious propaganda, the tribal-non-tribal affinity has not been snapped. A study of various historical accounts show that the tribes of Orissa were hardly influenced by the centrally organized movements sponsored by the Congress in the pre-independence period. The British rule has taken steps to protect the interest of the tribals in matter of paternalistic rule, relative isolation of the tribal areas, laying down a set of simple rules, making special agrarian laws, regulation of the entry of the outsiders into the tribal pocket, attaching due importance to the traditional leaders and institutions. The Agency System was introduced to pacify the tribes as the earliest mode of protective administration. An agency set up in the Meriah track (1839-65) to abolish the practice of human sacrifice was quite successful. The new system of administration had certain remarkable effects on the tribal life. Firstly it did away with the relative isolation of the tribal society, facilitated the growth of a market economy, put an end to the political dominance of the tribes in the regions and straightened the feudal crust of tribal societies and at the same time accelerated the pace of colonization of the tribal regions by non-tribes. The Zamindari and Ryotwari systems were introduced in the tribal areas and the tribal and the non-tribal chiefs were recognized as Zamindar, Ghatwals and Bisois, etc. The period of British rule also marked the breakdown of the communal mode of production and the emergence of the private right in land. The tribes of Orissa came under the sway of politics during the forties of the 20th century. They are, in the recent times, guided by the sentiment of "traditional loyalties" involving ethnic, linguistic, cultural and regional or sub-regional affiliations. Achievement of independence and integration of the native states were two outstanding political phenomena which evoked a revolutionary upsurge among them in their struggle for amelioration of their grievances. These may be viewed as the struggle which is essentially an extension of the earlier one but linked up with modernizing influences.

Since the promulgation of Constitution and implementation of Five Year Plans, the Government through various agencies has been making Herculean efforts for development of the scheduled masses of people. The inception of the First Five Year Plan initiated a number of developmental programmes for the socio-economic upliftment of the tribals. The introduction of 43 special multi-purpose tribal blocks during the Second plan and further expansion of blocks during the Third plan and the establishment of Tribal Development Agencies in the Fifth plan are some of the main efforts made by the Government to improve the tribals. The Tribal Development Blocks were more in the nature of welfare schemes and failed to become effective instruments for tribal development. The sub-plan approach did take into account the natural resources and the topography level of socio-economic development and aimed at balanced regional development. The Fifth plan had only very limited success. The administrative unpreparedness appeared to be the main constraint in implementation of programmes and protective policies. The Sixth plan inducted the sub-plan approach to include more and more tribes. It developed programmes to give benefit to areas of tribal concentration, dispersed tribals and the primitive tribes. MADA was added into the sub-plan approach. Added to this are many government sponsored schemes like DPAP, Micro Projects for specific tribes, ERRP (Orissa), Tribal Development Co-operative Corporation (Orissa), Integrated Child Development Scheme, etc, which touch the lives of tribes directly or indirectly. A number of non-governmental organizations like UNICEF, CARE, the Indian Red Cross Society, missionary institutions and many others, pump in partly or fully resources and efforts for improving the lot of the tribal people.

An examination of the nature of communication involved in the present pattern of development reveals that the tribal communities are not treated as equal partners in the process of development. They are merely passive recipients. The National Forest Policy of 1952 and the subsequent social forestry formulated in the 1970s clearly reflect this trend. Under external assistance of the Swedish International Development Agency (SIDA), Massive social forestry programmes have been taken up in Orissa since 1983. The project has achieved a coverage of 790 sq. k.m. of plantation and 228 sq.km. of rehabilitation in the degraded forests and distribution of 1,176.78 lakh of seedlings with the investment of 84.77 crores upto 1992-93. According to the report on the activities of the Forest and Environment Department, in 1992-93, the forest coverage of Orissa was 57,183 kms.

With vegetation coverage of 27,349 sq.kms, in order to

check the denudation of the forests, felling of trees has been banned in Orissa since November 1992 and large-scale plantation programmes have been undertaken for restoration of degraded forests and maintenance of ecological balance. However, these policies have substantially reduced the rights and privileges of the tribals on the use of forest produce on which they largely depend for their livelihood. Similarly, the decisions for construction of large-scale public projects which displace the tribals from their native land are communicated to them at the last moment without making suitable arrangements for their proper rehabilitation. Many of such large projects constructed do not help in any way for tribal development. "Development as it exists today has become an uni-directional flow of information from those with power and authority to those without power and authority.

After independence media technology has been developed and the AIR has become the instrument of development of communication. In Orissa, radio stations have been set up in the tribal belts of Jeypore, Keonjhar, etc. Television has become very effective and influential and the SITE, 1975-76, brought the message of education and modernization into the rural and tribal interior of several states including Orissa . After 1982 there has been unprecedented growth of television which has considerable impact on social change.

Mass Media, the main means of communication in developed societies, are a luxury for tribals. Poverty and to a lesser extent, illiteracy are responsible for why tribals have little access to newspapers, radio and television. Dwelling on the outcome of the forces of change is a tough task. Nobody can say it for certain that there have been no desirable effects on the well-being of the tribal communities. In an evaluative study (1985), sponsored by the Harijan & Tribal Welfare Department, Government of Orissa for the ITDA Koraput, it has been stated that "interaction of the tribals with the nearby towns including those of the adjoining state is quite good" 61 per cent of the sample families listen to radio and 15 per cent of the sample respondents pay attention to news items. Gadabas and Parajas are found to be exposed to newspapers. The study group found a large number of tribal women in the weekly markets wearing synthetic sarees. They used cheap cosmetics, scented hair oil and aluminium utensils for cooking. 44 per cent of the sample respondents wanted to send their children to school. Only 2 per cent of them wanted their children to follow their traditional occupation. Most favoured government jobs, and so on. It is possible to quote from other studies and assert that there are many indicators of desirable changes in the lives of tribes.

Government of India has recognized 12 primitive tribes of Orissa. Some of them are in tribal-plan and few are outside the sub-plan area. 15 Micro projects have been functioning for all-round development of the primitive tribes. District-wise distribution of these Micro Projects is given in Table 18.1.

TABLE - 18.1
DISTRICT-WISE DISTRIBUTION OF MICRO PROJECTS

Undivided District	*Micro Projects*
Mayurbhanj	1. Lodha Development Agency, Morada
	2. Hill-Kharia & Mankirdia Development Agency Gudugudia
Sundargarh	Paudi Bhuiyan Development Agency, Khuntagaon
Keonjhar	Juang Development Agency, Gonasika
Dhenkanal	Pauri Bhuiyan Development Agency. Jamardihi
Phulbani	Kutia Kondh Development Agency, Belghar
Ganjam	1. Saora Development Agency, Chandragiri
	2. Thumba Development Agency, Thumba
	3. Lajia Saora Development Agency, Serango
Kalahandi	Kutia Kondh Development Agency, Lanjigarh
Koraput	1. Bonda Development Agency, Mudulipada
	2. Dongria Kondh Development Agency, Chatikona
	3. Lanjia Saora Development Agency, Puttasingi
	4. Didayi Development Agency, Bayapada
	5. Dongria Kondh Development Agency, Parsali

That apart, various voluntary organizations are also engaged in the tribal development process. Some such active voluntary organizations, district-wise, are given in Table 18.2.

TABLE - 18.2
DISTRICT-WISE DISTRIBUTION OF VOLUNTARY ORGANIZATIONS

Undivided District	*New District*	*Voluntary Organisation*	*Aims & Objectives*
1	2	3	4
1. Balasore	i) Balasore	HEART	Mass Education Health care, Tribal Development
		JANSEVA	Women and Tribal Development.
	ii) Bhadrak	SWC	Tribal Development & Women & child welfare
2. Balangir	i) Bolangir	BIRA	Tribal Development & Child & Women's Welfare
	ii) Sonepur	RBSC	Health care for SC/ST
3. Cuttack	i) Cuttack	Five ways Rural Research Service	
4. Dhenkanal	i) Angual	BBS	Tribal Development and Social Service
	ii) Dhenkanal	BANYITAH	Tribal Development and Handicapped welfare
		Mother India	Mass Awarencess, SC & ST Drive
5. Boudh-Khondhmal			
	i) Boudh	Palli Seva Sansad	SC/ST Development
		YCDA	Development Alternative for the Tribals
	ii) Khandmal		
6. Ganjam	i) Gajapati	Gramodyog	Tribal Development, Income Generation
	ii) Ganjam	CEDA	Awareness, Education, Tribal Development
		Gram Vikas	Tribal Development, Income generation, community health
		MATA	Population Education, Social Forestry, Sanitation, Tribal Development
7. Kalahandi	i) Kalahandi	DISHA	Slum Development, Tribal Development, Sanitation

(Contd.)

1	2	3	4
		JANASAHAYA	Tribal Development, Bonded labour
		NILOTPALA	Tribal Development & Educational Programmes
		PARIBARTANA	Health & Education, Tribal Development
		SEBAJAGAT	Training, Education, Agriculture Environment protection, Community Health, Tribal Development
	ii) Nuapada	ITDC	Community Awareness, Vocational Training Elementary Education, Environment protection for Tribal Folks
		RTDA	Overall Development Programmes
8. Keonjhar		Adivasi Vikas Samiti	Tribal Development Education and Community organization
		AHWAN	—DO—
		CITARD	Education and Tribal Development
9. Koraput	i) Koraput	BCA	Development of Tribal, Women and children
		CRDS	Upliftment of SC/ST & Rural poor
		MARR-MUNNING ASHRAM	Educational promotion Among Tribal people
		SIDA	Health care for Tribal & weaker sections
	ii) Malkangiri	GARDEN	Environment and Tribal Development
		KOYA	Integrated Rural Tribal Development
		SOMKS	SC/ST, Women and Child Development
	iii) Nabrangpur	PVYP	Forest Protection, Women and Tribal Development
		IYSARA	Health, Education, Agriculture, forest protection
	iv) Rayagada	JAGARANA	Non-formal & Adult Education, Tribal Development

(Contd.)

1	2	3	4
		Servants of India Society	Vocational Training, Women, Children and Tribal welfare
		Utkal Jyoti	Tribal and Rural Development programmes
10. Mayurbhanj		AYUS	Smokeless Chullah and welfare of SC & ST
		CSZM	Socio-economic Development of Tribals
		PALLI VIKAS	Women and child Development for Rural Tribals
		SANSKAR	Tribal Socio-economic Development
		SEENSCAR	Tribal and Harijan Development
11. Puri	i) Khurda	CTRD	Tribal Development, Self-help Group
		CSP	Tribal Development, Consumer Protection
	ii) Nayagarh	BANCHHA	Agriculture, Women & Tribal Development
		SAMPARK	Rural and Tribal Development
	iii) Puri	Jana Kalyan	Health, Education, Environment,
		Jubak Sangha	SC, ST child & Women's Development
12. Sambalpur	i) Bargarh	Kharmunda Panchyat Adivasi Sangathan	Integrated Tribal Develpment Programme
	ii) Deogarh	VOICE	Development of Hill-Tribal and Economic Backward people
	iii) Sambalpur	Udiyaman Matru Kshetra	Agriculture and Spiritual Development and Tribal welfare
13. Sundargarh		AWDI	Welfare of Handicapped Tribals and working children
		LUCK	Promotion of Tribal culture, community development and self employment.
		YOUTH	Tribal Welfare and community Development

REFERENCES

Bailey F.G., 1971, "The Ganatantra Parishad" in *Economic Weekly*.

Govt. of India, 1980, Report of the working Group on Tribal Development during Sixth Plan. Ministry of Home Affairs, New Delhi.

Haimendorf, C.V.F., 1956, *The Descent Group System of the Raj Gonds*, London : School of Oriental and African studies, Vol.XVIII, Part-3.

Haribabu, E., 1989, "Communication in Tribal Development; Some Observations". In *Aspects of Human Communication* (Ed.) by L.Krishna, B.N. Pattnaik and N.K. Sharma, New Delhi: Mittal.

Mishra, Godabaris, Saraikella and Kharswan (in Oriya) Cuttack : Bharati Vihar.

Mohanty, P.C., 1993, "Environmental Pollution, Policies and Management", *Orissa Review* Vol. I No.1

Ray, S.C., 1912, *The Mundas and Their Country*.

———, 1961, Census of India, Vol. IV, Part VA

———, 1941, Census of India.

Ressell, R.V. and Hiralal, R.S., 1961, *The Tribes and Castes of the Central Provinces of India*, London; MacMillan & Co., Ltd.,

Singh, Suresh, 1966, *Dust-storm and Hanging Mist: Story of Birsa Munda and His Movement*, Calcutta.

———, 1977, Colonial Transformation of the Tribal Society in Middle India, Presidential Address, Indian History Congress, Bhubaneswar.

Varier, Elwin, 1950, *Bonda Highlander*, Bombay; Oxford University Press.

Nineteen

Habitat, Society, Economy and Development of the Tribes of Maharashtra

J.B. AMBEKAR

Introduction

The tribals are an important component of the Indian culture and civilization. They are one of the early settlers (*adivasis*), aboriginals of India (*adimjati*), live in forests (*vanvasi*) or/and in hilly, mountainous areas (*pahari*).[1] The Constitutional term used to refer to the tribal people who are racially, culturally and ecologically distinctive is Scheduled Tribes (ST). The resource habitat of the tribals have been cumulatively destroyed endangering their livelihood due to reasons such as was and invasions by Moghuls (historical); racial miscegenation (legal); the commercial nature of the British National Forest Policy of 1864 as well as the post Independent forest policy and the tensions and conflicts it created over the use of forest resources and hunting; increasing industrialization and urbanization and loss of forests. As a result some of the tribals like Katkaris, Mahadeo Kolis, Pardhis, Kanjarbhat, Yerukula (Kaikadi), were forced to engage themselves in criminal activities. As such, to keep a check over them, as many as 28 communities throughout India were declared as 'Criminal Tribes' during the British period. The ex-criminal tribes of Maharashtra communities are now included under the Denotified Tribes (DNT) category. This category is known as 'Vimukta Jati' (VJ).[2] There are also communities in or near the village settlements whose occupations are pastoral, hunting, semi-skilled services, entertainment, trading and religious services, which by their very nature make the practitioners move from one place/habitat to another periodically. Such communities are known as Bhatkya

TABLE - 19.1

DISTRICTWISE AND RURAL/URBAN DISTRIBUTION OF SCHEDULED TRIBE POPULATION IN MAHARASHTRA

Sl. No.	*Administrative Division and District*	*Total Population of STs*	*Tribes found*	*Percentage of ST to Total Population*	*Rural ST Population*	*Percentage of Rural STs Population*	*Urban ST Population*	*Percentage of Uban ST Population*
	Maharashtra	73,18,281	Bhils, Gond, Mahadeo Koli, Warli, Kokna, Katkari, Kolam, Korku, Thakar, Andh, Malhar Koli, Pardhan, Pardhi, etc.	9.27	64,05,814	13.24	9,12,467	2.99
Konkan Administrative Division								
1.	Greater Bombay	1,03,775	Warli, Katkari/Kathodi, Koli Malhar,etc.	1.05	—	—	1,03,775	1.05
2.	Thane	9,51,205	Kokna, Katkari, Koli Malhar, Koli Mahadev.	18.12	8,48,042	45.69	1,03,163	3.04
3.	Raigarh	2,33,953	Katkari, Thakar	12.82	2,12,762	14.22	21,191	6.45
4.	Ratnagiri	14,847	Thakar, Katkari.	0.96	13,968	0.99	879	0.64
5.	Sindhudurg	3,893	Kokna, Katkari.	0.47	3,656	0.48	237	0.38
Nashik Administrative Division								
6.	Nashik	9,31,069	Katkari, Pardhi, Kokna,	24.18	8,57,093	34.53	73,976	5.40
7.	Dhule	10,36,491	Kokna, Bhil, Koli Dhor, Naikda, etc.	40.88	9,95,180	49.37	41,311	7.95
8.	Jalgaon	3,13,551	Dhanka, Bhil, Koli Dhor.	9.84	2,79,843	12.10	33,708	3.85
9.	Ahmednagar	2,40,141	Thakar, Koli Mahadev, Koli Dhor, etc.	7.12	2,30,465	8.12	9,676	1.81
Pune Administrative Division								
10.	Pune	2,16,336	Thakar, Katkari, Koli sub-tribes	3.91	1,77,677	6.52	38,659	1.38
11.	Satara	18,342	Barda, Katkari, etc.	0.75	15,990	0.75	2,352	0.74

12. Sangli	10,784	Pardhi	0.49	9,262	0.56	1,522	0.34
13. Solapur	48,352	Barda, Pardhi	1.50	30,898	4.18	17,454	1.34
14. Kolhapur	14,789	Pardhi, Mahadeo Koli	0.49	12,832	0.58	1,951	0.25
Aurangabad Division							
15. Aurangabad	83,502	Bhils, Pardhan	3.77	73,401	4.93	10,101	1.39
16. Jalna	28,300	Bhil	2.07	25,132	2.22	3,168	1.37
17. Pardhani	1,11,470	Andh	5.27	1,03,564	6.31	17,906	1.65
18. Beed	20,515	Andh	1.13	18,012	1.20	2,503	0.77
19. Nanded	2,75,972	Pardhan, Andh, Gond, Kolam	11.84	2,49,970	13.70	26,002	5.14*
20. Osmanabad	22,463	Andh, Pardhi	1.76	19,608	1.81	2,855	1.47
21. Latur	37,527	Pardhi	2.24	33,282	2.49	4,245	1.24
Amravati Division							
22. Buldhana	95,389	Korku	5.06	89,423	5.97	5,966	1.54
23. Akola	1.55,695	Kolam	7.03	1,38,055	8.74	17,640	2.78
24. Amravati	3,16,448	Korku, Halba	14.38	2,85,469	19.25	30,979	4.32
25. Yavatmal	4,45,840	Kolam, Andh, Gond	21.46	4,17,965	24.30	27.875	7.81*
Nagpur Division							
26. Wardha	1,66,391	Kolam, Gond, etc.	15.59	1,42,677	18.20	23,714	8.36*
27. Nagpur	45,77,115	Gond, Binjhwar	13.92	2,35,616	18.76	2,22,099	10.94*
28. Bhandara	3,09,822	Gond, Korku, etc.	14.70	2,88,475	15.75	21,347	7.14
29. Chandrapur	3,49,157	Kolam, Gond, Pardhan, Halba.	19.70	3,03,045	23.77	46,124	9.28*
30. Gadchiroli	3,04,535	Gond and its various sub-tribes, Korku, Kolam, Bhunja, etc.	38.70	2.94,452	40.98	10,083	14.71*

Source: Census of India, 1991.

Jamati and are placed in the State schedule in the same reserved category as the DNT.

Many times there is confusion between usage as well as operationalization of the terms tribe and caste in the State schedule of the reserved communities. For instance Kaikadi is included as a Scheduled Tribe in Andhra, Tamil Nadu and Kerala. However, Kaikadi is declared as a Scheduled Caste for eight districts of Vidarbha region in Maharashtra while it is included as a Nomadic Tribe (NT) for Western Maharashtra region. Because of changing nature of tribes and castes, a tribe-caste continuum or model needs to be developed for different geographical regions and then to place the various communities on this continuum on the basis of selected variables like occupation, social units like caste, clan, phratry and lineages, habitat and resource use pattern. A socio-ecological approach to study castes like Kunbis and tribals like the Phasephardhis of Western Maharashtra was used by Gadgil and Malhotra.[3]

In this study, the author wishes to present a demographic and socio-economic profile of the Scheduled Tribes (ST), Denotified Tribes (DNT) and Nomadic Tribes (NT) in Maharashtra. This will then be followed by discussion on the transformation and changes taking place in them. The data used are primarily drawn from secondary sources, viz, Census Hand Books and Tribal Studies in Maharashtra as well as on the author's experiences of studying a few Nomadic Tribes like the Nath Panth, Davari Gosavi and the Dange Dhangars in Kolhapur district.

Demography

There are 47 tribes in Maharashtra and the districtwise/ distribution[4] of some of these tribes[5] are presented in the Table 19.1. Some of the districts of tribal concentration are Thane (18.12%) in Konkan administrative division, Nashik (24.18%) and Dhule (40.88%) in Nasik division, Gadchiroli (38.70%), Chandrapur (19.70%) and Wardha (15.59%) in Nagpur division and Yavatmal (21.46%) and Amravati (14.38%) in Amravati administrative division.

The total tribal population in Maharashtra according to the 1991 Census is 7,31,8281 which is 9.27% of the State population. Out of the total tribal population, 87.53% tribals are rural while 12.47% are urban based.[6] Some of the numerically dominant tribes in Maharashtra are Gonds, Bhils, Koli Mahadev, Warli, Thakar, Andh and Kathkari/Kathodi. The estimated projected population of the above seven tribes can be calculated on the basis of their previous census figures[7] and the percentage of increases of the tribal population per year. On this basis the population of the Gonds in Maharashtra in the year 2001 will be approximately 18,70,839, Bhils - 15,25,352, Koli Mahadev - 12, 11,056, Warli - 5,54,915, Thakar - 4,96,421, Andh - 3,56,153 and Kathkari - 2,68,188.

Denotified Tribes (DNT)

In the State reserved category of VJ/NT there are in all 44 communities out of which 14 communities are included in the Vimukta Jati (VJ) sub-category (see Table 19.2). The total estimated population of all the communities in the DNT/NT category during 1991 is 22,42,304.[8] Including the recently included two numerically, socially and politically dominant communities of Dhangar (23,31,241) and Vanjari (7,51,420), the total estimated population of 44 communities in the VJ/NT reserved category goes upto 53,24,966. These communities also known as 'Ex-criminal Tribes', exhibit tribal as well as caste/rural features in varying degrees and can be placed at different points of the tribe-caste continuum. The total population of the denotified tribes in Maharashtra during the 1931 Census was 3,72,937 and according to one estimate the population during 1991 is 13,15,398. Another estimate namely Vasantrao Naik Vimukta Jamati/Bhatkya Jamati Mahamandal[9] puts the DNT population at 18,91,455. The numerically dominant Denotified Tribes in Maharashtra according to above 1991 estimate are - Banjara (5,55,319), Ramoshi (2,06,284), Berad (1,08,107), Kaikadi (58,465), Rajpardhi (61,876), Waddar (1,00,000) and Rajput Bhamta (21,000). (Table 19.2).

Nomadic Tribes (NT)

At present there are in all 30 Nomadic Tribes (NTs). Their population during the 1931 Census was 2,62,793 and their estimated population during 1991 was 9,26,906 (Table 19.3). Some of the numerically dominant Nomadic Tribes as per the estimates for 1991 are Gosavi (2,61,120), Beldar (1,84,804), Bharadi (16,887), Gondhali (20,552), Golla (19,536), Gopal (18,859), Joshi (27,240) and Kolhati (12,933).[10]

TABLE - 19.2

DISTRIBUTION OF DENOTIFIED TRIBES (DNT) IN MAHARASHTRA ACCORDING TO THEIR POPULATION* AND OCCUPATIONS(S)

Sl. No. Name of the Tribe/Caste Included as DNT or VJ	Synomous group/ Sub-groups/ Endogamous Groups	Geographical Distribution in Maharashtra	Population in the State of Maharashtra 1931 Census	Estimated Population in (1991)	Occupation(s)	Remarks
1. Berad	1. a) Vagalle b) Naikwadi c) Talwar d) Walmiki	Kolhapur, Solapur, Latur, osmanabad and Konkan (sea-shore areas)	32,815	1,08,107	Hunting, agriculture, Semi-nomadic	Were ex-criminal tribe during the British period.
2. Bestar	2. Sanchalu Waddar	Solapur, Mundwa, Pune	—	100	Labour, Semi-nomadic, collection of scrap, arrack distillation, transportation of mud	Nomadic
3. Bhamta	3. a) Bhamti b) Girni Waddar c) Kamati d) Pathrut e) Takari f) Uchale	Pune, Satara, Solapur, Ahemadnagar, Nashik, Kolhapur.	9,398	33,148	Stone workers, preparation of grinding equipments, pickpocketing, robbery, cheating, labour, jobs.	Nomadic econo- life, ex-criminal tribe.
4. Kaikadi	4. a) Dhontale b) Korawa c) Makadwala or Konchikurva d) Pamlor e) Korvi	Mumbai, Thane, Colaba, Ratnagiri, Dhule, Jalgaon, Pune, Ichalkaranji, Sangli, Kolhapur, Solapur, Aurangabad,Beed, Pandharpur, Parbhani, Osmanabad, Nanded and Chandrapur	16,576	58,465	Manufacturing and sale of baskets, agriculture labour, domestication of pigs, picking or collecting scrap, jobs, distillation of arrack, playing band and musical instruments, transporation of goods with the help of asses, etc.	Also fund in government jobs.
5. Kanjar-bhat	5. a) Chara b) Kanjar c) Nat	Jalgaon, Nandurbar, Dhule, Solapur, Hatakanangale, Ichalkaranji, Ambarnath, Mundwa, Yerawada.	431	1,520	Collection of scrap, pick-pocketing, arrack distillation, sale of drugs, petty jobs, etc. (nomadic)	Criminal activities relatively more
6. Katabu		Migrated from Konkan to Belgaum, Bijapur adjoining districts of Karnataka.				Not found in Maharashtra criminal settlements present in Karnataka

7. Banjara	7. a) Gor Banjara b) Lambada/ Lambara c) Lambahane d) Charanbanjara e) Labhan f) Mathwa labhan, g) Kacki-wale banjara h) Laman banjara i) Laman/Lamani j) Laban k) (excluded), l) Dhali/dhaliya m) Dhadi/ dhadiya n)Singari o)Navi Vanjara p) Jogi Vanjara	Pune, Dhule, Jalgaon, Osmanabad, Chandrapur, Latur, Parbhani, Nagpur, Nashik, Miraj etc.	1,57,442	5,55,319	Fishing, tatooing, begging, shadow play, bullock cart transportation, agriculture, labour, jobs, petty business, etc.	Not engaged in criminal activities Nomadic
8. Palpardhi					Arrack distillation, sale of	Ex-criminal tribe.
9. Rajpardhi	9. a) (excluded) b) Gaon pardhi c) Haran Shikari d) (excluded)	Barshi, Hotgi, Kolhapur, Mundwa, Solapur, Pandharpur	17,543	61,876	Women's ornaments, begging, robbery, agriculture, labour, stone work, etc.	Nomadic
10. Rajput Bhamta	10.a) Pardeshi bhamta	Solapur, Ambarnath, Pune,	6,011	21,000	Cheating, pickpocketing, labour, petty jobs, distillation of liquour, robbery, etc. (nomadic)	Ex-criminal tribe. Nomadic
11. Ramoshi		Ambarnath	58,485	2,06,284	Hunting, labour (nomadic)	Not found in Ex-criminal tribe settlements.
12. Waddar	12.a) Gadi Waddar, b)Jati Waddar, c) Mati Waddar d) Patharvat	Solapur, Umedpur, Limayewadi, Undirgaon, Haregaon, Chakkanwadi, Karad, Pandharpur, Vijapur.		1,00,000	Agriculture, labour, digging of wells, making stone grinding implements, transportation and sale of mud, stone, criminal activities like pick-pocketing, distillation of liquor, etc.	Nomadic occupations Many sub-groups are settled in towns and cities. Approximate figure.
13. Vaghri	13.a) Salat b) Salat Vaghri					Not found in the ex-criminal tribe settlements of Maharashtra
14. Chappar-band		Jalgaon, Hotgi, Solapur and Mundwa	10	35	Making and circulating fake coins, notes, erecting tents and labour	Muslim Converts but exhibit also Hindu characteristics.

*Source: Bokil, Milind (1995).

TABLE - 19.3

POPULATION AND OCCUPATIONAL CHARACTERISTICS OF NOMADIC COMMUNITIES (NT) IN MAHARASHTRA

Sl. No. Name of the Tribe/Caste Included as 'NT'	Synonymous group/ Sub-groups/ Endogamous Groups Nomadic Tribes	Geographical distribution in Maharashtra	Population in the State of Maharashtra: 1931 Census	Population in the State of Maharashtra: Estimated Population in (1991)	Occupation(s)	Remarks
1. Gosavi	1. Bava 2. Bairagi 3. Bharti 4. Giri Gosavi 5. Bharti Gosavi 6. Saraswati Parvat 7. Sagar. 8. Ban or Van 9. Teerth Ashram 10. Aranya Gharbhari 11. Sanyasi 12. Nath Parvthi Gosavi	Kolhapur, Satara, Sangli and scattered in small numbers throughout Maharashtra.	74,032	2,61,120	Religious alms, presently service, collecting of scrap paper, plastic, umbrella and stove repair, begging, crime and petty traditional selling of various things.	Migrated from the Western Ghats and Northern area. Nomadic occupation.
2. Beldar	2. Oad		52,395	1,84,804		
3. Bharadi	3. A. Babsanthosi b. Kingiri-shle c. NathBava d. Nath-jogi e. Nathjagi f. Nath Panthi devari Gosavi.	Kolhapur, Sangli, Panhala, and distributed in other parts of Maharashtra and Karnataka	4,788	16,887	Religious alms, cultivation, government and private jobs.	Gosavi and Bharadi have similar priestly characteristics.
4. Bhutya	4. Bhope		120	423		
5. De;etd						
6. Chitrakathi			540	1,904		
7. Garudi	7. Ghisadi lohar, or Gadi Lohar, or Chitodi		141	497	Snake charming or play	Nomadic
8. Ghisadi	8. Lohar, Rajput Lohar		2,932	10,341	Blacksmithy, utensils repair, etc.	Nomadic
9. Golla	9. Gollavar, Goler, Gollar	Kolhapur, Sangli	5,539	19,536	Domestication of cows, buffaloes, labour, agri.	Nomadic
10. Gondhali		Sangli, Satara, Pune, etc.	5,827	20,552	Religious service during marriage (Gondhali), labour, etc.	Nomadic
11. Gopal	11. a) Gopal Bhorpi b) Khelkari		5,347	18,859		

12. Helave	12. Hilava	Kolhapur, Miraj, Pandharpur, Belgaum, Bijapur, Dharwad	—	—	Ancestral family, linkage, clan record keepers	Nomadic
13. Joshi	13.1) Budbudki 2) Damaruwale 3) Kudmude 4) Mendhagi 5) Sarode 6) Sahdev 7) Sarwade 8) Saroda	Solapur, Pandharpur, Osmanabad, Miraj, Latur etc.	7,723	27,240	Fortune telling, Astrology	Nomadic but not found in Maharshtra
14. Kashi Kapdi						
15. Kolhati	15. Dombari	Kolhapur, Solapur, Pandharpur, etc.	3,667	12,933	Acrobatics, labour	Nomadic
16. Mairal	16.1) Dangat 2) Veer		39	137		
17. Masanjogi	17 1) Sudagadsiddh 2) Mapanjogi	found in Karnataka				Nomadic (found in burial group)
18. Nandiwale	18. Tiramal		1,502	5,297	Bull performance, sheep keeping	
19. Pangul			99	349		
20. Raval	20. Rawul of Rawulgogi					
21. Sikkalgar	21.Katari	Found in Miraj, also found in Belgaum, Bijapur (Karnataka), etc.	154	543	Weaving mats, basket making, begging, labour	Nomadic
22. Thakar		Ratnagiri	1,551	5,470	Cultivation, forest resources, collection, sale of fuel wood, etc.	Nomadic
23. Vaidu			1,332	4,698	Herbal medicine men	
24. Vasudev			61	215	Religious alms	
25. Bhoi	25. 1) Zhinga bhoi, 2) Pardeshi bhoi, 3) Rajbhoi, 4) Bhoi, 5) Kahar, 6) Godia Kahar, 7) Dhuria kahar, 8) Kirat, 9) Hachna, 10) Manzi, 11) Jatiya, 12) Kevat, 13) Dhivar, 14) Dheevar,	Kolhapur, Radhanagari, Ratnagiri, etc.	94,894	13,34,703	Fishing in lakes, river and sea water.	

	15) Dheeman, 16) Palewar, 17) Machendra, 18) Navadi, 19) Malhar, 20) Malhao, 21) Boi, 22) Gadhav Bhoi, 23) Khadi Bhoi, 24) Khare Bhoi, 25) Dhevara					
26. Bhahurupi		Miraj, Pandharpur, Kolhapur, etc.	110	387	Religious alms, enacting roles pertaining to Maharashtra and Ranaya	Nomadic
27. Thelari		Dhule, Nasik, Jalgaon, Aurangabad				
28. Otari						
		Total Nomadic (1)	2,62,793	9,26,906		
		Total Nomadic - DNT	6,35,730	22,42,304		
29. Nomadic (2) Dhanagar	29. 1) Ahir, 2) Dange, 3) Gatri, 4) Hande, 5) Telwar, 6) Hatkar, 7) Haatkar, 8) Shegar, 9) Khutekar, 10) Telangi, 11) Tellari, 12) Kokani Dhangar, 13) Kanade, 14) Varhade, 15) Zhade, 16) Zhende, 17) Kurnaar, 18) Mahure, 19) Ladase, 20) Sangar, 21) Dhanwar	Kolhapur, Sangli, Solapur, Satara, Pune, Nasik, Ahmedanagar, Osmanabad, Bid, Nanded, etc.	6,60,945	23, 31, 241	Pastoral : Goat, sheep domestication, cultivation etc.	Found throughout Western Maharashtra Economic position better than other NT's
30. Nomadic (3) Vanjari	Vanjar, Vanjara	Nagpur, Nashik, Beed, Osmanabad, Satara, Kolhapur, Ahmednagar and Dhule.	2,13,040	7,51,420	Cultivation, labour, transportation, etc.	Economically more sound than other NT's
Total of all	Nomadic - DNT		15,09,715	53, 24,966	—	—

Source: Bokil, Milind (1995).

Habitat

In Maharashtra, we can broadly classify the habitats of places of dwelling of the two tribal categories (ST and VJ/NT) into the following types: a) Thick Forest habitat b) hilly/and Mountainous habitat and c) Plains and Semi-Arid Urban and Rural habitats.

Thick Forest Habitats

The Eastern district of Maharashtra viz. Chandrapur, Gadchiroli have thick forests and incommunicable roads and are known as Gondwana region after its tribal residents namely Gonds. The forests are rich in flora and fauna and support biodiversity among the plants as well as cultural diversity among its human or tribal population. The percentage of ST population in Gadchiroli district of this region is 37.70. This region comprises 7 districts and 16 tahsils.[11] The districts in the Nagpur administrative division : Wardha, Nagpur, Amaravati, Bhandara and Chandrapur also have tribals ranging from 14% to 20% of the district population. On an average this Eastern region of Maharashtra consists of 20% tribal population. Some of the significant tribes in this region are: Gond and some of its 59 sub-tribes like Rajgond, Bada Maria, Hill Maria, Koya, Bisonhorn Maria, etc, and Kolam, Korku, Baiga, Bhunja, Chodhara, etc. (see Table 19.1)

Hilly and Mountainous Habitats

This region refers to the Sahyadri and Satpura mountain ranges forming the western and north-western ghats They also consist of forests and a variety of plant species, animals, birds, and fishes which are the natural habitats of Bhils, Warlis, Katkaris, Mahadeo Kolis, Kolam, Naikada, Koli Malhar, Thakar, etc. This region includes districts like Dhule, Nasik, Jalgaon, Thane, Raigad, Ahmedanagar and Satara. The tribal population in these districts on an average basis is 17%. Dhule district in this region is the district of highest tribal concentration (40.88%) which is higher than the total population in the thick forest district of Gadchiroli in Gondwana region of eastern Maharashtra. (Table 19.1)

Plains and Semi-Arid Rural Habitats

The tribals especially the VJ like the Pardhi, Kaikadi, Waddar, Kanjarbhat, Mang Garudi, Makadwale, Takari, Takari Bhamta,

Chapparband and NTs like Thakar, Vanjari, Garudi, Golla, etc, are the Scheduled Tribes displaced from their original forest habitats. Due to their involvement in crime they were rehabilitated by the British in closed barbed wire fencing and open settlements in district of Central and North Western Maharashtra like Beed, Osmanabad, Solapur, Jalgaon, Dhule, Thane, Pune, Latur and Satara. These settlements are found both in urban, rur-urban as well as rural areas. They can also be seen living on the fringes and slums of towns and cities in the districts of central and north western Maharashtra. The economic, sanitation and hygienic conditions of these slums were found to be extremely poor. Besides, such slums and settlements are the homes of crime and social ills. Percentage of crime among these families ranged from 2% to as high as 60% among the Kanjarbhat according to a study conducted by Mane, Laxman. He studied 58 DNT settlements in Central and North Western Maharashtra. In all, 2500 families were studied out of which detailed data pertaining to 500 families were recorded. Out of these 500 families majority i.e. 74.12% lived inside the fenced wired settlements while 8.8% came from open settlements. In the rural and rur-urban areas these people live in huts, thatched houses or tents on the outskirts of the villages. But, the VJ/NT communities have various sorts of social, occupational, economic and religious relationships with the rural castes and rur-urban populations. Hence, now these communities exhibit both tribal as well as rural/caste characteristics due to their prolonged contacts with mainstream social groups.

The conceptual difficulties faced by the Government authorities in defining a group as a caste or tribe can be partly resolved with an ecological approach to caste/tribe. Gadgil and Malhotra (1994) view Indian Society as analogous to a biological community which is made up of a number of cultural species or endogamous groups. They studied castes like Kunabi and Gavali as well as tribe like communities namely Tirumal Nandiwalas, Fulmali nandiwalas, pastoral Vaids (medicine men), Phasepardhis (hunters), Hatkar and Gavalis (Pastoral). They divide these communities into three trophic levels:

(i) Cultivators pastorals and hunter gatheres who directly depend on the land, flora and fauna.

(ii) Artisans, entertainers and traders

(iii) Priestly caste and other communities.

The authors illustrate with the help of examples different levels of adaptation to their eco-systems. The last two groups are dependent upon the first group. In the case of pastorals and nomads they have demonstrated the principles of niche diversification and prudent use of natural resources.

Economy and Society

The occupations and economic activities of the different categories of Scheduled Tribes and VJ/NT communities can be classified broadly into the following types: a) food gathering and hunting; b) pastoral; c) agriculture; d) agricultural and non-agricultural labour; e) religious singers, priests and mendicants; f) skilled workers and entertainers; g) petty traders and businessmen and h) criminal activities. The work participation and occupational categories of the tribes reflect their economic conditions. According to the Census of India 1981, the work participation rate of rural tribals is found to be more than the urban tribals. The average percentage of 'main tribal workers' for the above seven numerically dominant tribes is 44.11% which is slightly higher than the corresponding figure of 42.63% for the general population in Maharashtra.[12]

As per 1981 Census, agriculture or cultivation is an important occupation of the tribals like Gonds, Andh, Koli Mahadev, Warli and Thakar. This occupational category constitutes an important occupation for the above tribes and constitutes about 25% of the total occupational categories. But if we compare the corresponding figures for the 1961 Census we see that 62% were cultivators among Warlis, 65.5% among Mahadev Kolis, 75% among Korkus and 54.66% among the Gonds. This means that cultivation among these tribes has decreased by 40-50% within a period of 20 years.[13]

Agricultural labour constitutes an important source of livelihood for almost all the rural tribals. On an average the percentage of above rural tribals in this category falls in the range of 15% to 35% (1981 Census). During the 1961 census only 11.67% worked as agricultural labourers among the Warlis, 25.5% among Mahadev Kolis, and 54.6% among Gonds. Among Gonds there is decrease in the agricultural labour by about 20%. 'Livestock, forestry, fishing, hunting and plantation activities are practiced comparatively more by tribes like Koli Mahadev (8.84%) and Katkari (8.67%) while only 0.5% to 2.0% population of Thakar, Warli, Bhil, Gond and Andh are involved in this economic activity. The corresponding figure for the general population is 1.52%. There is also a slight decrease in livestock, forestry, hunting and fishing occupation. All the above is an indication of the decreasing forest on account of the shifting cultivation and pressures of industrialization and urbanization and faulty National Forest Policy. A large percentage of population (40% to 60%) of all the tribes fall in the 'non-workers' category.[14] It is an indication of economic social and ecological crisis in the tribal society today. As a result many tribal communities have been displaced to various towns and cities. The nomadic communities like Nandiwale have settled as agriculturist in different villages of Western Maharashtra.

As mentioned earlier in an extensive and independent study[15] conducted by Laxman Mane (1995) who incidentally comes from a Denotified Tribe : 500 families from 58 different settlements in Maharashtra were studied in depth and it was found that out of the total families studied, 53.75% families worked as labourers and 9.22% families were involved in thefts, robbery, illicit distillation of liquor, etc. The livelihood of majority (85%) of the families is of very low standard and uncertain. This boils down to the question of identity of the indigenous communities. Destruction of their culture is taking place at a rapid pace. However, we do find 2% to 24% families among these DNT belonging to upper middle class. Among some tribes like Kanjarbhat as high as 60% families who were primarily hunters are now involved in criminal activities. But among Takari, Kaikadi, Mang Garudi, criminal activities are in the range of only 1.0% to 3.0%. This indicates that conflicts and tension are more visible among Kanjarbhats. Both women and children among the VJ/NTs have to do gainful work and fight against unemployment and poverty. Literacy is very low. In the urban families it is 10% while in the rural areas it is less than 1.5%.[16] Cultural adaptation is equally important as is economic security.

Mahadev Koli

There are no sub-divisions in the Mahadev Koli tribe. Professor Ghurye studied this tribe in great details.[17] It consists of Gotri-bhau — a certain grouping of families whose members cannot inter-marry among themselves. In other words the Gotri-bhau is an exogamous group consisting of families numbering between 2 to 12 who need not necessarily have same surnames. The exogamy of the Mahadev Kolis is based on Devaks (totem) rather than family surnames. The family is patrilineal and patrilocal. The Mahadev Kolis have no connection with the Koli castes from districts of Western Maharashtra and Kolis of Konkan area in Maharashtra such as Son Koli or Macchimari Koli (fishermen), Panbhare Koli (water carrier).[18]

The Mahadev Kolis are agriculturists and agricultural labourers. Padkai is an important cooperative social institution used for carrying out agricultural activities.[19]

Gonds

They have been considered as one of the principal tribes of the Dravidians and the language is similar to that of Tamil, Telugu or Kannada. They are divided into more than 50 sub-groups or sub-tribes such as Raj-Gond, Bada-Maria, Bisonhorn-Maria, Gond-Gowari, Maria Gond, Hill Maria, etc. They are divided into 4 *sagas* or *phrataries* which are exogamous and each divided into a number of clans. Traditional agriculture and agricultural labour is their main occupation.[20] Collection of *mahua*, gum, and other forest produce is their secondary occupation. Some of the sub-tribes who live in thick forests still practice shifting cultivation. Gotul-ghar is an important social institution in many Gond villages.

Varlis

They are known as Varlis or uplanders because they lived in the Northern part of the Konkan. The tribe is sub-divided into three groups : Murdes, Devars and Niners which are further divided into 200 exogamous groups or clans. They generally believe in Hindu gods like Ram, Siva and deities like Hanuman and also worship their own deities like Vaghya and Bhairav. Their dialect is a mixture of Warli, Marathi and Gujarati. Their main source of livelihood is agricultural and forest labour.[21]

Katkari/Kathodi

They are mainly found in Thana and Kolaba districts. The word seems to come from the word Kath/Kat which means the thickened juice of the catechu tree. Dhor Katkari and Son-Katkari are the two divisions of the tribe. The exogamous divisions of the tribe are represented by different family surnames. They are one of the primitive tribes of the State. They were once known as a criminal tribe.[22] The Katkari settlements are on the outskirts of the village and town settlements and they have established various sorts of relationship with the land owning castes like Brahmins, Marathis and Kunbis and with artisan castes like carpenters, barbars and blacksmiths as well as with the other tribes like Thankars, Warlis and Kolis. Katkaris are engaged as tenants, agricultural labourers and as seller of forest produce and as fisherman. They worship tribal gods such as Supali, Gavdeo as well as Hindu gods of the region.

Development Pattern

The tribal sub-plan approach has been adopted for achieving faster socio-economic development of the tribal people. Integrated Tribal Development Project (ITDP) has been one such planned development programme. Many areas of development are involved in the tribal sub-plan. Some of the important areas of development programmes are in the field of health, education and irrigation. In an evaluation study conducted by Aphale and Bairagi (1988) in Thane it was found that out of 265 villages surveyed Primary Health Centres, 101 villages (38%) had no State Transport facility.[23] Case studies of PHCs also revealed that there is no awareness among tribals to attend the PHCs. But this fact is belied by the work of some of the voluntary organizations run by Dr Vikas Amate for the tribals in Chandrapur district. Many tribals wait for hours together to take medicines from him. A residential school is also maintained by this voluntary organization.[24]

As regards, the irrigation sector, it was observed that due to poor economic conditions individual cultivators cannot avail the benefits of irrigation schemes. In a survey conducted by the Tribal Development Officer, Thane, it was noted that out of 493 pumps surveyed 264(54%) were in not in use, further, out of 12 irrigation wells supported by subsidy, 6 could not be put into use due to non-availability of pump sets. Hence, repair and maintenance should become part and parcel of the tribal or rural subsidy programmes.[25] Money or cash economy is totally an alien system of economic transaction for the tribes whose economy is based on subsistence and barter.

Agriculture is one of the most crucial activities of the tribals in Maharashtra. However, indebtedness, fragmentation of land and land alienation in spite of the Land Restoration Acts are some of the problems faced by the tribals. A survey[26] in indebtedness and bonded labourers in Thane District indicates that 31.19% tribal families were found indebted in contrast to 11.6% non-tribals. The Katkaris are more indebted than Malhar Kolis and Warlis. It was also observed that the number of indebted families were more (56.38%) among cultivators than among agricultural labour families (22.22%). 7.8% of the sample families were found to be bonded labourers. This is due to the primitive nature of their technology which was more adapted with the forest eco-system. The forest cover is constantly eroding in Maharashtra to well below 10% of its total geographical area. A tribal cannot easily adjust to the changing lifestyle. The other tribes for example Mahadev Kolis who are at higher technological and cultural level interact comparatively more with their neighbouring caste and communities and assimilate many new cultural elements. Welling A.N. (1934) a student of Professor G.S. Ghurye, pioneer of Indian Sociology conducted a detailed anthropological study of the Katkaris.

Welling describing the tribes wrote:

> Katkari culture is peculiar in its own way. It is so simple, so rudimentary and at times so primitive. The Katkari builds a hut, can make fire with the help of flint and iron, makes his own bow and arrows (not the arrowblade) and hunts singly or in a group, can construct fishing dams and weirs, basket traps, nets and can catch fish, eats cooked food, uses cloth and covers his body and nakedness with corresponding ideas of modesty and shame, has a marriage institution, is monogamous in practice and lives in his own hut with wife and children, has a tribal council and has to obey to some

> extent its decisions regarding social matters. He celebrates some Hindu festivals but primarily worships animistic gods. Believes in black magic and its efficacy in doing harm to others, has some folk tales, folk songs and folk dances, cremates his dead and cares not for life after death.

The above description and physical type of the Katkari gives us an idea of his aborginality, technology, social organization and culture of the Katkaris. During 1930 they were purely in hunting and pastoral sage. At the same time because of contacts with caste[27] Hindus during the last 65 years he has also gradually adopted Hindu cultural elements. But in comparison to tribes like Mahadev Koli who are at the cultivator stage of technology and economy the process of acculturation or assimilation of new technological or urban cultural elements among Katkaris is slow and many times creates conflicts resulting in their displacement, deepening of economic crises, and crises of cultural identity.

A notable and welcome feature is that the moneylender as a dominating agency of loan is reduced at present to 2%. The government societies and banks are proving to be useful sources of economic support. This survey also reveals that out of 63%, borrowing co-operative societies account for 36%, banks account for 14% and Government for 13%.

The Adivasi Co-operative Societies under the Tribal Development Corporation are another important source of development in the 10 tribal districts of Maharashtra : Pune, Ahmednagar, Amaravati, Nashik, Thane, Dhule, Bhandara, Nagpur, Yavatmal and Chandrapur. The scheme is meant to help the small land holders and the landless in the form of providing loan for their economic upliftment in the field of dairy, agriculture, purchase of forest produce, providing grains, etc. However, the impact of tribal development programmes has been negligible because of a number of barriers like faulty nature and implementation of programmes, lack of sincerity, etc. The Forest Labourers Co-operative Societies rose from 11 to 422 during a period of 30 years with membership increase from 508 to 56,400. This is a basic indicator of there increasing development participation.

As regards development of tribal education in the Thane Block there was a slight increase of 3.77% literacy for census period of 1971 to 1981. As far as the reservations of jobs are concerned, the State government has reservation quota of 7% for Scheduled Tribes (ST) and 4% for VJ/NT which is based on the proportion of each category to the total population.[28] However, low level of literacy is an inhibiting factor for all the tribal categories to avail this facility. The Government should concentrate on primary education of VJ/NT and ST children along with providing appropriate occupational support.

Conclusion

We have so far examined the demographic, social, occupational and development aspects and problems relating to the Scheduled Tribes. The Denotified Tribes and Nomadic Tribes of Maharashtra. These communities fall at different points of tribe-caste continuum. The demographic and geographical concentration of the tribals in the forest and hilly mountainous districts of Dhule, Thane, Nashik in the Western region namely in the Sahayadri and Satpura range and in the Northern and Eastern region of Gondwana belt indicates an organic linkage between the Scheduled Tribes and the forest, mountainous isolated habitats. They are one of the earliest aboriginal, indigenous communities of the region. Tribes in Maharashtra today are at different levels of technology, economy and sociocultural organizations. There are hunting and pastoral tribes like Katkari and Pardhi as well as agricultural tribes like Gond, Mahadev Koli, Warli and Bhil. Majority of tribes in Maharashtra belong to the Dravidian stock which have migrated from Southern regions and a few from the Western and Northern regions of India.

The Census figures indicate a decline of 30 to 40% in the cultivators or agriculture occupation. Several factors like: primitive shifting cultivation; Slash and burn cultivation; growing industrialization; river valley projects and large dams; Urbanisation, commercial nature of National Forest Policy; Non-recognition and lesser importance to tribals; and lack of a cultural-ecological perspective of tribal development together have been responsible for this situation. A disastrous, consequence of all these cumulative factors has been the emergence of conflicts, and tension, ultimately displacing the tribals to the urban centers in search of new sources of livelihood like non-agricultural labour in: construction, industries, quarrying, jobs, nomadic business, and criminal activities. The percentage of urban tribals is relatively more in districts like Nagpur, Yavatmal, Chandrapur and Greater Bombay. Various rulers and kings belonging to Moghuls and Rajputs and Marathas have also pressurized the tribes like Gonds, Pardhis, Kaikadi and Bhil to move into the interior regions. The social organization of the tribes reveals the presence of social units like *phratry*, clan, exogamous practices of marriage, practices of taboo, totemic and magical practices and beliefs in tribal as well as Hindu Gonds. Preserving the habitats and forests should therefore be a top agenda in tribal development.

The 14 denotified tribes (VJ) were once the criminal tribes during the British period. Out of the 14, two namely Kaikadi and Raj Pardhi are the Scheduled Tribes in the Southern and Western India Region. The remaining 12 are tribes who have migrated into Maharashtra from the Southern states largely because of their hunting, pastoral and artisan skills and occupations which by their very nature are nomadic. A large majority of these people live in abject poverty in slums and settlements in various cities and towns of Western and Central Maharashtra. These settlements in the slums of various towns and cities reflect the picture of indigenous nomadic communities whose socio-economic health and cultural life is a broken one. Loan facilities are provided to the needy by the Vasantrao Naik Vimukta Jati and Bhatkya Jamati Mahamandal. But unfortunately, the impact of these schemes is negligible. Manual labour both by men, women and children and petty jobs, business and criminal activities are the hallmarks of these people. Socially and culturally they are more akin to the Scheduled Tribes than the Nomadic Tribes.

The Scheduled Tribes can be represented on one end of the continuum or model while the Nomadic Tribes can be represented at the other. The Denotified Tribes of Maharashtra who exhibit both tribal as well as caste characteristics can be placed in between the two ends of the continuum. In a nutshell, the poor economic state of affairs of the Denotified Tribes and Nomadic Tribes of

Maharashtra is directly related to the collapse of the forest and natural resource base of the Scheduled Tribes, commercial bias of the National Forest Policy and various push and pull factors such as rapid industrialization and urbanization and simultaneous decrease of cultivation.

There are 28 small nomadic communities who practice occupations of pastoral, religious services and alms, entertainment weaving of mats, etc. They have reciprocal social and economic relationships with the cultivator caste thereby they even exhibit certain rural or caste characteristics. Some of the NTs have settled down in the villages of Western Maharashtra and are treated as a caste with a social position in the village social structure. In the changing circumstances many nomadic communities can no longer sustain on their primitive traditional occupation because of the growing trends of urbanization as a way of life especially in the developed villages of Western Maharashtra. Various conflicts and tensions among rural cultivator castes and the pastoral nomadic communities like the Golla, Gavalis, increasing popularity of TV/ Films and the decreasing importance of traditional skills and acrobatics have caused problems of adjustments. As a result there are negative effects as well as positive shifts in the occupations. For instance some NTs like Nandiwale originally from Andhra Pradesh who have migrated to Maharashtra have now settled down as cultivators. Educational facilities and reservations in jobs are being utilized by these communities. Many families among the Nath Panth Davari Gosavi are working as primary school teachers, clerks and officials in the state/private organization and even as doctors in Kolhapur district. Caste organization of NTs are helping them to organize themselves and fight for their rights. However, a few numerically dominant as well as electorally, politically and economically well-off communities have staked a claim as NTs and are now competing with the numerically small NTs who are economically poor and needy. The State government must give due weightage to claims of genuine communities from these reserved categories on the basis of sociological and anthropological community studies. Exact Census figures of the communities are not available. The State government, research organization and universities should come forward to conduct scientific studies of these communities and suggest programmes for their implementation and upliftment. An important future thrust area of the anthropological/sociological studies should be on studying the socio-ecological adaptation patterns in the context of their natural habitats as well as there social interaction and social environment.

Hence, the development of various categories of tribals in Maharashtra today requires a perspective which should be economic as well as socio-ecological or cultural-ecological. The bottlenecks involved in the various development programmes need to be carefully addressed to and corrected with the help of a team of interdisciplinary social-scientists.

NOTES AND REFERENCES

1. Vidyarthi, L.P. and B.K. Rai, 1976, *The Tribal Culture of India*, New Delhi: Concept.
2. Mane Laxman, Vimuktyan (Marathi), 1997, *A Study of Denotified Tribes in Maharashtra*, pp. 1-10, pp. 181-286. Yeshwantao Chavan Pratishtan, Mumbai.
3. Gadgil, Madhav and K.C. Malhotra, 1994, "The Ecological Significance of Caste", pp. 27-38, in *Social Ecology* (ed) Ramachandra Guha, Delhi: Oxford.
4. Maharashtra Census Directorate *District Census Hand Book* (Kolhapur) Series-14 Part XII A & R, Government Central Press, Mumbai, 1991.
5. Director of Census Operations, *Census of India Maharashtra*, 1991 Series-14 Part-II (i) Primary Census Abstract General Population, Bombay.
6. District Census Hand Book (Kolhapur), 1991 op.cit.
7. Director of Census Operations Maharashtra, *Census of India*, 1981. Series-12, Maharashtra special Tables for Scheduled Tribes, Part IX (iii), Bombay.
8. Bokil, Milind, 1995, 'Bhatkya Vimuktnachi Lokasankhya Nemaki Keeti' (Marathi) in *Saptaljk Sakal*, 92-100, 21st October.
9. Vasantrao Naik Vimukta Jati and Bhatkya Jamati Vikas Mahamandal, Information Booklet on DNT and NT, (Marathi) Bombay, 1984 (pp. 19-25)
10. Bokil, Milind op. cit., pp. 92-95.
11. Jain, Navinchandra, "Land Reforms, Prevention of Atrocities and Ameliorative measures for Tribal in Maharashtra State" in *Tribal*

Research Bulletin, Vol.SVII, No2, Sept, 1995,pp115. Also see Singh, Indrajeet, 1994; pp. 4-8. *The Gondwana and Gonds*, for his description of climatic condition, vegetation, birds and animals, fish, minerals etc.

12. Census of India, 1981 on Scheduled Tribes, op cit.
13. Ibid.
14. Ibid.
15. Mane, Laxman, op. cit
16. Mane, Laxman, op. cit., p. 188-200.
17. Ghurye, G.S., 1963, *The Mahadev Kolis* (A Scheduled Tribe), pp. 1-60, Bombay: Popular Prakashan.
18. Gare, G.M. and M.B. Aphale, 1982, *The Tribes of Maharashtra*, Tribal Research & Training Institute, Pune, 1982,
19. Gare, G.M. and M.B. Aphale op. cit., pp. 35-39.
20. Ibid, pp. 11-15.
21. Ibid, pp. 60-65.
22. Ibid,.
23. Aphale M.B. and K.V. Bairagi, 1988, "Evaluation Study of Integrated Tribal Development Project, Thane-I, Jawahar". In Gare, G.M. (ed). *Review of Tribal Studies*. op. cit., pp. 60-67.
24. I personally visited this Health Centre during the Marathi Sociological Conference held at Chandrapur.
25. Aphale M.B. and K.V. Bairagi in Gare G.M. (ed). op. cit., pp. 63-66.
26. Surana, M.B., "A Survey of Indebtedness and Bonded Labour in Thane District (Maharashtra) in 1979" in Gare, G.M., Govind (ed). op. cit., pp. 25-27.
27. Gare, G.M. and D.T. Biragi "Contribution of Forest Labourers Co-operative Societies, Their Limitations and Possibilities" in *A Review of Tribal Research Studies* (ed.) by Gare, G.M., Govind, Tribal Research & Training Institute, Pune, Maharashtra, 1988, pp. 1-3.
28. Government of Maharashtra. A Booklet on Reservations for Backward Communities, General Administration, Government Press, Mumbai, 1992.

[illegible] Programme [illegible]
[illegible] Tamil Nadu and the [illegible]
of [illegible] and [illegible]

[illegible] Technical [illegible]

[illegible]
[illegible]
[illegible] Engineering [illegible]
[illegible]
[illegible] Research Institute, Pune, 1983.
[illegible]

[illegible] 1986 [illegible]
[illegible]
[illegible] during [illegible]
[illegible] Conference [illegible]
[illegible] survey of [illegible]
[illegible]

[illegible] Central Board of Irrigation and Power [illegible]
[illegible]
[illegible]
[illegible]
[illegible]

Twenty

Identity and Development of the Scheduled Tribe, Scheduled Caste and Other Backward Class in MP

T.K. VAISHNAV

I
SCHEDULED TRIBES

Madhya Pradesh has the largest tribal population in India. The population of Scheduled Tribes in the State is 1,53,99034 which works out to 23.27 per cent of the total population of 6,61,81,170 according to the census 1991. 22.73 per cent tribal population of the country lives in Madhya Pradesh. The Scheduled Tribes living in the State have been categorized in the 46 groups according to the Scheduled Tribes order Amendment 1976. The population size, socio-economic activities and education level of these also varies considerably. On the one hand there are groups like Gonds and Bhils who respectively have population, exceeding 53.5 lakhs and 25 lakhs, while on the other hand there are some tribal groups like Birhor, Karku, Mina, Kolam, Andh which in 1981 had a population less than one thousand. The level of development, acculturation, and assimilation also varies from group to group and also from area to area. So a short introduction and classification of the tribes of the State can be stated as below:

1. Introduction - based on cultural & geographical area
2. Introduction - based on population
3. Introduction - based on economical life
4. Introduction - based on development
5. Introduction - based on language
6. Introduction - based on racial characteristics
7. Introduction - based on educational level

1. Introduction based on Cultural and Geographical classification

The tribal population of the State can be divided into 5 cultural and Geographical zones based on their bonafide residential area.

(a) North-Eastern Tribal zone

This zone is densely forested and it is a hilly area and includes the tribal area of Surguja, Sidhi, Raigarh and Bilaspur districts. The inhabitants of this zone are Oraon, Kanwar, Kol, Dhanwar, Korwa, Bhaina, Saonta, Gond, Munda, Nagesia, Bhumia, Panika, Biyar, Khairwar, Majhwar, Majhi, Kharia, Saora and Birhor Tribes.

(b) South Tribal Zone

This is densely forested and it is a hilly area and includes the tribal area of Bastar Raipur, Durg, and Rajnandgaon districts. The inhabitants of this zone are Madia, Muria, Gond, Halba, Bhatra, Dorla, Parja, Kamar, Bhujia, Binjhwar, Sawara, Kanwar, Kondh, Gadaba and Shikari-pardhi tribes.

(c) Central Tribal Zone

This zone is also densely forested and it is a hilly area. It includes the tribal area of Mandla, Shahdol, Sioni, Chhindwara, Betul, Balaghat, Hoshangabad and Jabalpur districts. The inhabitants of this zone are Gond, Baiga, Kol, Pardhan, Bharia, Bhumia, Korku, Mawasi, Pao and Agaria tribes.

(d) Western Tribal Zone

This zone includes the tribal area of Jhabua, Dhar, Khargoan (West Nimar), Khandwa (East Nimar) and Ratlam districts. Inhabitants of this zone are Bhil, Bhilala, Barela Damor, Karku and Patelia tribes.

(e) North - West Tribal Zone

This zone includes the tribal area of Morena, Shivpuri and Guna districts. The inhabitants of this zone are the Saharia tribe.

2. Introduction based on Demographic Classification

Tribal groups of MP are divided into following categories based on their population of Census 1981.

(a) More than 50,00,000 : This Category includes Gond and sub groups (53,49,883)

(b) 25,00,000 to 50,00,000	:	This Category includes Bhil and sub groups (25,00,530)
(c) 1,00,000 to 25,00,000	:	This Category includes Kanwar and sub group (5,62,199) Saharia (2,61,816), Baiga (2,48,948), Halba (2,36,376), Bharia and sub group (1,95,490), Kol (1,23,810) and Bhatra (1,17,297).
(d) 75,000 to 1,00,000	:	This Category includes Oraon and sub group (88,817) and Binjhwar (92,080),
(e) 50,000 to 75,000	:	This Category includes Saur (68,034), Korku (66,781), Sawara (63,774), Agaria (55,757), Panika (52,980) and Sonr (48,658).
(f) 25,000 to 50,000	:	In this Category major tribes are Bahina (39,135), Dhanwar (34,386) tribe.
(g) 1,000 to 25,000	:	In this Category includes Pardhan (18,234), Kamar (17,516), Korwa (15,341), Nagesi (14,473), Khairwar(14,375), Mahji (11,074), Mawasi (11,011), Keer (9,893), Bhunjia (9,524), Pardhi, Bahalia and Shikari (8,065), Pao (7,222), Kharia (6,892), Majhwar (6,509) Bhil Mina (5,358), Gadaba (3,255), Saunta (3,173), Pardhi (1,830), Kondh (1,670), Munda (1,579), Parja (1,409) and Damar (1,110).
(h) Less than 1,000	:	Birhore (561), Karku (470), Mina (382), Kolam (299) and Andh (151).

3. Introduction based on Socio-economic Activities

Classification based on Socio-economic Activities of the tribal groups of MP are given below:

(a) Food gathering, hunting & fishing

The most undeveloped tribe like Birhore and Pahari Korwa belong to this category. Their economic life depends on the collection of roots, tuber, fruit, leaf and other forest products. They hunt rabbit, rat, deer, bear, wildcat, monkey and birds. They also catch small fish, crab, tortoise, Pila and Unio for their own food.

(b) Primitive agriculture, hunting and food gathering

This tribal category are mainly dependant on primitive cultivation, hunting and forest products collection. In some isolated area they are doing 'Jhum' cultivation even know. Abujhmaria and Kamar tribes are examples of this group. Baiga, Pando, Kol, Majhi and Bharia of Patalkot also belongs to this group.

(c) Settled Cultivation

This tribal category depends on settled cultivation, collection, of forest products. They are Bhinjhwar, Sawara, Muria, Halba, Bhil, Bhatra, Bhunjia, Bhumia, Korku, Kanwar, Oraon, Majhwar, Majhi, Mawasi, Munda, Nagesia, Bhaina, Sour, etc. Before 3-4 decades hunting was also in their practice. At present in some occasions they hunt rabbit, wild cat, boar, deer and birds.

(d) Advanced cultivation

This tribal group are in contact with other advanced communities. They have learnt advanced cultivation technique and nowadays they are doing advanced cultivation. They are Tanwar, Bhilala, Rajgond, Mina, Kir, etc.

(e) Urban Migrated, & Mining labour

The tribes of this category are mainly Bhil and Saharia. The Bhil of Jhabua, Ratlam, Dhar and Khargone district, migrated for labour in nearest urban areas like Bhopal, Indore, Ujjain, Ahmedabad, Baroda, Dewas, etc. The Saharia of Shivpuri, Guna and Morena districts become Agricultural and Mining labour. Some tribal people also become labour in industries, coal mines and iron mines.

(f) Artisans

Some tribal groups like Kamar, Kandara, Dhanwar, Saunta, Saur, Baiga, Majhi, Pando, Bharia, Dhulia, etc, are doing basketary work along with primitive cultivation, hunting and gathering. 'Shikari Pardhi' tribe also make looms, mats and baskets from palm leaves. Birhor and Khond make rope with bark and grass. Agaria tribe in Mandla, Shahdol and Bilaspur districts melt iron ores and make some agricultural equipments. Khairwar makes Catechu from Khair tree.

(g) Other Works

Bhaima, Koilabhuta, Pardhan, Ojha are sub groups of Gond. Their main occupation is folk dance and folk song through which they earn food grains. Dhulia, Nagarchi, play folk, musical instruments for tribal ceremonies. Badigond and Ojha Gond women make tatoo on other tribal women and get some money.

4. Introduction based on Development

Classification based on development of tribes of MP are described below:

(a) Undeveloped tribal group

They are economically, socially and educationally undeveloped as compared to other tribal groups. This group includes Kamar, Abujhmaria, Pahadi Korwa, Birhore, Saharia, Baiga, Bharia of Patalkot, Pando, etc.

(b) Developing tribal group

These tribal groups are not fully developed. At present they are on the process of development. They are Muria, Madia, Agaria, Bhatara, Bharia, Bhumia, Bhil, Dhanwar, Kharia, Kol, Majhi, Majhwar, Mawasi, Nagesia, Pao, Pardhi, Parja, Saunta, Saur, etc.

(c) Developed tribal groups

These tribal groups are nowadays socio-economically, educationally and politically developed. They ar Rajgond, Bhilala, Mina, Kir, Oraon, Tanwar, Andh, etc.

5. Introduction based on Linguistic Classification

Linguistic classification of tribes of MP are given below:

a) Aryan linguistic group

This tribal group has forgotten their own traditional dialect and nowadays speaks dialects of Indo-Aryan language. For example, Kanwar, Binjhwar, Bhunjia, Dhanwar, Bhaina, Baiga, speaks Chhatisgarhi. Halbi is spoken by Halba. Bundelkhandi is spoken by Saur and Saharia, Bhili dialects are spoken by Bhil, Bilala, Barela, Patelia, Bhil, Mina, etc. Bagheli dialects are spoken by Kol, Bharia, etc.

b) Austric Linguistic group

This group includes Kolarian and Mundari Language speaking tribes. They are Munda (Mundari); Korwa (Korwa dialect); Majhi (Majhi dialect); Korku (Korku dialect); Kharia (Kharia dialect); Gadaba (Gadaba dialect); Birhor, Sawara, etc.

c) Dravidian Linguistic groups

This category includes Gondi or Koya dialects spoken by Gond and sub groups; Kudukh dialect spoken by Oraon, Kui by Kondh and Parji dialect by Parja.

6. Introduction based on Racial Classification

Tribal groups of MP are classified on the basis of racial characteristics they are:

a) Cacasiod mixed racial groups

This group includes those tribes who were originated from the Rajput and tribals. They are Bhil Mina, Bhilala, Patelia, Mina, etc.

b) Proto-Australiod racial group

Other tribal groups belong to Proto Australiod race, some members of this group are Munda, Oraon, Baiga, Korku, Gond, etc.

7. Introduction based on Literacy Percentage

Total literacy per cent of MP is 28.87 according to the census 1981 and 44.2 percent according to the census 1991. Tribal literacy per cent was 10.68 according to 1981 and 21.54 per cent according to 1991 census but the literacy rate is not equal in case of all tribals. So the classification based on the literacy per cent is given below (Census 1981).

a) More than 20% literacy

This group includes Halba (28.76%), Oraon (22.61%), Andh (22.22%), Pardhan (21.93%), and Keer (20.15%), etc. Rajgond, Tanwar, Bhilala sub-group also belong to this group.

b) 15 to 20 per cent literacy

This group includes Kanwar (19.03%), Kondh (17.84%), Munda (17.82%), Sawara (16.41%), Damor (16.28%) and Mina (14.36%).

c) 10 to 15 per cent literacy

This group includes Gadaba (14.87%), Karku (14.71%), Kolam (13.16%), Binjhwar (12.66%), Gond (12.46%), Bhunjia (11.94%), Majhi (11.63%), Bhaina (11.24%), Bhil Mina (10.92%), etc.

d) 5 to 10 per cent literacy

This group includes Panika (9.59%), Shikari Bahelia (8.58%), Nagesia (8.44%), Khairwar (8.38%), Kharia (8.28%), Parja (7.17%), Pao (6.98%), Biyar (6.94%), Bhumia Bharia (6.7%), Korku (6.54%), Bhatara (6.23%), Saur (5.5%), Agaria (5.4%), Kol (5.4%), Bhil (5.38%), Dhanwar (5.35%) Sonr (5%), etc.

e) Less than 5 per cent literacy

This group includes Kamar (4.5%), Mawasi(4.08%), Majhwar (3.92%), Baiga (3.62%), Saunta (3.43%), Korwa (2.83%) Saharia (2.74%), Birhor (1.6%) Pardhi (1.42%) etc.

II
SCHEDULED CASTE

The population of Scheduled Caste in Madhya Pradesh is 96,26,679 which works out 14.55 percent of the total population of 6,61,81,170 according to the Census 1991. The Scheduled Caste living in the State have been categorized into 47 groups according to the Scheduled Caste Order, Amendment 1976. The population, size, socio-econimic activities, education level and development stages of these caste also vary considerably. On one side there are groups like Chamar and sub group whose population is more then 38.45

lakh (52.25% of total SC population in MP). Their literacy per cent is 16.56. (1981). They are more developed as compared to other groups, while on the other hand there are some Scheduled Caste groups like Dhed, Muskan, Chitar, etc, which had population less than one thousand in 1981. Their literacy percentage is very low and they are undeveloped. A short introduction, of the Scheduled Castes of the State are given below :-

1. Introduction based on population and inhabitation
2. Introduction based on traditional economic activities
3. Introduction based on literacy

1. Introduction Based on Population and Habitat

According to the Census 1981 their population and inhabitant area are given in Table 20.1.

TABLE - 20.1
POPULATION AND INHABITATION AREA OF SC OF MP

Population Group	*SC (Population)*	*% of Total SC Population*	*Inhabitat Districts*
1	2	3	4
1. More than 35 lakhs	1. Chamar & sub groups (3,845106)	52.25	All districts of the State.
2. 10 lakhs to 35 lakhs			
3. 1 lakhs to 10 lakhs	2. Balahi (7,15,435)	9.72	Distt of old Madhya Bharat region and Bhopal state, Hoshangabad.
	3. Mahar group (577151)	7.84	All districts of the State.
	4. Koli (3,79,137)	5.15	All districts of the State.
	5. Bhangi group (2,22,039)	3.02	All districts of the State.
	6. Ganda (2,05166)	2.79	Mainly Chhatisgarh region.
	7. Basor group (1,64,630)	2.24	All districts of the State.
	8. Bagari (149080)	2.03	Distts of old Madhya Bharat.
	9. Kumhar (1,21,876)	1.66	Distts. of old Vindhya Pradesh.
4. 75 thousand to 1 lakh	10. Khangar group (96,530)	1.31	Mainly Bundelkhand, Beghelkhand & Old Bhopal state.

(Contd.)

	11. Katiagroup (95,678)	1.38	Mainly Chhindwara, Seoni, distt.
	12. Ghasi group (76,320)	1.04	Chhatisgarh region.
	13. Khatik (75,068)	1.02	All districts of the State.
5. 50,000	14. Barhar (60,789)	0.83	All districts of the State.
6. 25,000 to 50,000	15. Dhanuk (49,391)	0.67	Bhind, Gwalior, Sagar, Jhabua, Indore, Raisen, Vidisha, etc.
	16. Natgroup (44,127)	0.60	Mandsor, Ratlam, Ujjain Shajapur, Indore, Rajgarh.
	17. Chadar (41527)	0.56	Sagar, Damoh, Jabalpur, Narsinghpur.
	18. Dom group (39,873)	0.54	Jabalpur, Raigarh, Satna Rewa, Sidhi, etc.
	19. Dahait Group (37,706)	0.51	Jabalpur, Satna, Panna.
	20. Chidar (35,532)	0.48	Guna, Vidisha, Raisen, Sagar, Shivpuri, etc.
	21. Pasi (30,310)	0.41	Indore, Jabalpur, Chindwara, Ratlam E.N, etc.
	22. Chikawa (27,311)	0.37	Raigarh, Sarguja, Rewa, Satna
7. 10,000 to 25,000	23. Silawat (23,832)	0.32	Raisen, Vidisha, Bhopal. Ratlam, Sehore, Rajgarh etc.
	24. Dhobi (22.487)	0.30	Old Bhopal State.
	25. Moghia (21,487)	0.29	Old Madhya Bharat region
	26. Mano group (17,738)	0.24	Indore, E.Nimar, Betul, Chhindwara, etc.
	27. Beldar (17,617)	0.24	All districts of the state
	28. Banchhada (14,151)	0.19	Mandsor, Indore, Ujjain, Ratlam, Shajapur.
	29. Bargunda (13,626)	0.18	Ujjain, W.Nimar, Indore, Dewas, Ratlam.
	30. Bedia (13,302)	0.18	Guna, Morena, Sagar, Rajgarh, Vidhsha, etc.
	31. Meghwal (11.945)	0.16	Mandsore, W.Nimar, etc.
	32. Daohor (10,836)	0.15	Bhind, Satna, Sehore, Bhopal.
8. 1,000 to 10,000	33. Kanjar (8,554)	0.12	Jabalpur, Shajapur, Dewas, Guna, Rajgarh.
	34. Kotwal (8,362)	0.11	Jhabua, W. Nimar.
	35. Pardhi (7,518)	0.10	Old Madhya Bharat region.

(Contd.)

	36. Dewar (6,568)	0.09	Chhatisgarh region.
	37. Kuchabandia (5,694)	0.08	Sagar, Bhopal, Damoh, Bhind, Jabalpur.
	38. Zamral (3,961)	0.05	W. Nimar, Dewas, Dhar, etc.
	39. Holia (3,363)	0.04	Balaghat, Seoni, Hoshangabad, etc.
	40. Sansi (3,043)	0.04	Rajgarh, Guna, Dewas etc.
	41. Audhelia (2.994)	0.04	Bilaspur
	42. Bahana (1,835)	0.03	Seoni, Sagar, Hoshangabad, Jabalpur.
	43. Rujjhar (1,720)	0.02	Hoshangabad
	44. Bhanumati (1,106)	0.02	Rajgarh, Shajapur, Ujjain etc.
9. Less than 1,000	45. Dhed (886)	0.01	Indore, Dewas, etc.
	46. Chitar (423)	0.006	Raisen, Jabalpur, etc.
	47. Muskan (416)	0.006	Rewa, Satana.

The traditional occupation and literacy per cent of the Scheduled Castes of Madhya Pradesh are given in Table 20.2.

TABLE - 20.2
TRADITIONAL OCCUPATION AND LITERACY PER CENT OF SCHEDULED CASTES IN MP

Caste	*Traditional Occupation (1981)*	*Literacy % (1981)*
(1)	*(2)*	*(3)*
1. Audhelia	Labour & Piggery	22.44
2. Bagri, Bagadi	Robbery, Labour & Basketry by palm leaf.	10.91
3. Bahna, Bahana	Cotton cleaner	25.82
4. Balahi, Balai	Weaver, Village watchman & Messenger	16.91
5. Banchada	Prostitution	8.33
6. Barhar, Basod	Bamboo work and to play on musical Instrument like drum	17.93
7. Bargunda	Making baskets, brooms and mats	10.21
8. Barsor & group	Like S.No. 6	13.24
9. Bedia	Robbery, labour and prostitution	16.69
10. Beldar	Digger and Navvy	20.07
11. Bhangi, Mehtar	Sweeper	24.93
12. Bhanumati	Magician, Fumna bulist and prostitution	17.19
13. Chadar	Weaver and Village watchman	24.29
14. Chamar group	Leather work	16.56
15. Chaidar	Weaver and Village watchman	18.64

(Contd.)

16.	Chaikwa, Chikvi	Weaver	18.74
17.	Chitar	Calico Printing	22.66
18.	Dahait etc.	Village watchman and weaver, labour	23.20
19.	Dewar	Piggery, Beggar and Women do tatoo work.	9.59
20.	Dhanuk	Cotton Cleaner, labour	14.45
21.	Dhed, Dher	Weaver, Labour, Watchman, Scavenger	10.27
22.	Dhobi (Old Bhopal state)	Cloth washing	20.78
23.	Dohor	Leather work	11.18
24.	Dome, Dumar	Village musician & labour, Scavenger	33.06
25.	Ganda, Gandi	Play on drum & weaver, labour	19.96
26.	Ghasi	Grass cutting, labour, sweeper	52.14
27.	Holia	Labourer, Curing hides	18.94
28.	Kanjar	Robbery	22.02
29.	Kotia, Patharia	Spreening, weaver and labour	29.56
30.	Khatik	Butcher, work	34.82
31.	Koli, Kori	Weaver, Labour	26.33
32.	Kotwal	Village watchman, Weaver	8.02
33.	Khangar, Kanera etc.	Village watchman, labour	20.25
34.	Kuchbandhia	Brush maker by pig hair	15.07
34.	Kumhar	Pottery maker	9.37
36.	Mahar	Weaver, Watchman, labour	31.66
37.	Mang group	Drum player, Beggar and mate, Loom maker, etc.	27.58
38.	Meghwal	Weaving, making mats and Labour	18.31
39.	Moghia	Robbery	22.00
40.	Muskhan	Making Leaf cup and Leaf Plate and Rat hunter	6.95
41.	Nut, Kalbelia etc.	Rope dance, Snake catcher, Beggar	6.67
42.	Pardhi	Hunter and fowler	8.76
43.	Pasi	Labour & Piggery	42.65
44.	Rujjhar	Agricultural Labourer	6.66
45.	Sansi	Robbery	18.80
46.	Silawat	Stone work	22.10
47.	Zamral	Basketary	8.28

Development

The Scheduled Caste of MP can be divided into three categories on the basis of their socio-economic and educational development. They are given below:

(a) Developed Scheduled Caste

They are Pasi, Mahar, Katia, Khatic, Ghasi, Dhobi, Kumhar. etc.

(b) Developing Scheduled Caste

They are Audhelia, Bahana, Balahi, Basod, Beldar, Bhangi, Bhanumati, Chadar, Chamar, Chidar, Chikwa, Chitar, Dahayat, Dhanuk, Dhed, Dohar, Dom, Ganda, Holia, Kanjar, Kori, Kotwal, Khangar, Kuchbandhia, Mang, Meghwal, Moghia, Sansi, Silawat, etc.

(c) Undeveloped Scheduled Caste

They ar Banchada, Bedhia, Dewar, Muskan, Nat (Kalbelia, Kobootar, Sapere, etc.) Pardhi, Rujjar, Bagri of old Madhya Bharat region, Bargunda, etc.

Other Backward Class

Madhya Pradesh has the largest number of other backward classes. Latest census figure is not available but according to Directorate of Backward Class Welfare, Govt. of MP their population is 256.93 lakhs in 1982. It is 48.08 per cent of the total population of the state. According to the Ministry of other Backward Classes and Minority Welfare, Govt. of MP Order No. 23-4.97-54-1 dt. 2.4.1997, the OBC's are categorized into 87 groups.

The level of development, acculturation educational status, traditional occupation and assimilation also varies from group to group and area to area.

The names of the caste and their traditional occupation are given in Table 20.3.

TABLE - 20.3
NAME OF CASTES AND TRADITIONAL OCCUPATIONS

Sl. No.	*Name of the Caste, Sub-caste & Groups*	*Traditional Occupation.*
(1)	*(2)*	*(3)*
1.	Ahir, Brajwasi, Gavali, Goli, Jadav (Yadav), Bargahi, Bargah, Thethawar, Raut, Gowari (Gwari), Gobara, Gwara, Mahakul, Mahkul, Gop, Gawali, Lingayat,	Animal husbandry, Cow herds & milk seller (milkman)
2.	Asara, Asada	Cultivation, labour
3.	Bairagi (Vaishnav)	Religious mendicants, Priest and Beggar.

(Contd.)

4.	Banjara,Banjari, Mathura, Naik, Naikada, Dhuria, Labhana, Labaria, Lamane.	Pack carrier, Salt, Palm and Sugar seller
5.	Barai, Tamoli, Tamboli, Kumawat, Kumavat, Chaurasia.	Betel - wine grower and seller
6.	Barhai, Sutar, Dawej, Kunder (Vishvakarma)	Carpenter.
7.	Bari	Maker of Leaf plates
8.	Vasudeo, Basudeo, Basudewa, Vasu-dewa, Harbola, Kapadia, Kapadi, Godhali, Tharwar.	Religious beggar, Glory singer, cattle dealer
9.	Bhadbhunjia, Bhunjawa, Bhurji.	Grain parcher
10.	Bhat, Charan, Sutia, Salwi, Rao Janmalodi, Jasodhi, Maroosonia.	Bard and genealogist.
11.	Chhipa, Bhavasar, Nilgar, Jingar, nirali, Rangari, Mandhav	Dryer and Calico-printer,
12.	Dhimar, Bhoi, Kahar, Dhiwar, Mallah, Navada, Turha, Keot (Kashyap, Nishad, Raikwar, Bathan) Kir (excluded Bhopal, Sehore & Raisen distt.) Britia, Singaraha, Jalari (Jalaranalu in Bastar) Sondhia.	Fisherman, Boatman, Water carrier, household servant, palanquin bearer.
13.	Pawar, Power, Bhoyar	Cultivator
14.	Bhutia, Bhurtia	Animal husbandry and milk seller
15.	Bhopa, Manbhaw	Religious beggar
16.	Bhatiara	Meals cooked by Bhatthi in communal use
17.	Chungar, Chunkar,Kulbandhia, Rajgir	Mason work
18.	Chitari	Wall painting
19.	Darji, Chhipi, Shipi, Mawi (Namdeo)	Tailoring
20.	Dhobi (Excluded Bhopal, Sehore, Raisen distt.)	Washerman
21.	Mina (Rawat), Deshwali, Mewati, Mina (excluded Sironj sub division of Vidisha distt.)	Cultivation
22.	Kirar, Kirad, Dhakad	Cultivation
23.	Gadaria, Dhangar, Kurmar, Hatgar, Hatkar, Gadari, Dharia, Ghoshi (Godaria), Gari, Gairi, Gadaria (Pal, Gaghel).	Shepherd
24.	Kadere, Dhunkar, Dhunia, Dhanka, Kodar.	Cotton cleaner
25.	Koshta, Koshti (Dewangan), Kosta, Mala, Padmsali, Sali, Sutsali, Salwar, Salvi, Dewang, Jandra, Koskati, Koskati (Lingayat), Gadwal, Gadewal, Garewal, Garwal, Dukar, Kolhati	Weaver

(Contd.)

26.	Dholi, Dafali, Dafali, Dholi, Damani, Gurao	Shiv temple priest and Dhol (Drum) player.
27.	Gusai, Gaswami	Religious medicant, Shiv temple priest & religious bagger.
28.	Gujar (gurjar)	Pastoral and cultivation.
29.	Lohar, Luhar, Lohpita, Gadole, Hunga, Lohar, Lohpatha, Gadola Lohar (Vishwakarma)	Blacksmith.
30.	Garpagari, Nathjogi, Joginath, Haridas.	Averter of hailstorms and religious beggar.
31.	Ghoshi	Buffalo, herdsman
32.	Sonar, Sunar, Jhani, Jhadi Swarnakar, Awadhia, Audhia, Soni.	Goldsmith (Ornament made by Gold & Silver).
33.	(a) Kachhi (Kushwah, Shakya, Mourya), Koirior Koiri (Kushwaha), Panara, Murai, Sonkar. (b) Mali (Saini), Marar	Vegetable cultivator
34.	Joshi (Bhaddari), Dakocha, Dakota	Astrology and get *shani* alms.
35.	Lakhera, Lakher, Kachera, Kacher	Maker of glass bangles and Lac work
36.	Thathera, Kasar, Kasera, Tamera, Tambatkar, Otari, Tamrakar, Tamer, Ghadawa, Jharia.	Copper, Brass & Bronze, Utensil maker
37.	Khatia, Khatis, Khati.	Cultivator
38.	Kumhar (Prajapati), Kumbhar (Chhatarpur, Datia, Panna, Tikamgarh, Satana, Rewa, Sidhi and Shahdol distt. are excluded)	Pottery maker
39.	Kurmi, Kurmar, Kunabi, Kurmi, Patidar, Kurmvanshi, Chandrakar, Chandnahu, Kulmi, Kulami, Gavel (Gamel), Kumbhi, Sirvi.	Cultivation
40.	Kamaria	Pastoral, milk seller.
41.	Kaurav, Kavare	Cultivation
42.	Kalar (Jaysawal), Kalal, Dadsena	Liquor vendor
43.	Kalauta, Kalauta, Kolata, Kolata	Cultivation
44.	Lonia, Lunia, Od, Ode, Odia, Naunia, Muraha, Muraha, Mudaha, Mudaha.	Digger, Navvy and salt-refiner
45.	Nai (Sen, Savita, Usarete, Shrivash) Mhali, Nahvi, Sarete.	Barber (Hair cutting)
46.	Nayata, Nayada.	Agriculture Labour, small farmer
47.	Panaka, Panika (excluded Chhatarpur, Panna, Datia, Tikamgarh, Satana, Rewa, Sidhi, Shahdol distt.	Weaver, Village Watchman & labour

(Contd.)

48.	Pataka, Pataki, Patawa	Maker of Silk braid and thread
49.	Lodhi, Lodha, Lodh	Cultivator
50.	Sikaligar	Armourers and Knife grinders
51.	Teli (That, Sahu, Rathaur)	Oilman Oil grinder and seller)
52.	Turha, Tirwali, Vaddar, Mirdha	Digger and stone carving
53.	Tavayaf, Kisabi, Kasabi	Prostitution and dance (Mujra)
54.	Bavaria	Agricultural labour
55.	Rotia Rautia	Cultivator and formerly soldier
56.	Mankar, Nahal	Forest product collection, cultivation
57.	Kotwal, Kotwal (Bhind, Dhar, Dewas, Guna, Gwalior, Indore, Jhabua, Khargone, Mansor, Morena, Rajgarh, Ratlam, Shajapur, Shivpuri, Ujjain, and Vidisha distt. are excluded).	Village watchman & labour
58.	Khairuwa	Boilers of Catechu
59.	Kodha (Tanwar)	Cultivation, Labour
60.	Mowar	Cultivation
61.	Rajwar	Agricultural labour
62.	Agharia	Cultivation
63.	Tior, Turi	Bamboo worker, fishing & Boating
64.	Bharud	Transportation of cattle
65.	Sut, Sarthi, Sais, Sahis	Horse keeper and Charioteer.
66.	Telanga, Tilaga	Agriculture Labour
67.	Raghavi	Cultivation
68.	Rajbhar	Agricultural labour
69.	Kharol	Agricultural labour
70.	Sargara	Dhol (drum) player
71.	Golan, Gaolan, Golan	Cattle hards and milk seller.
72.	Rajjad, Rajjhad	Agricultural labour
73.	Jadam	Agricultural labour
74.	Dangi	Cultivation
75.	Gyar, Parghania	Agricultural labour and fowler.
76.	Kudami	Cultivation
77.	Mer	Agricultural labour
78.	Baya Mahara, Kaushal, Bayer	Weaver
79.	Pinjara (Hindu)	Cotton cleaner
80.	(Delete)	
81.	Scheduled Caste who change religion Hindu to Christian or Muslim.	
82.	Anjana	Cultivation
83.	Dhoria	
84.	Gehlot, Newada	Cultivation
85.	Rewari	Shephard
86.	Ruala, Ruhela	Cultivation

(Contd.)

87. Muslim religion groups

1.	Rangrej	Calico dyer
2.	Bhisti	Waterman.
3.	Chhipa	Dyer and calico printer
4.	Hela	Sweeper
5.	Bhatiyara	Cook
6.	Dhobi	Washerman
7.	Mewati	Cultivation & Pastoral
8.	Pinjara, Naddof, Fakir, Behana, Dhunia, Dhunkar	Cotton cleaner
9.	Kunjada, Rain	Vegetable seller
10.	Manihar	Glass bangles seller
11.	Kasar, Kasab	Mutton butcher
12.	Mirasi	Barad, Singer, Genealogist
13.	Mirdha	Watchman
14.	Barhai (carpenter)	Carpentery Work
15.	Hajjam (Barbar)	Hair cutting
16.	Hammal	Labour
17.	Julaha, Momin	Weaver
18.	Luhar, Nagori	Black smithy
19.	Tadavi	Cultivation
20.	Banjara	Pack carrier, cattle seller
21.	Mochi	Shoes maker
22.	Teli, Nayata, Pindari (Pindara) Kankar	Oil man
23.	Pemadi	Nursery work (Plant beeding)
24.	Kalaigar	Tin coat on utensil
25.	Halband	To shoe a horse & bullock
26.	Shishgar	Glass work

Twenty One

Development of Scheduled Tribes in Andhra Pradesh: An Overview

D. RAJESHWAR *and* **K. SUMAN CHANDRA**

Introduction

Andhra Pradesh, the fifth most populous State of India spreads over an area of 27,000 Sq. Kms. covering 8.7. per cent of the country's geographical area, accommodating 7.9 per cent (665 lakh) of the country's population. The population is pivotally rural and the principal economic activity of 73 per cent of the State population is agriculture.

In the State of Andhra Pradesh the population of Scheduled Tribes is 41.99 lakh (6.20% ofAll-India tribal population) comprising of 33 Scheduled Tribal Groups (Table 21.1) dispersed throughout the State in varying concentrations. Of the 71 Primitive Tribal Groups in India, eight are found in the State (Table 21.2). The levels of literacy among the tribals in the State is depressing, though recording a percentage increase from around 7.80 per cent in 1981 to around 14 per cent as made available in the 1991 Census.

The tribe wise population of the tribes of Andhra Pradesh is given in Table 21.1.

TABLE - 21.1
POPULATION OF EACH SCHEDULED TRIBE IN ANDHRA PRADESH 1961, 1971 AND 1981 CENSUSES

Name of the Scheduled Tribe	*1961*	*1971*	*1981*
1. Andh	1468	2405	5994
2. Bagata	55154	71657	87994
3. Bhil	83	560	259
4. Chenchu (PTG) Chenchwar	17609	24178	28434
5. Gadaba	1840	25108	27632
6. Gond Naikpod Rajgond	143680	157489	169477

(Contd.)

	Name of the Scheduled Tribe	1961	1971	1981
7.	Goudu*	3392	N/A	8962
8.	Hill Reddi	3894	4306	398
9.	Jatapu	62794	74310	86506
10.	Kammara	24629	35679	36548
11.	Kattunayakan	74	289	399
12.	Kolam (PTG) Mannevarlu	16731	26498	21842
13.	Konda Dora	86911	101556	131238
14.	Konda Kapu	29823	38126	28033
15.	Konda Reddi (PTG)	35439	42777	54685
16.	Kondh Kodi, Kodhu, Desaya Khond, Dongria Khondh (PTG), Kutia Khondh (PTG), Tikiria Kondh, Yenity Khondh.	21754	34375	39408
17.	Kotia, Bentho Oriya, Bartika, Dhulia, Dulia, Holva, Paiko, Putiya, Sanrona, Sidhopaiko	11008	17888	31466
18.	Koya, Goud, Rajah, Rash Koya Lingadhari Koya (ordinary), Kottu Koya, Bhine Koya, Raj Koya	220146	285226	359799
19.	Kulia	85	188	413
20.	Malis @	1433	1978	2467
21.	Manne Dhora	8476	9372	18964
22.	Mukha Dhora, Nooka Dhora	9965	13235	17456
23.	Nayak*	2902	3971	6532
24.	Pardhan	9701	11407	16023
25.	Poroja, Parangi Poroja (PTG)	9350	12357	16479
26.	Reddi Dhora	3132	5254	5281
27.	Rona, Rena	23	12	232
28.	Savara, Kapu Savara, Maliya Savara, Khutto Savara, Konda Savara (PTG)	68185	81227	82101
29.	Sugali, Lambada	96174	132468	1158342
30.	Thoti #(PTG)	546	1785	1416
31.	Vaimiki*	22354	28967	42944
32.	Yanadi	205381	239403	320444
33.	Yerukula	128024	162560	300557
34.	Unspecified	2198	11050	59276
	Total	1324368	1657657	3176001

* In the agency tracts.

@ Excluding Adilabad, Hyderabad, Karimnagar, Khammam, Mahabubnagar, Medak, Nalgonda, Nizamabad and Warangal Districts.

\# In Adilabad, Hyderabad, Karimnagar, Khammam, Mahabubnagar, Medak, Nalgonda, Nizamabad and Warangal Districts.

TABLE - 21.2
LIST OF PRIMITIVE TRIBAL GROUPS IN ANDHRA PRADESH

1.	Chenchu
2.	Gadaba - Bodo Gadaba Gutob Gadaba
3.	Kolam (Mannevarlu)
4.	Khond - Kutia Khond Dongria Khond
5.	Konda Savaras
6.	Konda Reddis
7.	Poroja - Bondo Poroja Khond Poroja Parengi Poraja
8.	Thoti

Classification

Considering the areas of habitation and the levels of development, the tribal groups are classified as:

1. Living in areas of tribal concentration (ITDAs)
2. Small pockets of tribal concentration (MADA)
3. Dispersed Tribal Groups (DTG)
4. Primitive Tribal Groups (PTG)

The development strategy for these groups varied from area to area and group to group depending on the local potentialities, economy and human resources. The Scheduled Tribes of the State of Andhra Pradesh are being assisted under various designs, in view of their social, political and economic conditions.

- Under the Integrated Tribal Development Project Approach for the core groups living in identified contiguous areas of tribal concentration in the eight districts of Adilabad, East Godavari, Khammam, Srikakulam, Visakhapatnam, Vizianagaram, Warangal and West Godavari, of the State.
- Tribals living outside the TSP area with a percentage of acclimatization to the outside world characterized with their agriculture being more advanced to that of the shifting cultivators and better responses to external development intervention, found in concentration in smaller area i.e. 41 MADA pockets and 17 clusters.
- Primitive Tribal Groups who are at the extreme end of the scale who survive on pre-agricultural pursuits like food gathering, hunting, collection of non-timber forest produce (NTFP), etc, eking out their living with pre-agricultural levels of technology inhabiting remote, inaccessible areas far away from the mainstream.

- Dispersed Tribal Groups living all over the State, scattered amidst plains population are assisted in a different approach as they are more responsive to development initiatives and their needs are in parallelism to other weaker sections of the general population of non-tribals.

Occupations

According to their traditional occupations the tribal groups can be categorized into:

1. Food gathering and hunting communities (eg: Chenchu)
2. Shifting cultivators (eg: Savara, Khond, Konda Reddii, etc.)
3. Pastorals (eg: Gond, Banjara)
4. Traders (eg: Valmiki); and
5. Settled agriculturists (eg: Jatapu, Bagata, Koya, Gond, etc.)

In the recent decades, there are perceptible changes in the occupational structures of the tribal groups. While the groups from category (1) to (4) have taken up or are slowly moving towards settled agriculture, the settled agriculturists are taking up cultivation of irrigated crops and commercial crops.

Social Organization

The tribal society is often characterized by divisions based on kin groups ranging from family, lineage, clan and sometimes to Phratry. The tribal heads in a village are differently called as Patels, among Gonds; Pedda Manishis among Chenchus and Naidu, among Savaras. Whatever may be the title, the headman's wish is most often than not, the final word after the discussions. In a multi-tribal village and for a group of villages it is found that inter-tribal and intra-tribal council exist (e.g. : Rai centres of Adilabad District), to maintain the social order and to resolve issues and a common platform with mutually agreeable terms.

The tribal groups do differ in their cultural practices, however, they do have similar patterns of social organization, which emphasize a communal spirit and the existence of democratic village institutions centering on a Village Council/Village Elders Committee composed of the traditional elders of the community, which provides a framework for community decision making. In several tribal pockets, these traditional institutions of the tribes still continue to exert/command considerable influence. These institutions are deeprooted in the sociocultural ethos of the tribal society. The traditional tribal institutions continue to command widespread respect in a number of areas, not withstanding the new democratic Panchayatiraj institutions attempting to provide representation to the local tribal population.

Language

Different language groups can be found among the tribals of Andhra Pradesh. The Sevaras of Srikakulam district speak a language traced to Austro-Asiatic family of languages, while the Khond, Koya and Gond, etc., speak a language belonging to the Dravidian family. The Lambada (Banjara) speak an Indo-Aryan language. Groups like Konda-Reddii and Chenchu speak a dialect of Telugu. In spite of the variations in their languages, all these tribal groups now speak Telugu also, due to the regular interaction with the people of the plains, education, etc.

Culture

The Revenue, Police and Excise administration introduced in tribal areas by the British and the development administration by the popular governments of the post-Independence period contributed to various perceptible changes in the tribal way of life. Nevertheless, the tribal still endeavours to continue their dying art forms of dance and dance and music (Dhimsa and Ghusadi dances are one of the most popular versions), their fairs, festivals and festivities.

Policies and Issues

The Constitution of India had, provided for reaching out to the tribal people much before the ILO Convention of 1957. However, neither the Tribal Panchasheel nor the concept of trusteeship nor the spirit of the Constitution have gone down or were being appreciated by the over governance of the administrative systems in the State of Andhra Pradesh, as elsewhere in the country.

The present levels of development and socio-economic conditions in different tribal areas of the State and even among the tribal groups vary considerably. The present planning process, does not take note of the different levels of development of these groups, as a result of which the gulf between the different groups is getting further widened*. The situation, pervading all over the country in the tribal development scenario has been aptly described by Dr Brahma Dev Sharma, former Commissioner for Scheduled Castes and Scheduled Tribes, Government of India in the following words:

> Because supplementary safeguards cannot make good the initial handicap besides countering the adverse processes intrinsic to the system as also the general slide back which the members of the Scheduled Castes and Scheduled Tribes may experience as members of the larger community of weaker sections, their position will be like that of a person who tries to climb up a downward moving escalator and is required to make increasing effort even to maintain his position not to go down. (highlighted)

Special plans to identify the priorities of development of tribal areas, were late arrivals, as a result of which, the general State plan priorities have also continued to be the priority needs of the tribals areas. Thus, there is growth in physical infrastructure in the tribal areas, with not much to do about the needs and aspirations of the tribal people.

Early Development Strategy

Several approaches have been introduced to take the mainstream development impulse into the tribal areas since the inception of the concept of Community Development in the country. These include (i) the policy of isolation, (ii) policy of assimilation of cultures, (iii) policy of intervention and (iv) the policy of revitalization. The sustained effort under the policy of revitalization is conspicuous by its very absence. The policy implies that special attention be given to each tribe to preserve the good elements of its culture and to extenuate the not so good ones. It proposes the development of the capacities and willpower of the tribes in

* as is acknowledged by the Working Group on Development and Welfare of Scheduled Tribes (1989).

resisting the temptations and clutches of exploitative individuals, groups and agencies. There appears a pertinent need to redefine our developmental objectives and link economic plans with an imaginative and thoughtful cultural policy. The tribes cannot continue to live indefinitely in their isolation when the physical, economic and cultural environment around them is changing rapidly.

Socio-economic Scenario in Tribal Areas

To fathom the concerns of tribal development in Andhra Pradesh it is pertinent to browse through the recognized issues in the tribal areas of the tribal people which can be broadly classified into economic and social spheres. Under the economic realm, issues of land, utilization of natural resources, maximization of utilization potential, Disastrous development and other related issues take the cake for as much as in the social sphere the major issues remain in the fields of education, health, housing, social institutions, etc.

The Economic Scene

The tribal communities represent one of the most under-developed sections of the society. Due to various historical processes of stress, strain and change over the centuries, they had to retreat to the relative safety of the inhospitable hilly areas and forest regions to subsist. It is understood that due to these reasons of existence, poverty is widespread in the tribal areas. Tribal society does aspire for augmented standards of living but its approach to the question is typical and sagacious. Tribal life by and large is permeated with a culture that has a personality of its own pervading every aspect of their life and activities.

More than 80 per cent of the tribal people depend on agriculture for their livelihood and most of them are landless agricultural labourers. The population growth has made the land available for agricultural purposes quite insufficient to provide a standard of living which bears any comparison to that enjoyed by any other group of people. Even among the lucky landed tribals, the average landholding is 0.4 ha and quite troubled is the conscience to realize that only 25 per cent of such land is in the actual possession and cultivation of the tribal.

The indebtedness and poverty forced many a tribal — first to lease, then hypothecate and later to part with his land to the ever intelligent non-tribal. The land reforms which have been, by and large, based upon landlord-tenant relationship, cannot help the tribal who leased, mortgaged or otherwise hypothecated land against debts contracted to the outsiders, who live in their midst such as the trader-cum-moneylender, for gratification of credit needs for consumption or ritual purposes, due to non-availability / inaccessibility of formal credit programmes. Table 21.3 indicates the Land Transfer Regulation Act cases and explicitly clarifies the point.

TABLE - 21.3
POSITION OF LAND TRANSFER REGULATION - ANDHRA PRADESH

(Figures as of December, 1996)

I.	Total No. of Cases detected	66,284
II.	Total No. of Cases disposed	53,431
III.	Cases disposed in favour of Tribals	26,456
IV.	Cases disposed in favour of Non-Tribals	26,975
V.	Cases pending disposal	12,853*
	Total Area of disputed land	2,79,088.87 acres
	i. Total Area disposed	2,36,807.19 acres
	ii. Area awarded in favour of tribals	1,06,228.31 acres
	iii. Area awarded in favour of non-tribal	1,30,578.88 acres
	iv. Extent still held under dispute	42,281.68 acres*
	v. Extent actually restored to tribals	N/A*

* Inferences

Source: Performance Budget, Tribal Welfare Dept., GOAP, 1997-98.

TABLE - 21.4
PROGRESS UNDER LAND TRANSFER REGULATION IN BHADRACHALAM AGENCY*

(as of August, 1997)

I.	Cases filed from inception to 31.1.1991	27,317	1,02,577.33
II.	No. of cases disposed off	23,572	89,410.36
	In favor of tribals	10,462	35,791.36
	In favor of non-tribals (Cases dropped)	12,946	53154.18
	Cases Where Land restored to tribals	9,882	34,323.39
III.	Cases pending disposal	3,745	13,166.37

Source: o/o Special Deputy Collector (LTR), Paloncha;
Figures show discrepancy indicating a serious lack of networking - to be reconciled.

Adding to this penury the tribal communities, by and large, are in the habit of growing only one crop (either paddy or the lesser millets) and given their landholding resort to the slash and burn mode of cultivation referred to as "Podu". The modern agriculture is yet to reach the real tribal who still depends on the vagaries of nature for his life sans facilities of improved seed, fertilizer, technological packages, irrigation facilities and the like. Thus, agriculture, the only viable economic activity, for the tribals has thus slipped away from even subsistence level to mere trail.

The Social Scene

Major importance has always been attributed to education and health by the Government donors to the tribal beneficiaries. The concept of education of today is so universal that - neither the curricula nor the language and systems of teaching prefer any differentiation between the less exposed tribal ward of illiterate parents from the hilly terrain and the better exposed ward of the educated bourgeoisie from the plains. This has led to a difference in the appreciation of the concept of education by students and their parents alike in most of the tribal regions.

The education levels have been worked upon by bringing in concepts like single teacher schools, employing tribal teachers though with a lower educational background, establishment of residential institutions of learning and the like. But it is overt that the major factor of the tribal way of life and their work culture has been ignored. The tribal child's environment is exhaustively different and the education he is afforded does not arrive at his levels of need and priority, leading to dropouts and an aversion to education itself.

Health institution of the government commands the tribal to it's doorstep and not vice versa.The inaccessibility of the areas, the shortage of extension staff added with the superstitious rites and beliefs of the tribal make health a system with only the skeleton but neither the muscles to stretch nor the beauty to reach for. So is the case with many of the extension departments/agencies or arms of the government which have solemnly pledged itself in the Constitutional Articles 244,330,332,334 and 335 read with the 5th and the 6th Schedule of the Constitution, for protection and advancement of the tribal groups.

Tribal Development in Andhra Pradesh

The original approach to tribal development has been unsatisfactory in the State of Andhra Pradesh like in any other State of the country. Whilst considerabe development efforts and government resources (largely in the form of grant assistance) were directed towards the tribal farmers, the expected impact was late in coming. The general and much preferred assumption that the provision of infrastructure facilities would be the stimulus for general and overall development of all the tribal households in the region in question proved to be unfounded and far from truth. Beneficiary oriented schemes, failed largely because of their piecemeal approach which depreciated the tribal communal tradition and the failure to identify and include key members of the village society in early planning and decision making. There has been little focus on the integrated development of the tribal communities, which combine social, economic and perceived technical needs of the villages, leading to the " Dependency Syndrome", with the Government taking up the role of the benevolent benefactor or "cherub".

With the exodus of *a la mode* scheme and major policy initiatives taken up during the Indira era, the major being the 20-Point Programme, meant to creat certain preconditions for mass-oriented and participatory development on one hand and introdution of a "new agricultural strategy" on the other. This brought about the sharpening of differentiation between the developed and backward region and rich farmers and poor peasants. It was during this era that large-scale influx of non-tribals into the tribal areas was seen creating situations of confrontation and exasperation.

With the passing times, it became apparent that the only way of averting the drift towards a crisis of confidence among the weaker sections of the society, tribals included, is to take effective steps on a comprehensive front to arrest the process of the marginalization and initiate mass participation, with the application of participatory approach to development. For, many a time, it is discerned that a development process which initiated without adequate thoughtfulness, negating the very concept of welfare of the tribal community and depraving the appetite of the tribal for social and technological change has been ambushed, having denied the right to choose and participate in their own development. Instances of these types are found in contexts where tribal land is acquired for the purpose of various projects (irrigation, power, industry, mining, education, health, infrastructure, etc) for the purpose of benefiting the tribals, but strike at the root of their living when their only earning source i.e.land is snatched away.

Implementation Strategies

G.O.Ms.30

The pivotal strength for participation and execution of works by the communities is provided through an Executive Order popular as G.O.Ms. No. 30 of 17th February, 1994. The orders read that "in the interest of speedy and quality execution of work and also to ensure the accrual of benefits to the local tribals themselves and to inculcate a sense of belonging through participatory approach, Government has decided to entrust the execution of all civil works benefiting the tribals in tribal area and other areas to Village Development Committees/Mahila Sanghams/ Society comprising of the local tribals, etc, on nomination basis irrespective of financial limits and depending on local initiative and discretion of the Project Officer, integrated Tribal Development Agency/ District Collector concerned."

The Executive Order is innovative for it provides for appropriately training the participant beneficiaries on the planning, execution and monitoring and evaluation of the civil works, and this training has been made the responsibility of the executing agency, namely the Engineering department in addition to providing for joint signatory account operation for withdrawal of funds pertaining to such works. Also the Order provides for considerable leeway for modification in the work proceedings for modifications as according to the requests of the village Committee, while ensuring that all the plans with schematic diagrams be explained to the Village Committee for them to appreciate the components and a copy of such plans also needs to be handed over to the committee well before the actual commencement of the works. Another unique feature of the Executive Order is that it ensures that after completion of the work entrusted, Project Officer,

Integrated Tribal Development Agency/ District Collector of the concerned area many allocate 50 per cent of the unspent balances, if any, to the Committee/Sangham which executed the work to be matched with contribution from the beneficiaries. 50 per cent of such savings will be deposited in a joint account to be used towards periodical maintenance of the structures/assets created and the balance 50 per cent of such conserved funds may be spent for such other community requirements, etc, as the Village Development Committee or Sangham, etc., may decide.

VTDAs

The Village Tribal Development Associations (VTDAs) are the village/habitation level committees which would include each and every male and female resident of the habitation. The VTDAs have been conceived as the local ITDA based in the habitation, the unit of planning for all development intiatives including planning, implementation, monitoring and initiating remedial action. The entire community is thus involved in the inventory of the resources endowment, the status appraisal of the utilization of these resources, utilizaton, analysis of the Strengths, Weaknesses, Opportunites and Threats (SWOT Technique) for optimal utilization of resources and securing better productivity. The VTDA are in the process of evolving as the umbrella organization for various subgroups functional in the habitation like Self-help Group, Youth Group, Water Users Committee, Mothers Committee, Vana Samrakshana Samiti, etc. (See Annexure 1)

Multi- Disciplinary Teams

All the functionaires operating at the Watershed level have been constituted as a Multi-Disciplinary Team (MDT) to formulate plans and programs as per the covet of the habitation level institutions and for collective responsibility to the community for implementation of the plans and programs as per schedule and design. This arrangement provides for convergence of basic development services, transparency and continuous interaction.

Programmes and Schemes

Presently, for a good number of programmes/schemes concentrating on the social, economic development of tribals,

Andhra Pradesh has taken to the Participatory approach as a strategy with encouraging results.

The Government of Andhra Pradesh, during the Sixth Plan period, had provided for the Single - line system of Administration with all functional departments of the Government of Andhra Pradesh, functioning in the TSP area, placed under the control of the Project Officers of the (8) ITDAs in the Scheduled areas. Apart from the regular programmes of these line departments like Agriculture, Horticulture, Sericulture, Minor irrigation, Soil Conservation, Animal Husbandry, Medical and Health departments to name a few. The Tribal Welfare Department of the Government of Andhra Pradesh is promoting the following Schemes/programmes:

Education

The Tribal Welfare Department has established 3727 Single teacher primary Schools (as of 1996-97) manned by local educated youth (matriculates) to take primary education to the thresholds of the tribal habitations and a further 540 new primary schools of the order are being started in a phased manner this academic year (1997-98). Additionally, about 830 Maabadi (Community Schools) are being co-financed with the parents of children contributing 50 per cent of the costs of maintaining the school.

The Tribal Welfare Department has also established Ashram Schools with attached hostel facilities in 481 clusters for ST children accommodating 79,789 boarders (1996-97) and 20 New Ashram Schools are on the anvil with proposals to convert 60 of the 504 ST hostels accommodating 63,095 boarders, into Ashram Schools duly upgrading the Ashram Schools to upper Primary and High Schools.

Special hostels for ST students studying intermediate (10+) and its equivalent or higher course are to be accommodated in 27 Special Hostels (20 for boys and 7 for girls). In fifteen districts of the State (43) Residential School (30 for boys + 13 for girls) have been established, accommodiating 15,252 students. Of these (10) Residential Schools (8 PTG boys + 2 PTG girls) are exclusively for the children of PTG families.

Additionally, the Government is also providing for incentives like text books, notebooks & uniforms, pre-matric scholarships for pre-matric boarders/students; book bank schemes, scholarships, mess charges, merit scholarships, etc, for post-matric students. Admission for bright children among STs selected by a District Selection committee, into the Best Schools recognized by the Education Department is also being taken up and presently there are 4692 children continuing in this category. Five Regional Pre-Examination Training Centres are functioning to prepare unemployed tribal youth for various State, Central, Bank competitive exams and job-oriented course.

Health

The Tribal Welfare department was running (60) institutions in the tribal areas, apart from the regular hospitals, dispensaries and Primary health Centres maintained by the medical and health Department. Of these (16) hospitals, (16) medical dispensaries, and (22) Mobile Medical units (MMUs), have been transferred with budget to the Medical and Health Department. Further the Government, through the Tribal Welfare Department is maintaining (6) Mother and Child Welfare Centres, staff of 18 Public Health Units in 4 districts and seven Family and Child Welfare Units with five Sub-Centres each in six districts.

IFAD

To improve the food security, ecological protection, economic development through natural resources development and human resource development with technological, social and political innovations, two projects with a total outlay of 293.50 crores are being assisted by the International Fund for Agricultural Development (IFAD) having co-financing arrangements with the Government of Netherlands.

The projects, Andhra Pradesh Credit and Tribal Development Project — {APCTDP (IFAD - I) since 1991 and the Andhra Pradesh Participatory Tribal Development Project APPTDP (IFAD -II) since 1994-95 are intended to benefit 6.60 lakh tribals in 3093 villages of 44 watersheds under 9 ITDAs in the areas of:

(i) Natural Resources Development and off-farm activities for income generation;

(ii) Community participation and development including health and education;

(iii) Marketing and credit support with strengthening of Research and Development efforts for value addition in minor forest produce and agricultural produce; and

(iv) Project Management Support.

The lessons learnt from the IFAD-1 Project (Andhra Pradesh Tribal Development Project) encouraged both the Department of Tribal Welfare and the IFAD to promote together the Andhra Pradesh Participatory Tribal Development Project (IFAD II) in the other remaining ITDA areas of Warangal, Adilabad, Khammam, West Godavari and Chenchu project.

The projects have brought in perceptible transformation in many arenas, apart from being a force to reckon with in the context of Participatory Development. Some of the key physical consummations are soil and moisture conservation measures in 34,581 ha of more than 30,000 families. Irrigation facility has been provided for 8025 ha of 7873 beneficiaries through 584 structures like check dams, minor irrigation tanks, lift irrigation schemes, CI Wells, etc, constructed through community labour and covet. More than 6249 Agricultural Demonstration Plots to induce the ripple effect of modern agricultural techniques combined with 2240 Seed Production Sites for providing of quality seed material to the tribal farmers were also introduced, including Tree Crops in 25,080 ha of 48,964 families by establishing 780 Satellite nurseries for efficient delivery of required plant material and providing employment opportunity to the tribal farmers and 341 demonstration Orchards supplementing the Horticultural Nurseries and Training Centres existing in various ITDAs. One indicator of the increase in the savings capacity is the evolution of (946) Women's thrift Societies with 22,050 members with saving of over 25 lakh and to tide over the lean season food grains crisis (466) grain banks have emerged by peoples contribution with 96.7 tons of grain.

The local village level (traditional) institutions have been acclaimed and taken into confidence thus providing to harness the opportunities this unique endowment offers, by focusing on the development of sustainable Modern Village Institutions on the available community structutes. The considerations of these institutions are contemplated while formulating plans and programmes for tribal development and reinforcing them, as requited, to respond to the developmental opportunities offered for better (equitable ?!!) utilization of common assets and management of local resources.

Lessons

Role modification

The tribal village level institutions which have never been consulted earlier with regards to their preferences to the nature of the developmental programmes, have now been acknowledged and their consideration contemplated before embarking on any developmental program. This unique arrangement has gone into improving the sufficiency, efficacy and efficiency of the schemes launched or introduced in the context of the village/habitation.

- the emphasis is on Community Participation with the key to this process being the development of capable and sustainable village institutions which itself has to become the forum for community decision making, comprising of representatives from every household.
- The concepts of Participatry Resource Appraisal (PRA) and village level micro-planning have been brought into practice replacing the desktop planning processes.
- The concept of the Community Development Coordination Teams (CDCTs) with the admixture of professional proclivity and youthful ebullience of the young professionals, working in a contiguous concentrated cluster of villages for reasons of sharp focusing in generating, promoting and sustaining appropriately the participatory approaches of the communities, came to be the mainstay of all Tribal Development strategy under the IFAD project.
- The change agents, herein above mentioned, brought about well defined and strategic changes in the entire service delivery and beneficiary roles and renditions. It was now the community that would choose deliberately and the VTDAs shall execute and the earlier givers would guide in the technical details.

Summing up

The concept of Participatory Methodologies and VTDAs + MDTs, can be reckoned as an innovative approach worth replication. The positive side of this approach and its usefulness, as demonstrated, in the context of Tribal Development has been placed below:

1. *Timely execution of works:* with proper planning of manpower and man days and period of workforce availability. For example: The seasonal diagram indicates the period of lean season and each farmer/member of the community ranks the period of lean season by the marking dots technique. The larger number of dots during a particular month/period shall indicate the larger availability of manpower during the period and the works that need maximum labour can be taken up.
2. *Identification of priorities and execution:* thereof independent of schemes and other quibbles has been made possible, for the finances are available with the village community and the community shall decide when and where and how to take up a programme. The priorities of the functionaries viz., targets and dates can in no way interfere with the priorities of the community.
3. *Reduction of Leakage (Transparency):* There has developed a feeling of our asset within the community and therefore there is a continuous vigil or the physical and financial progress of the works by the community, the liaison agents, the youth groups and the traditional leaders so also with the the young professionals. The estimated costs and the nature of work is known to all and made understood to all thus eliminating suspicion of leakage or actual leakage.
4. *Reduction in Migration:* With the availability of wage employment at the village level appropriately as to the requirement in both time and available manpower the out migration has been reduced to less than 5 per cent.
5. *Elimination of Middlemen:* is ensured by providing for self-labour by the community and "Shramdan", thus reducing the overall unit cost. This proves as a deterrent for the middlemen as there could be no profit with reduced and transparent estimates. The modus operandi is: 'Reduce the

rate prescribed by the SSR for any item of works' for example: if the SSR would indicate say 25 rupees per cubic meter of earth excavation, the unit cost would be for say Rs 12 and the balance of the work estimate ploughed back into the village for providing of a common asset or for meeting a community need.

6. *Increased interest:* is observed, as the beneficiary, who is no more a passive onlooker of bulldozers running into his field and doing the work for him without his consent or asking for his/her opinion. The beneficiary has donned the role of the planner, director and actor of the scene of development and has started utilizing his/her capacities and capabilities, thus raking his/her interests.
7. *Power to the People:* The rule of financier dictating the terms has changed and thus has the power of the financier to rule. The functionaries once and even today in most parts make the commoner run between pillar and post and the illiterate tribal most often than not falls prey and also sometimes, in fits of exasperation takes to arms. With the advent of the VTDA concept, the funds are with the village and the functionary is now at the mercy of the village if (s) he has to show the results expected of him/her by the higher-ups.
8. *Involvement of the Traditional Institutions:* The traditional Institutions which have been *per se* neglected in the development process have been accommodated and these institutions for example the Rai Centres in the district of Adilabad have ascribed themselves the role of monitoring agents and guiding forces and at times questioning a non-functional VTDA and its representatives, heretofore unknown.

ANNEXURE — 1

Inferences on the effective functioning of the habitation level ITDA have been arrived at as:

- *Territorial Jurisdication:* VTDA is either for a single habitation or for more than one habitation, as according to the wishes of the residents.
- *Homogeneity:* The VTDA may be homogeneous tribal group

or a mix of tribal groups. The revenue village may thus have a single VTDA or more but all the "tribal" families of the habitation are members of the VTDA.

- *Constitution:* All the male and female residents of the habitation being the members of the VTDA, they constitute the General Body and select a five member Core Group of Executive Committee with atleast two women, who are generally not necessarily, selected from the Women's thrift Group to review the status of all developmental programmes, with a President and a Secretary. The elected tribal representative of the village for example, a Sarpanch or Mukhya, though is a member but not necessarily needs to be designated the President or member of the Executive Committee.
- *Meetings:* The Core Group is required to meet every week generally the night after the shandy day and the General Body meets once in a month a fixed day. At places, it is the full moon night and in some other habitations the no moon day. During peak working season some VTDAs have claimed to have 4-5 meetings in a month.
- *Peoples representative:* The Sarpanch of the Gram Panchayat, the President of the Mandal Parishad, the MPTC, ZPTC members and the MLA of the concerned constituency are permanent invitees to the meetings of the VTDAs as are the local level government functionaries of Development Departments., as per design so as to allow the former to appreciate the concerns of the habitation.
- *Tenure:* Unlike the traditional institutions, the tenure of office is not hereditary for the office of President/Secretary of the VTDA. The tenure of Office is annular (in principle) and the principles that governed the selection of tribal elders in the traditional tribal societies, is also seen to be followed in the selection for the above offices by the general body, purely on the person's merits and demerits.
- *Village Development Fund:* The VTDAs have opened Savings Bank Account at the nearest branches as per the prescription of the General Body. The ITDA remits each and every paisa that is meant for the development of the village from which the community can draw funds for the creations of the community assets.

I. The Accounts are being operated jointly either by the President and Secretary of the VTDA or the Village Headman (sometimes observed), but only with prior discussions and concurrence of the General body as contained in the minutes, the accounts are being maintained by the Village Teacher/Anganwadi Worker/VLWs.

II. For any activity that would benefit an individual or the community, 25 per cent of the total estimated cost, prepared through participatory process and approval by the VTDA, is released to the VTDA as advance.

III. Once 80 per cent of such advance is utlized and utilization certificate furnished another 25 per cent of the unit cost is released to the VTDA and the process continued with the Sectoral Officer and Task Force Officer being responsible jointly and severely for timely execution of the programmes, proper utilization of funds, furnishing the utilization certificates to the ITDA and timely release of funds to the VTDAs.

IV. To eliminate the leakage at any point certain norms have been evolved over a period of three-four years for the delegation of financial sanctions. For withdrawal of amounts over and above Rs 10,000 but below Rs 15,000, the VTDA shall withdraw with the concurrence of the Agricultural Coordinator/Sectoral Officer and above Rs 15,000 with the concurrence of the Project Officer.

V. Service Cost: 6% of the total cost of every work is earmarked for monitoring and establishment costs and half of it is remitted in the VDF and the remaining half retained with the ITDA. This amount is deducted at source by the ITDA, by costing the Monitoring Costs/Petty Supervision charges over and above the amount due to the participant beneficiaries. Monitoring charges thus accrued by the VDF is utilized for payment of honorarium to the Liaison Worker/Development Organiser. *For example*: If the commuted cost of Soil Conservation Works in a village is Rs 10 lakh, it is estimated for Rs 10.60 lakh, out of which Rs 2.50 lakh is released as advance to the VTDA and Rs 0.30 lakh released towards monitoring cost to the VDF and the 0.30 lakh of the monitoring costs deposited by the ITDA under the head of Watershed Development Fund to meet the honoraria of the Agricultural Coordinators and other Professionals.

VI. Village Organizer/Development Organizer: The VTDAs select a reasonably educated and articulate young man as the Village Organizer in the Governing Body, to liase between the Governmental functionaries and the village community and is made responsible for the Natural Resources Development of community. Similarly, a lady is selected as Development Organizer responsible for the Human Resources Development and promotion of Women and Child Development Programmes.

VII. Convergence of Basic Development Services: The primary objective of the VTDAs is to secure convergence of Community based development services by a network of trained tribal extension workers located within the village context and young professionals providing support to monitor and bring to the village a sustained utilization of available services.

REFERENCES

Appraisal Report, Andhra Pradesh Credit and Tribal Development Project, 1991-1997, International Fund for Agricultural Development, Rome, 1991

Appraisal Report, Andhra Pradesh Participatory Tribal Development Project, 1994-2001, IFAD, ROME, 1994.

Development Perspectives for Tribals, Subhendru Bhattacharya and Dr T. Lakshmaiah, *Girijana Samskruti*, Vol. 2, No. 1 , TCR&TI, Hyderabad, January, 1994.

Participatory Management of Tribal Development Programmes, K.A.S. Hussain, ibid.

Note on Activities, Girijan Cooperative Corporation Limited, Visakhapatnam, September 1994.

Report of the Working Group on Tribal Development during Seventh Plan, 1985-90, Planning Commission, India, December, 1994.

G.O.Ms. No. 30, Social Welfare (v2) Department, GOAP, 1994.

Guidelines for Participatory Development, Tribal Welfare Department, Government of Andhra Pradesh, Hyderabad, 1996.

APPTDP - Supervision Mission Notes, UNOPS, Kualalumpur, July, 1997.

Twenty Two

Development of Scheduled Castes and Scheduled Tribes: An Assessment of UP

A.K. SRIVASTAVA

Developmental activities under planning, are directed towards the provisions of social services like health, education and housing for all and of social justice for socially disadvantaged and deprived sections such as Scheduled Castes, Scheduled Tribes, other backward classes, women, children and old people. Though these provisions only may not constitute social development as such, however, they certainly lead to it. Delimiting our study to census data, we find literacy rate and employment pattern as reliable indicators for the development of any section of society. Singh (1989) while considering the status of the Scheduled Caste and Scheduled Tribe women in Punjab, also took these two variables in her study.

Thus, the paper examines the development of Scheduled Castes and Scheduled Tribes in Uttar Pradesh in terms of their educational status and employment pattern. For this purpose, the changes occured during the decade of 1981 to 1991 have been taken into account. The census data of 1981 and 1991, available on these two aspects, have been analysed as to assess the situation existing there in the state of Uttar Pradesh.

The Demographic Profile

As per the Census 1991, the total population of Scheduled Castes and Scheduled Tribes (hereinafter SC and ST) in UP is 21 and 0.2 per cent of the total population as compared to 16.7 and 8 per cent in India respectively. Thus, the SC population in UP is 4.3 per cent more than that in India, whereas the ST population is much less. Comparing these data with Census 1981, we find no significant change in their population. (21.2 and 0.2 per cent for SC and ST in UP and 15.7 and 7.8 per cent in the country as a whole respectively).

As regards the growth rate in SC and ST population, it is seen that in India, the growth rate in both the segments is on an increase (32.5 and 31.1 for SC and ST respectively as compared to 25.5 for all). In UP the SCs maintain the balance with the total (24.5 per cent for SC and 25.5 per cent growth for total) whereas the growth rate among STs is about 5 per cent less. As per the Census 1991, in UP 88 per cent of SCs and 94 per cent of STs as against 80 per cent of total population live in rural areas.

On the basis of sex-ratio, the population in UP has a higher proportion of males (879 females in UP as compared to 927 per 1000 males in India). The SC population in UP also follows the same pattern (877 females per 1000 males). The STs however, show a better sex ratio, i.e. (914 females per 1000 males) as compared to their SC counterparts.

Literacy

Among other factors, education is basic in bringing about social and economic transformation in any community. This is more so for the Scheduled Castes, who appear to be socially and economically depressed and have remained under supression for centuries,and also the Scheduled Tribes who have long been isolated from the mainstream culture and whose economic activities have remained at subsistance level. Table 1 depicts the percentage distribution of literacy among SCs, STs and those not belonging to these categories in UP in 1981 and 1991 Census.

According to Census 1991, the literacy rate for the country is 64.1 per cent, whereas it is only 41.6 per cent in Uttar Pradesh. Comparing the data among those belonging to SC, ST and Non-SC & ST categories, we find sufficient gap. Establishing educational backwardness in SCs and STs. The literacy among SCs is 21.1 per cent, while in ST, it is 28.4 in comparison to 36.4 per cent belonging to those of non-SC & ST category. Thus, SCs are lagging behind by more than 15 per cent and STs by 8 per cent from others.

On the level of rural-urban variation though there is a yawning gap throughout, but the situation among SC and ST population, in this regard, is worse than those not belonging to these categories. It is noticed that whereas 19.4 per cent of SCs and 26.8 STs are literate in rural areas the percentage of such non-SC & STs is 32. The better percentage of literate STs in urban areas (54.1 per cent as compared to 33.6 per cent of SCs and 52.1 of those of non-SC & STs) suggest that the STs who migrate to urban areas, sufficiently avail the existing better educational facilities. In rural areas too their need for education is better catered due to their comparatively less population.

TABLE - 22.1

PERCENTAGE DISTRIBUTION OF LITERACY IN CENSUS 1981 AND 1991

	1981		*Literate*	*1991*	
	Total	*Female*		*Total*	*Female*
			SCHEDULED CASTE		
Total	15.0	3.9		21.1	8.3
Rural	13.5	2.7		19.4	6.6
Urban	27.4	14.3		33.6	21.5
			SCHEDULED TRIBE		
Total	20.4	8.7		28.4	15.7
Rural	18.9	7.3		26.8	14.1
Urban	50.7	38.1		54.1	42.3
			NON SC & ST		
Total	30.4	16.8		26.4	23.2
Rural	25.9	11.5		32.0	17.5
Urban	48.5	38.4		52.1	43.5
			TOTAL		
Total	27.2	14.0		33.2	20.0
Rural	23.1	9.5		29.1	15.0
Urban	45.9	35.4		49.8	40.7

Population in the age group of 0-6 has not been deducted while computing the literacy percentage as the same is not available in census 1981.

As regards the female education, we find that though they are throughout in a worse position as compared to their male counterparts, their sisters in SC and ST category are much worse. Female literacy among SCs is only 9.4 per cent and STs 15.7 as compared to other women having more than 23 per cent of literacy. Further, among all the women, the rural-urban variation is also present in each category i.e. the urban women are throughout more literate than those of rural background. But the women belonging to SC and ST categories are more backward in regard to education than their other counterparts. Comparing the level of literacy among SC & ST women in rural society, we find 14.1 per cent of STs in comparision to only 6.6 of SCs while in urban centres, there are 42.3 per cent of STs in relation to 21.5 SCs. It appears that because of their less population, the STs and consequently their womenfolk remain relatively much in the focus of governmental efforts made in this direction. Further, among STs the regional variation is also present (which is at present not the focus of study).

Putting the data parallel to those available from Census 1981, the scenario does not exhibit any change even after passing one full decade. In 1981 Census, the literacy among SCs was 15 per cent in comparison to 20.4 among STs and 30.4 among non-SC & STs. Thus, the difference of literacy of non-SC & STs with SC was 15.4 and with ST 10 per cent in 1981. In Census 1991, this difference with SC remains 15.3 per cent and with ST, it reduces to 8 per cent (SCs and STs are less in percentage).

Taking the rural population into account, we find that the gap between literacy percentage among SC and non-SC & ST category is 12.4 per cent and among ST and non-SC & ST as 7 per cent in 1981, which in Census 1991 becomes 12.6 and 5 per cent respectively. The urban population follows the similar pattern.

As regards the percentage of female literacy in the Census 1981, among SC females, it was 12.9 per cent less and among those of STs 8.1 as compared to those not belonging to these categories, which in the year 1991, becomes 14.9 and 7.5 per cent respectively. Among the rural women in 1981, this gap was 8.8 and 4.2 per cent respectively with their non-SC & ST counterparts, which in the year 1991, in regard to SCs videns and becomes 10.9 and among STs it reduces to 3.4 per cent. However, in the case of urban SC women this gap reduces by 2 per cent.

Thus, it is clear that the literacy percentage among SCs and STs is throughout lower than the non-SC & STs. The state of female literacy among SCs and STs is worse in their own category and also in comparision to their non-SC & ST sisters. Literacy percentage among SC and STs in rural areas is significantly low than others in the area. The comparative picture of the gap existing between SCs and STs on the one hand and non-SCs & STs on the other in the years's 1981 and 1991, exhibit the non-occurence of any significant change. However, relatively better show by the ST population may be attributed to its regional variation, where the STs of hill areas who constitute the majority, have higher literacy rate than those in the plains.

This brings us to conclude that of course, due to various governmental and non-governmental efforts for making education for all, some changes are taking place as natural consequences but such changes have not yet succeeded in reducing the gap considerably between SCs & STs and those of non-SC & ST category in regard to the expansion of education. This may either be because of our efforts not being sincere enough and effective or among SCs in particular, we have yet not been able to create in Maclland's terminology, the sufficient 'need for achievement'. Thus, more focused literacy programmes are needed for the females who as mothers are the source of inspiration for their children and motivation for other members of the family, should in particular, be concentrated in the programmes.

Employment Pattern

Employment is another basic input that leads to the development of any community. Hence, the economic backwardness of Schedule Castes and Scheduled Tribes is to be seen in the light of their employment pattern.

Uttar Pradesh is predominantly an agricultural State with little more than 80 per cent of its population living in rural areas. Agriculture is the single largest sector that employs 72 per cent of the labour force.

Table 22.2 presents the comparative percentage distribution of the main workers among SC, ST and those not belonging to these categories in UP in Census 1981 and 1991. On the basis of comparison of main workers, we find no such change in the per cent figures as to deduce any directional conclusion, neither on basis of male-female distribution nor on rural-urban variation among SC, ST and others. Surprisingly, we find a better participation of the SCs & STs as main workers than their counterparts. However, an observation of the variety of work among the mainworkers does exhibit a better comparable employment pattern (Table 22.3).

TABLE -22.2
PERCENTAGE DISTRIBUTION OF MAIN WORKERS IN CENSUS 1981 AND 1991

	1981		*Literate* *1991*	
	Total	*Female*	*Total*	*Female*
SCHEDULED CASTE				
Total	31.6	9.1	32.2	11.9
Rural	32.0	9.5	33.0	12.6
Urban	28.6	5.7	27.5	6.0
SCHEDULED TRIBE				
Total	36.9	17.4	35.9	19.3
Rural	37.1	17.4	36.3	19.7
Urban	32.3	16.9	29.3	12.4
NON SC & ST				
Total	28.5	4.3	29.0	6.2
Rural	29.0	4.8	29.7	7.0
Urban	26.8	2.6	26.4	3.4
TOTAL				
Total	29.2	5.4	29.7	7.4
Rural	29.7	5.9	30.5	8.4
Urban	27.0	3.0	26.6	3.7

As per the Census 1991, it is seen that STs have a high percentage of cultivators (69.5 per cent in comparison to SCs 42.6 and 53.3 for all). But in regard to their total population in the State (.02 per cent), the type of their social organization and the subsistence level of their agriculture, this high percentage may not be treated as an indicator of their better economic position. However, a comparison of total workers and those belonging to SC suggests that the SCs are sufficiently low in percentage as cultivators. It is also evident from the fact that when only 18.9 per cent of total main worker are agricultural labours, the percentage among SCs in this category is 38.8. Similarly, those who are engaged in other services are less in SCs than the total percentage (16.5 as against 25.4 per cent of the total).

TABLE - 22.3

PERCENTAGE DISTRIBUTION OF THE TYPE OF WORK OF THE MAIN WORKERS IN CENSUS 1981 AND 1991

		1981						*1991*					
		SC		*ST*		*Total Workers*		*SC*		*ST*		*Total Workers*	
		T	F	T	F	T	F	T	F	T	F	T	F
Cultivators	Total	47.7	28.4	78.7	76.2	58.5	47.8	42.6	30.9	69.5	71.2	53.3	4.8
	Rural	51.9	30.0	81.7	79.1	68.4	52.4	46.7	32.5	72.5	73.4	63.0	5.3
	Urban	7.2	4.5	10.0	12.0	8.7	5.1	6.5	5.3	10.2	9.7	8.1	0.6
Agricultural Labourers	Total	35.0	58.9	7.2	7.6	16.0	35.2	38.8	57.7	13.0	13.3	18.9	35.8
	Rural	37.1	61.5	7.4	7.9	17.9	38.0	41.3	60.0	13.3	13.7	21.5	38.6
	Urban	14.7	21.0	3.0	0.5	6.2	9.2	15.7	21.8	0.4	2.2	7.2	10.3
Household Industry	Total	3.1	3.5	4.8	11.8	3.7	5.2	2.0	2.4	3.4	9.0	2.4	3.5
	Rural	2.6	2.9	4.1	9.2	2.8	3.7	1.8	2.0	3.0	7.7	1.8	2.4
	Urban	7.4	12.0	22.7	67.6	8.1	18.8	4.4	8.9	13.3	43.9	5.2	13.8
Other Workers	Total	14.2	9.2	9.2	4.4	21.8	11.7	16.5	9.0	14.1	6.5	25.4	12.4
	Rural	8.7	5.5	6.8	3.7	10.8	5.8	10.2	5.5	11.1	5.1	13.7	6.2
	Urban	70.5	62.6	64.3	19.9	76.9	66.9	73.3	64.1	72.4	44.2	79.5	69.7
Marginal Workers	Total	6.4	41.1	7.3	27.6	5.1	49.5	8.9	48.3	20.9	70.0	8.3	65.3
	Rural	6.8	42.6	7.4	28.9	5.9	53.2	9.6	49.8	21.6	71.6	9.6	69.5
	Urban	2.3	19.7	5.1	17.0	1.1	15.8	2.9	24.2	7.5	36.9	2.1	27.5

T = Total; F = Female

The difference in the employment status also becomes clear when we compare in terms of rural-urban distribution. In rural areas, only 46.7 per cent of SC main workers are categorized as cultivators in comparison to 63 per cent of cultivators among total workers. Similarly, among total workers, only 21.5 per cent are agricultural labourers, whereas among SCs this percentage is 41.3. In urban areas, the situation is relatively less imbalanced, in service sector, the percentage of the total workers is 6 per cent more than the SCs in this sector (79.5 per cent total workers as compared to 73.3 per cent SCs).

Economic activity of women as per the Census 1981, was lower in UP (5.4 per cent) as compared to nation as whole (14.4 per cent). According to Census 1991, women's participation in economic activity in UP is throughout lower. They are only 7.4 per cent as compared to 29.7 per cent of total main workers and 49.3 per cent male workers. However, when a decrease of 5 per cent is noticed among the female main workers, an increase of 2 per cent is observed in comparison to their share in 1981 census.

On the basis of type of economic activity, we find more SC & ST women in agriculture sector. As against only 4.8 per cent of total women as cultivators, there are about 31 per cent of SC and more than 71 per cent ST women in this category. Similarly, in comparison to 35.8 per cent of female agricultural labourers in all, among SC women it is 57.7 per cent. Among the ST women, the situation is a bit different (13.3 per cent), there the women work more in their own small lands than as labourers. Though their cultivation is at subsistance level. This is supported by their participation in household industry (9 per cent in comparison to 2.4 per cent SC women and 3.5 total female workers in this sector). It appears that the women belonging to upper caste do not participate in agricultural activities due to some cultural taboos and lack of freedom and inability to participate in outdoor activities. The adversly affected economic condition is also reflected by the fact that in the category of other workers, the percentage of SC and ST women is less than the total women (9 and 6.5 per cent of SCs and STs as compared to 12.4 per cent of total women). This is true for both the rural and urban areas. As regards the marginal workers, we find more than 65 per cent of total female main workers in this category whereas this percentage among those of SC and ST is 48.3 and 70 respectively. This is how a large section of women remain deprived of economic activity throughout the year. Though SC women are relatively less in this category, they are much in the category of agricultural labourer which is low paid and of low status. However, this marginality is low throughout in the urban sector (all 27.5, SC 24.2 and ST 36.9 per cent).

Going back with the data of main workers to those available in census 1981, we do not find any significant change in the scenario. However, on the basis of type of economic activities they do, some changes appear. It is seen that throughout there is significant reduce in the percentage of those categorized as cultivators. Among all the workers as cultivators, the reduce is by 5 per cent, among SCs, it is again 5 per cent and STs it is more than 9 per cent. Among the agricultural labourer category, there is an increase of 3 to 6 per cent in SC and ST and total workers. In household industry, we find a decrease in all the sections. In the service sector, among SCs there is increase by more than 2 per cent, among STs by more than 14 per cent in comparison to 4 per cent in all. Thus, the gap of SCs with all other workers which was 7.6 in 1981 increases to about 9 per cent. The STs in this sector, however, maintain the proportional ratio in 1991 too. Again, there is growth in the percentage of marginal workers too throughout. Same pattern appears on the basis of rural-urban variation in Census 1981 as well as 1991.

Taking female workers specifically into account, we find that females as cultivators have reduced from 47.8 per cent in 1981 to 4.8 in 1991. In the agricultural labour category, though SC and total female workers maintain the pattern, there is increase among ST women from 7.6 to 13.3 per cent (this indicates the turning of ST women as cultivators to agricultural labourers). As regards those in the household industry, there is decrease among female workers, making some proportion among SC, ST and all female workers. In the other workers category, there is an increase in ST and total female workers. This exhibits the widening of gap with SC females. The percentage of marginal female worker is at substantial increase, i.e. among total females workers it is 49.5 per cent in 1981 and 65.3 in 1991. Although there is an increase of marginal workers in SCs by 7 per cent, the gap is more pronounced among STs as it researches from 27.6 in 1981 to 70 per cent in 1991. This shows that the percentage women getting work throughout the year is dropping at a significant rate, the ST women have been marginalized at very high rate in the Census 1991.

Thus, we find that though some changes are occuring in 1991 census, the gap of SCs and STs with their counterparts in 1981 does not show a considerable reduce in Census 1991. For the development of STs and SCs, this must come down and nearer to the percentage that the total workers have in various categories of work. Again the lower percentage of females among total workers as well as among SC and ST also needs attention. The increased percentage of SC and ST females in the labour category shows that their economic status is lower than the women in general.

These observations question the achievements of the various governmental programmes for improving the economic status of the STs and SCs. In respect of the utilization of the reservation, the sociological studies reveal that these have benefited only a tiny fraction of the SCs and STs (Sharma, 1990). Generally, the benefits of reservation have gone to the already better-off among the SCs and STs and most of the beneficiaries, are urban based (Sharma, 1989: 37-53). As regards the situation in UP, Sharma mentions that SCs accounted for 18.1 per cent in Class-IV employees while their representation in Class-I jobs was just 8.1 per cent as against their reserved quota of 20 per cent. Thus, reservations have had only a marginal impact on reducing the status gap between Scheduled Castes and the non-scheduled castes.

Thus, to sum up, it is proposed that the government in its plans, should focus on SCs and STs in such a way as to reduce the gap between them and those not belonging to these categories. The womenfolk in these categories should also be taken care of in the governmental efforts.

REFERENCES

Census of India, 1981 Series 1 India Part II B (ii), Primary Census Abstract for Schedule Caste.

———, Series 1 India Part II B (iii), Primary Census Abstract for Schedule Caste.

———, Series 22, Uttar Pradesh, Primary Census Abstract of Schedule Caste and Schedule Tribe.

———, Series 22, Uttar Pradesh, State Primary Census Abstract.

Census of India 1991, Series 22, Uttar Pradesh, Primary Census Abstract of Schedule Caste and Schedule Tribe.

———, Series 22, Uttar Pradesh, State Primary Census Abstract.

National Family Health Survey 1992-93, Population Research Centre, Lucknow University and International Institute for Population Sciences Bombay, 1994.

Sharma, S.L., 1989, Social Development: Reflections on the concept and the Indian Experience, *Guru Nanak Journal of Sociology*, Vol. 10, Nos. 1-2, April-October.

———, 1989, 'A Tiny Fraction Benefited', *Indian Express*, April 16, 1990.

Singh, K.P., Women and Development: Gender Concerns'. In P.N. Pimpley, K.P. Singh and A Mahajan, (ed.), *Social Development: Process and Consequences*, Jaipur: Rawat Publications.

Index